IMAGINATION

WILKIE COLLINS: THE CRITICAL HERITAGE

THE CRITICAL HERITAGE SERIES

GENERAL EDITOR: B. C. SOUTHAM, M.A., B.LITT. (OXON.)
Formerly Department of English, Westfield College, University of London

For a list of books in the series see the back end paper

WILKIE COLLINS

THE CRITICAL HERITAGE

Edited by
NORMAN PAGE
Associate Professor of English
University of Alberta

ROUTLEDGE & KEGAN PAUL: LONDON AND BOSTON

First published in 1974
by Routledge & Kegan Paul Ltd
Broadway House, 68–74 Carter Lane,
London EC4V 5EL and
9 Park Street,
Boston, Mass. 02108, U.S.A.
ISBN 0 7100 7843 9
Library of Congress Catalog Card No. 73-92987

Set in 'Monotype' Bembo type
and printed in Great Britain by
W & J Mackay Limited, Chatham

General Editor's Preface

The reception given to a writer by his contemporaries and near-contemporaries is evidence of considerable value to the student of literature. On one side we learn a great deal about the state of criticism at large and in particular about the development of critical attitudes towards a single writer; at the same time, through private comments in letters, journals or marginalia, we gain an insight upon the tastes and literary thought of individual readers of the period. Evidence of this kind helps us to understand the writer's historical situation, the nature of his immediate reading public, and his response to these pressures.

The separate volumes in the *Critical Heritage Series* present a record of this early criticism. Clearly, for many of the highly productive and lengthily reviewed nineteenth- and twentieth-century writers, there exists an enormous body of material; and in these cases the volume editors have made a selection of the most important views, significant for their intrinsic critical worth or for their representative quality—perhaps even registering incomprehension!

For earlier writers, notably pre-eighteenth century, the materials are much scarcer and the historical period has been extended, sometimes far beyond the writer's lifetime, in order to show the inception and growth of critical views which were initially slow to appear.

In each volume the documents are headed by an Introduction, discussing the material assembled and relating the early stages of the author's reception to what we have come to identify as the critical tradition. The volumes will make available much material which would otherwise be difficult of access and it is hoped that the modern reader will be thereby helped towards an informed understanding of the ways in which literature has been read and judged.

B.C.S.

Contents

The Queen of Hearts (1859)

The Woman in White (1860)

No Name (1862)

CONTENTS

Preface

Wilkie Collins was one of the most popular novelists of the second half of the nineteenth century; yet of all his large output—the results of forty years spent in the pursuit of literature as a career—only two novels have achieved undisputed classic status. A handful of others (*Armadale*, for instance, and *No Name*) still retain some kind of currency; the rest are forgotten by all except the most dedicated specialists. In spite of this, the contemporary reception of his books offers much of interest to the student of English fiction, and of its critics and its reading public, between 1850 and 1890. As a young writer, Collins was widely reviewed in journals of the highest standing and was frequently hailed as a novelist of exceptional promise; his early novels were given close and serious attention, and he was held up for comparison with Dickens, Thackeray, Charlotte Brontë, Mrs Gaskell, and others. He became, and remained, one of the most widely-read authors of his day throughout the English-speaking world, and he was widely translated. Though there were fluctuations in popularity during his long career, these were nothing like so dramatic as has sometimes been suggested. More significantly, however, there were at times disparities between the enthusiasm for his work manifested by the book-buying and book-borrowing public and the pronouncements of the usually anonymous arbiters of taste who reviewed for the leading newspapers and journals. In a shrewd obituary assessment (28 September 1889), the *Spectator* suggested that 'the position of Mr. Wilkie Collins in literature was a very unusual one. He was an extremely popular writer—deservedly popular, as we think—who was not very highly esteemed. . . . That is an odd position, and we do not know that it has been quite satisfactorily explained.' If this is not the whole truth about Collins's reputation, it is certainly an interesting and suggestive part of it. What it demonstrates is that his novels posed certain distinctive critical problems which made the placing of them a delicate and controversial operation—a task for which Victorian reviewers were not always adequately equipped.

As the acknowledged leader of what came to be known as the 'sensational novel', he unavoidably associated himself with the purveyors of a proliferating sub-literature, feeble in quality and ephemeral in nature; yet there were, as Dickens and others were quick to recognize, unmistakable qualities in Collins's novels which raised them high above most other specimens of the class to which they appeared to belong. In his hands, fictional sows' ears were apt to turn out as silk purses; and the reviewer was faced with a problem which may be put briefly in some such form as 'Under what circumstances can a third-rate literary genre accommodate a first-rate work?' The modern reader, trained by such modern instances as the thrillers of Graham Greene, takes the paradox in his stride; but Victorian men of letters, many of them with a classical background, entertained stricter notions of a hierarchy of genres, and felt a genuine puzzlement at the difference between the kind of novel Collins appeared to be writing and the powerful and unignorable response of the reader.

Again, he was generally admitted even by hostile critics to be a supremely skilful fashioner of plots, and this inevitably raised the question of the importance of plot in the novel and its relationship to other elements—a question which had had a long innings in criticism of the drama, but which the nineteenth century found itself called upon to grapple with in relation to fiction. Yet again, Collins's remarkable experiments in narrative technique, though they offer no problems to the competent undergraduate of today, provided another test of critical understanding which Victorian reviewers did not always pass with honours. As late as 1889 a writer in the *Academy* could still urge that 'unbroken sequence of narrative is one of the greatest charms of a work of fiction', and the originality of Collins's use of multiple viewpoints had evidently taken his contemporaries by surprise.

Whatever our final estimate of Collins may be (and the implicit judgment of the *New Cambridge Bibliography of English Literature* in classifying him as a minor novelist, while granting major status to such writers as Borrow, Marryat and Reade, seems an extraordinary one), it cannot be disputed that he was widely read and widely reviewed during a longer period than almost any other novelist of his time. For this reason I have sought in this collection to illustrate, however incompletely, the reception of his books over his entire career. The novels of the 1860s, some at least of which have earned a permanent place among the acknowledged masterpieces of Victorian fiction, are represented relatively fully; the earlier and later works deserve and receive less space, but they have not been ignored. For while it may be argued that there is little profit or excitement to be gained from learning what an obscure or unknown reviewer thought of a forgotten novel, there is a sense in which the shape of the whole justifies by its interest a modicum of attention to even the apparently insignificant parts. The pattern of Collins's career in its entirety, that is, is unusually interesting as a case-study of the critical fortunes of one who would certainly not have objected to being described as a dedicated professional novelist.

The items in this collection have been drawn from a wide variety of sources—from dailies, weeklies, monthlies and quarterlies of various circulations and persuasions, as well as from private documents such as letters and diaries. Of special interest are the informal but often pene-trating judgments of fellow-novelists—Thackeray, Trollope, Meredith, Stevenson, James, and most notably Dickens, who was not only a fellow-craftsman and colleague but an intimate friend of Collins. There are some substantial essays, including survey-articles which attempt to assess his career as a whole; but most of the extracts are brief, and many have been abridged more or less drastically. The elbow-room enjoyed by the Victorian reviewer, though understandably the object of bitter envy by his present-day counterpart, was not an unmixed blessing: the articles of 2,000 words and upwards which were habitually devoted to a single novel encouraged prolixity, and the modern editor finds it necessary to prune, often ruthlessly. Moreover, Victorian reviews were often seen as serving a somewhat different purpose from those of our own time: they were apt to devote much space to lengthy quotations from the work in question and to summarize its plot in detail—a practice deplored in the 1860 preface to *The Woman in White* and else-where. Nearly all the reviews given appeared anonymously, but where it has been possible to determine an attribution with reasonable confi-dence the authorship has been noted. Attention has been confined to Collins's novels and short stories; the journalism, plays and public readings which were further outlets for his considerable energies are briefly discussed in the Introduction.

Collins was even more widely reviewed than this anthology suggests, and inevitably in assembling a collection of documents of this kind many will be culled and relatively few chosen. Even so, it cannot be claimed that the result is a body of consistently first-class criticism. Collins's critics were not all as intelligent, or as well-informed, as Swinburne and Henry James; yet a surprising number of unremembered reviewers wrote shrewdly and incisively, and even the limitations and prejudices of the more pedestrian pieces are revealing of the general context of taste and ideas within which the Victorian novelists, major and minor, worked. In understanding the climate of an age, the failures of comprehension and judgment among a writer's contemporaries may be as illuminating as the successes.

For willingly replying to my queries in the course of preparing this volume, my grateful thanks are due to Professor Alec Brice of the University of Saskatchewan, Professor Philip Collins of the University of Leicester, Professor Juliet McMaster of the University of Alberta, Professor Robert Patten of Rice University, Professor Gordon Ray of New York University, and Professor Robert Tener of the University of Calgary. The *Spectator* generously provided, through its Librarian, Mr C. A. Seaton, some useful information concerning the attribution of reviews; the assistance of the *New Statesman* is also gratefully acknowledged in respect of reviews which appeared in the *Athenaeum*. Two works of reference—the *Dictionary of National Biography* with its supplements, and the *Wellesley Index to Victorian Periodicals*—have been particularly valuable. Finally, my thanks are due to the staffs of various libraries—the Cameron Library at the University of Alberta, the Cambridge University Library, and the Library and Newspaper Library of the British Museum—for patiently searching out much dusty and unwieldy material on my behalf.

Introduction

I

The original publication of Wilkie Collins's novels covers exactly forty years, from *Antonina* in 1850 to *Blind Love*, left unfinished at the author's death in 1889, completed from his notes by Sir Walter Besant, and published in the following year. His career is thus longer than that of Dickens, Thackeray, Trollope, Hardy, and nearly every other Victorian novelist of note. Moreover, it straddles two distinct epochs in the history of fiction which the undiscriminating application of the label 'Victorian' should not be permitted to obscure. When Collins began to write, Dickens and Thackeray were at the height of their success; Trollope, Mrs Gaskell and Kingsley had been recently launched as novelists; George Eliot and Charles Reade were still to make their appearance. By the mid-1880s all of these writers were dead, and a new generation who were infants or unborn when *Antonina* appeared—a generation which included Hardy, Stevenson, Moore, Gissing and Kipling—had arrived on the literary scene or were on the point of doing so. Among these Collins remained, a lonely survivor of the mid-century generation, still prolific and, in spite of a widely-current posthumous legend to the contrary, still receiving his share of attention from both readers and reviewers. A study of his reception, therefore, affords a conspectus of four decades of periodical criticism, with their inevitable modifications in critical standards and attitudes. Reviewers of his early novels, for instance, instinctively turned to the 'Waverley Novels' as a fictional yardstick; a generation later, Collins has himself become a remnant of a disappearing tradition, and reviewers of the 1880s on occasion hold up his well-made plots for praise as something all too rare in the novels of the day. Nor is there any shortage of material for such a study: though the quantity and quality of critical attention were subject to variations, and though some of his books were damned as enthusiastically as others were praised, he was discussed, often at length, in several of the most influential journals right to the end of his life.

Professor Jump has argued that, partly thanks to the promptness with which they reviewed new books, the three principal weekly papers—

the *Athenaeum*, the *Spectator* and the *Saturday Review*—exerted an important influence on the reading public in the mid-Victorian period.[1] The first two of these journals both reviewed Collins's first novel, and both were still devoting space to his books forty years later; the *Saturday Review* was not founded until 1855, but it too soon became a regular recorder of his achievements and failures,[2] and the *Academy*, started in 1869 and widely read, also gave a full share of attention to the later novels. These were some of the journals which, through their articles and reviews, contributed so largely to the formation of contemporary ideas and tastes; and Collins received from them and others an impressive amount and continuity of critical attention. Even his disasters were apparently deemed interesting enough to be the subject of extended discussion: *The Fallen Leaves*, for instance, though by general consent then and now a dismal failure, received a 2,000-word examination by the vigorous and intelligent *Saturday Review*. One of the incidental interests of a collection of documents such as the present one is that it provides a convenient opportunity to estimate the consistency of critical attitudes, and at times to detect shifts of principle and tone, in a given journal over a considerable period of time.

During the generation before 1850 the annual output of fiction in England had steadily increased, and it has been estimated that about 100 novels were published in that year—four times as many as in 1820. (By 1864, less than halfway through Collins's career, the number had grown to 300.[3]) A reviewer in the *Spectator* on 10 April 1852 complained of the 'incessant production' of three-volume novels catering for the circulating libraries and accumulating on the jaded critic's desk like 'Chancery-suits'.[4] Yet the reviewer himself had come into existence precisely in response to the growth of the book-trade and the swelling weekly tide from the presses. Michael Wolff has suggested that the 'interposition of the reviewer between the important writers and the significant audience was a phenomenon of the middle third of the nineteenth century',[5] and the reception of Collins's novels offers an interesting and well-documented case-study in the triangular relationship between author, reviewer and public.

Nor, to vary the metaphor, did the current flow in only one direction, for where Collins was concerned the reviewers were not always allowed to pronounce judgment without contradiction, though it would be difficult to argue that he came off best in the long run. On at least one occasion his rejoinder took the form of direct protest, as when he wrote to the *Athenaeum*, in a letter published on 29 October 1859, indignantly pointing out the inaccuracy of their reviewer's description of the stories in *The Queen of Hearts* as reprinted 'from the pages of *Household Words*'. On the other hand, he showed a willingness to profit by well-founded criticism when the inconsistencies in *The Woman in White* pointed out by *The Times* reviewer (No. 30) were quickly corrected in a second edition. Habitually, however, he used the prefaces to his novels to anticipate or reply to critical objections: 'Mr. Wilkie Collins is fond of challenging his critics', said the *Spectator* in 1866, and others recognized the same trait in more astringent terms. His polemic is often vigorous and not without justification, though perhaps ill-advised, since the reviewers were generally in a position to have the last word, and his aggressive self-justification, so far from forestalling their attacks, merely provided them with a stick with which to beat him the more soundly.

But his statements concerning the principles and practice of his art have at least the merit of consistency. He repeatedly insisted, for instance, on his scrupulous adherence to what he called, in the preface to *Basil*, 'the Actual': 'Is not the noblest poetry of prose fiction', he demanded there, 'the poetry of everyday truth?' Similarly he announced in *No Name* 'a resolute adherence throughout to the truth as it is in Nature', and claimed in the dedication to *Poor Miss Finch* that the subject of blindness, previously treated by imaginative writers from 'the ideal and the sentimental point of view', was depicted in that novel 'as it really is'. He is also fond of citing legal and scientific authorities as a guarantee of the authenticity of his material: the legal points in *The Woman in White* have been checked, he assures the reader, by 'a solicitor of great experience in his profession', and the medical issues raised by *Heart and Science* have been 'submitted for correction to an eminent London surgeon'. The master of the sensational, it would seem, was also a dedicated exponent of realism. All these claims, however, did not prevent reviewers from finding many of his stories improbable and untrue to human nature, or from attacking his accuracy on matters of fact— indeed, his occasionally truculent tone may positively have encouraged them to take pains to do so.

The other main issue raised in Collins's prefaces concerns the integrity of his moral purpose. As early as *Basil* he refers scornfully to the disciples of Mrs Grundy, 'whose morality stops at the tongue, and never gets on to the heart'; and the battle with the Grundyites was to continue throughout his career. Nearly twenty years later, in the preface to *The Fallen Leaves*, he states, in tones worthy of G. B. Shaw, that he has 'nothing to explain' and 'nothing to excuse'; and in *Jezebel's Daughter* he points out bitterly that 'there are certain important social topics which are held to be forbidden to the English novelist . . . by a narrow-minded minority of readers, and . . . the critics who flatter their prejudices'—words that Hardy and others might still have been prepared to endorse after Collins's death. As the *Academy* observed (1 May 1880) of the dedication of the latter novel, Collins '[threw] down the gauntlet to his critics with appalling fierceness', and not surprisingly it was promptly seized by many reviewers: see, for example, the discussion below (p. 18) of the reception of *Armadale*. It is entirely to his credit that Collins was unwilling to accept what has been termed the 'young girl' standard of fictional reticence (one recalls, in the same period, not only Mr Podsnap but Leslie Stephen's advice to the young Hardy to bear in mind the 'country clergymen's daughters' into whose maidenly hands the *Cornhill* might fall); but his boldness in tackling unconventional topics undoubtedly provoked much critical hostility.

Another quotation from the prefaces—which collectively constitute a more interesting body of documents than those of most pre-Jamesian novelists—will illustrate a further aspect of Collins's relationship to his critics and readers. The preface to *Armadale*, dated April 1866, addresses itself to two distinct classes of reader: 'readers in general' and 'readers in particular'—that is, the public at large and the professional critics. His consolation for rough treatment on the part of the latter was to maintain the Johnsonian principle that it is, in the long run, the approbation of the former that is alone worth having. This consolatory reflection is one that he returns to more than once. The limited success of *The Fallen Leaves*, for example, prompts the remark (in the preface to its successor, *Jezebel's Daughter*) that its true recognition is yet to come: 'When the book is finally reprinted in its cheapest form—then, and then only, it will appeal to the great audience of the English people.' (The shade of Collins is still, one fears, awaiting that happy outcome.) In the assessment of his contemporary success, however, the implicit caveat ought not to be disregarded: he was keenly aware of the vast and growing mass of readers and potential readers who were deaf to the pontifications of the reviews; he was concerned to reach as much of that public as possible; and there were occasions on which a novel condemned by the critics nevertheless achieved a popular success. We must not make the mistake of supposing that published criticism is an infallible guide to the reception of these novels in the wider sense, by public as well as reviewers.

After the early novels, most of Collins's work appeared initially in

4

serial form in a wide variety of English and North American periodicals. His most enduring allegiance was to Dickens's two weeklies, *Household Words* and *All the Year Round*, in which most of his best work during the eleven years from *The Dead Secret* (1857) to *The Moonstone* (1868) was published; the only exception during that period was *Armadale*, which appeared as a monthly serial in the *Cornhill*. It might be supposed that serialization in a popular magazine would have an adverse effect on the subsequent sales of a novel in volume form, and on the demand for it by subscribers to the circulating-libraries. However, the *Athenaeum* reviewer's comment on *The Moonstone* (No. 54) suggests that careful timing by the publisher may often have produced a situation in which the unfinished serial actually helped to promote the sales of the complete work by reducing readers to a state of intolerable curiosity: the serial ran in *All the Year Round* until 8 August 1868, but the novel was published by Tinsley in three volumes the previous month, leading the reviewer to predict that 'those readers who have followed the fortunes of the mysterious Moonstone for many weeks, as it has appeared in tantalizing portions, will of course throw themselves headlong upon the latter portion of the third volume, now that the end is really come, and devour it without rest or pause . . .'. The novel of mystery and suspense as practised by Collins was obviously well adapted to retaining the attention of readers throughout a long run; but he rejected the charge of deliberately contriving cliff-hanging instalment-conclusions in order to hold his audience captive from week to week, claiming rather that his aim was 'to keep the story always advancing, without paying the smallest attention to the serial division in parts, or to the book publication in volumes'—a denial that should probably be taken with a generous pinch of salt.[6] From the reader's point of view, serialization seems unquestionably to have acted as a sharpener of the appetite. 'The weekly numbers of his tales', wrote a reviewer in *Harper's Weekly* (22 August 1868), 'are seized with the eagerness with which an important letter is opened and read, or rather devoured', whilst the *Athenaeum* reviewer of *Poor Miss Finch* made the interesting observation that 'his tales read best when we get them by instalments of three or four chapters at a time' (No. 63). In spite of his disclaimer, however, it says much for Collins's powers of construction that he contrived to execute his best work not only under the exacting conditions of the serial novel, but customarily in the brief instalments of the weekly serial.

II

THE EARLY NOVELS

At the outset of his career, Collins did not immediately discover his own supreme gifts for the novel of mystery and suspense. 'The biography and the classical romance', as Holman Hunt later observed somewhat grandiosely, 'were the trial pacings of his Pegasus.'[7] After a couple of preliminary canters, however, the young writer wisely decided to change his mount for a humbler beast. His first book was the *Memoirs of the Life of William Collins, R.A.*, a pious filial memorial in two volumes, published in 1848. It was reviewed with enthusiasm and at length— *Blackwood's*, for instance, gave it sixteen pages—but its favourable reception must be taken as a tribute to the father's celebrity as an artist rather than to any outstanding skill on the part of his biographer; and the prediction of the *Gentleman's Magazine* in April 1849 that it would 'soon take its place among our standard English books' has not been fulfilled. It has been plausibly suggested, however, that its detailed descriptions of the elder Collins's paintings constituted a kind of apprenticeship to the art of landscape description that was later to be a feature of the son's fiction.[8] The other book referred to by Holman Hunt was *Antonina, or the Fall of Rome: a Romance of the Fifth Century*, which was completed in 1848 and, after being refused by two publishers, was issued by Richard Bentley as a three-decker early in 1850. It represents Collins's single venture into a genre popularized by Bulwer-Lytton, the classical romance; and it was greeted, as its author later recalled, 'with such a chorus of praise as has never been sung over me since'.[9] When Bentley advertised it in the *Athenaeum* (16 March 1850) two weeks after publication, he was able to quote a full column of effusive praise from nine dailies and weeklies. The *Observer*, for instance, described it as 'a remarkable book', and the *Morning Post* hailed it as 'sufficient to place [its author] in the very first rank of English novelists'. In addition to these, *Harper's* (July 1850) lauded its 'splendour of imagination', and the *Athenaeum* (No. 2) and the *Eclectic Review* (April 1850) both compared Collins to Shakespeare. The *Edinburgh Review* (October 1850) referred to its great popularity with the public. All this represented an extraordinary triumph for the first novel of a young man in his 20s, though the voice of criticism was not altogether silent. The *Spectator* (No. 1), though praising his descriptive powers and 'painter's eye', found the heightened rhetoric wearisome and deplored the lack of 'nature'. In similar terms the *Eclectic Review* (April 1850) commended the descriptions but regarded the element of 'pictorial display' as 'frequently detrimental to the dramatic character of the work—causing the action to halt'; and, whether or not Collins consciously took its advice to heart, it was sound enough and strikingly prophetic of the direction his talents were to take:

Let him study thoroughly the art of construction, especially in making his story more compact and rapid in action, avoid excess of description to the exclusion of dialogue, and curb a slight tendency of redundancy to expression . . . and he will, undoubtedly, take a very high place in English literature as a romancist.

More sternly, H. F. Chorley in the *Athenaeum* warned him against 'the vices of the French school'. Nevertheless, Collins had every reason to feel satisfied with his first attempt at fiction; and when, a dozen years later, he wrote at the request of an unidentified French admirer a short account of his life and work, he commented of *Antonina* that its success 'decided my career'.[10]

Two unimportant books followed. *Rambles Beyond Railways* (1851) is an account of his peregrinations in unknown Cornwall; according to the preface Collins wrote for a second edition in 1852, it was 'very kindly received by the public'. *Mr. Wray's Cash-box* bears the date 1852 on the title-page but was actually published in December 1851—in time, that is, for the seasonal trade, for this is a Christmas story in the Dickens manner. *Basil: a Story of Modern Life* (1852) received more critical attention and is important as evidence of its author's growing awareness that 'modern life'—specifically, the Victorian middle-class domestic scene— was a rich source of material for fiction of a melodramatic cast. The novel of sensation, unlike the Gothic novel, was to exploit the notion that drama and mystery need not be sought beyond the Alps or in the past, but lie hidden beneath the surface of contemporary English life— 'the terrors of the cheerful country-house and the busy London lodgings', as Henry James was later to put it (No. 36). Many of the reviews of *Basil* were favourable, and *The Times* was much later, in its obituary notice of Collins, to refer to its 'deserved success' and to describe it as 'certainly the best of the early works of the writer' (24 September 1889). Among contemporary reviews, however, the *Examiner* commented on 'the skill with which Mr. Collins has wrought out a plot that in worse hands would be nonsense' (27 November 1852)—the kind of double-edged tribute that was to become standard treatment in later years. At the same time it is worth noting that the *Examiner* (under John Forster's editorship) was prepared to take Collins seriously as a writer of considerable promise in its discussions of his early novels: the review of *Basil* concludes by remarking that 'it points ... to a future in the writer's power that is no mean object of ambition'. Two dissident voices of some weight call for mention. The *Athenaeum* took up its earlier warning and deplored Collins's adoption of the 'aesthetics of the Old Bailey' (No. 6); not unlike a magistrate reproving a young man who had gone temporarily astray, it expressed the hope that he would put his undoubted gifts to better use. The schoolmasterly reproof that 'he *could* do better' was also the verdict of the *Westminster Review* (No. 9), where the attack was more forceful: it found the central incident of the novel, in which the hero learns of his wife's infidelity, 'absolutely disgusting', and was dismayed to find the author apparently writing without any moral purpose. This was the first of many attacks by the Grundyites, and Collins's note added to the original preface in 1862 seems to constitute a delayed reply to the *Westminster*'s criticisms: recalling that on its first appearance the novel was condemned 'by a certain class of readers as an outrage on their sense of propriety', he rejoices that, ten years later, it has succeeded in winning a place in the favour of the public at large. This was not the last time that he was to appeal to the verdict of the common reader in defiance of professional critics.

Two years after *Basil*, *Hide and Seek* again shows the influence of Dickens, to whom it is dedicated; the theme of the child of unknown parentage may well have been owed to the recent example of *Bleak House* (1853). Britain's entry into the Crimean War some ten weeks before the publication of Collins's novel caused readers to neglect novels in favour of newspapers, and its success was limited. When, seven years later, another edition was at last called for, he took the opportunity to add a preface blaming its lukewarm reception on the war. Disappointing though sales were, however, he had no grounds for complaint concerning the reception accorded to it by the reviewers. W. M. Rossetti gave it high praise in the *Morning Post* (No. 14), ranking it with the best of Dickens and Thackeray; the *Athenaeum* (No. 11) welcomed its more healthy atmosphere and expressed satisfaction that the author had 'ceased walking the moral hospital to which he has hitherto confined his excursions'; the *Spectator* (No. 10) also found it a great improvement on *Basil*, whilst the *Examiner* deemed it 'a delightful novel' and paid tribute to its humour and originality, concluding of the author that 'We designate him a true artist, and have faith in his future' (8 July 1854).

The same reviewer, however, found it necessary to sound a tactful warning against 'unconscious imitation' of Dickens ('an imitation of the part that is not imitable in the works of Mr. Dickens'). A later comment came from the *Saturday Review*, which greeted the revised edition with a marked lack of enthusiasm (5 October 1861), finding the novel 'feeble and forced, though not unpleasant'; while recognizing certain negative virtues—the absence of sermonizing, sentimentalism and bad jokes—it complained that Collins's method was 'too businesslike', and regretted the absence of lively dialogue and vivid descriptions.

Three years passed between *Hide and Seek* and his next novel. In the meantime he had become a frequent contributor of stories and articles to *Household Words* under Dickens's editorship. The two men had met as early as 1851, at which time Collins, still in his 20s, had recently published his first novel, whilst Dickens, the elder by twelve years, had just produced *David Copperfield* and was at the height of his success. Collins contributed to *Household Words* from 1852: his first contribution was the short story 'A Terribly Strange Bed' on 24 April, and a stream of others followed. Five stories which appeared between 1852 and 1855 were collected in *After Dark* (1856): among them, 'A Terribly Strange Bed' is probably his best short story; 'A Stolen Letter' may owe something to Poe but has also been described as 'the first *British* detective story'; and 'Sister Rose', though an insignificant tale, is noteworthy for its possible influence on *A Tale of Two Cities*. (Dickens described it, in a letter to Collins (19 March 1855), as 'An excellent story, charmingly written, and showing everywhere an amount of pains and study in respect of the art of doing such things that I see mighty seldom.') The collection was well received, the *Leader* (8 March 1856) observing of its author that 'no man tells a better story'. A second collection, *The Queen of Hearts*, followed in 1859: eleven stories, several of which had appeared in *Household Words*, are linked by a connecting narrative. Worthy of special mention are 'Anne Rodway', which was much admired by Dickens (see No. 20) and 'The Biter Bit', both experiments in the emerging genre of detective fiction; 'The Dead Hand', a horror story; and 'The Dream Woman', which looks forward to *Armadale* in its use of a dream as a foreshadowing of future events. In what was to become a familiar vein of criticism, the *Saturday Review* (No. 21) acclaimed the writer's skill as a story-teller while disparaging his conception of the novelist's vocation as confined to 'setting and solving a puzzle': his technical ingenuity savoured too much of calculation ('he never rises above a machinist'), and his stories suffered from a deficiency of 'characters which appeal to our feelings'. The 'pains and study' which Dickens, as a fellow-professional, had admired were seen as producing brilliant story-telling at the expense of the development of human interest; and the verdict, not entirely justified, that Collins's work combines masterly plotting with vapid and inadequate characterization was to become a commonplace of later criticism.

In addition to these two collections of stories, many of the articles and sketches written for Dickens's magazine were later salvaged for the two volumes of *My Miscellanies* (1863). A number of other contributions have never been reprinted.

By 1856, Dickens had come to regard Collins as a valuable contributor who had begun to command respect for his literary wares on the open market, and on 16 September of that year he informed his sub-editor Wills of his proposal to take Collins on to the staff of the magazine, adding revealingly that 'He is very suggestive and exceedingly quick to take my notions'. By the end of the year Collins had joined his staff of writers, and he remained there for more than four years, serving Dickens on *Household Words* and its successor *All the Year Round* until January 1861. Apart from the short pieces already referred to, four of his best novels appeared for the first time under Dickens's editorship. They collaborated regularly over the production of Christmas numbers, and Collins was later described by Percy Fitzgerald, a devoted disciple of Dickens, as 'perhaps of all his followers the most useful and valuable to Dickens'.[11] The relationship of the two writers, and the extent of the influence of each upon the other, have been the subject of extensive discussion and radical disagreement. Collins makes few appearances in Forster's *Life of Dickens* (though there is a brief but striking reference to him as 'one of [Dickens's] dearest and most valued friends'[12]); and some later Dickensians have been accused of following Forster's example in playing down the closeness of the association between the two novelists. On the other hand, Dickens's sister-in-law and eldest daughter, in editing his letters, referred to 'the affectionate friendship he had for [Collins]' and 'the high value in which he held him as a brother-artist'; and an ardent Dickensian, J. W. T. Ley, devotes a chapter to Collins in his account of Dickens's friendships, describing him as 'the great friend of Dickens's later years', and observing (though somewhat disapprovingly) that the latter 'came under Collins's spell to a remarkable degree'.[13] Edmund Yates claimed that Collins was Dickens's most intimate friend to the last;[14] and of their close personal friendship and the compatibility of their temperaments there can be little room for doubt. On the more difficult question of literary influence and indebtedness, there seems to be no consensus. K. J. Fielding has argued that 'from first to last there is no reason to think that Dickens owed anything in his development as a novelist to Wilkie Collins'—a view shared by Philip Collins and others. There are reasons for supposing, however, that the more elaborate plotting of Dickens's later novels was, in part at least, stimulated by Collins's rousingly successful example.[15] A tenable view is that 'influence', though difficult to demonstrate conclusively, was mutual, though not equally powerful in both directions. (Nor, indeed, is this suggestion a startlingly original one: as early as 1901, Thomas Seccombe wrote in the Supplement to the *Dictionary of National Biography*: 'The influence of Dickens is very clearly traceable in Collins's work, yet there is reason to believe that Collins had nearly as much influence upon the latest works of the greater writer as Dickens had upon him.') Incidental and minor debts are easy enough to trace—the reminiscence of the third chapter of *Little Dorrit* in the opening of *Hide and Seek*, for instance, or Dickens's use of situations from 'Sister Rose' in *A Tale of Two Cities* and the often-noted reappearance of the oriental elements of *The Moonstone* in *The Mystery of Edwin Drood*. More important and more pervasive, however, are Collins's imitations of Dickensian techniques of humour and caricature, and Dickens's adoption of the complex constructional qualities of the novel of sensation. His later novels, particularly *Our Mutual Friend* and *Edwin Drood*, show him moving more closely towards the class of fiction popularized by his friend. (T. S. Eliot is guilty of confusing the issue, however, in referring to *Bleak House*, written when Collins had scarcely begun his career as a novelist, as 'the novel in which Dickens most closely approaches Collins'.[16])

It was *Household Words*, again, which saw the first appearance of Collins's final novel of the 1850s, *The Dead Secret*. The reviewers were unenthusiastic when it appeared in volume form in 1857, the *Athenaeum* judging it 'only . . . moderately-successful' (No. 18), and the *Saturday Review* finding it 'scarcely equal to its predecessors' (No. 19). Both, however, deemed it worthy of serious and lengthy discussion.

Before the end of the decade, therefore, and after nearly ten years as a writer of fiction, Collins, now in his mid-30s, was an established author whose work was granted a full measure of attention by some of the most prominent and influential periodicals. Two notable tributes belonging to this period call for special mention. As early as 1855 the French critic É. D. Forgues, editor of the famous *Revue des deux mondes*, had published there a substantial essay, running in the original to thirty-four pages, on Collins's work to date (No. 16)—evidence of his growing European reputation. Forgues's criticism has been described as 'the most intelligent and constructive that Wilkie ever received',[17] and he seems to have recognized its value: 'I read that article', he wrote in 1859, in the 'Letter of Dedication' to *The Queen of Hearts*, 'at the time of its appearance, with sincere pleasure and sincere gratitude, and I have honestly done my best to profit by it ever since'. Forgues includes long analyses of the first three novels; he clearly regards Collins as a writer of exceptional promise, and his approach is enthusiastic though not uncritical. *Basil* is favourably compared with two other contemporary novels, *Jane Eyre* and *Mary Barton*; especially striking is the comparison of Valentine Blyth in *Hide and Seek* with a character in Balzac, not at all to the disadvantage of the English novelist. At home, two years later, Edmund Yates accorded him high praise in the *Train* (No. 17), ranking him fourth among living novelists, and drawing particular attention to his professionalism. It was the next decade, however, that was to see the production of the novels which made him one of the most popular of mid-Victorian writers and which have best stood the test of time.

III

THE NOVELS OF THE 1860s

Properly speaking, the new phase opens in the last weeks of 1859. Dickens had launched his weekly magazine *All the Year Round* on 30 April of that year with *A Tale of Two Cities* as the lead-story; four weeks later he was able to boast, in the concluding number of *Household Words* (28 May 1859), that the circulation of the new magazine 'moderately stated, trebles that now relinquished'.[18] As Dickens's serial neared its end, it was obviously crucial for him as editor to find a successor to the *Tale* which would hold, if not actually increase, this gratifyingly large audience. His choice fell on Collins, and in the issue of 26 November the final instalment of his own novel was followed by the opening pages of *The Woman in White*, which thereafter became the lead-story for the rest of its run. Between the two, Dickens inserted the following announcement (*All the Year Round*, ii, 95):

We purpose always reserving the first place in these pages for a continuous original work of fiction, occupying about the same amount of time in its serial publication, as that which is just completed. The second story of our series we now beg to introduce to the attention of our readers. It will pass, next week, into the station hitherto occupied by *A Tale of Two Cities*. And it is our hope and aim, while we work hard at every other department of our journal, to produce, in this one, some sustained works of imagination that may become a part of English Literature.

Dickens's hope and aim, although not consistently fulfilled throughout the magazine's career, were not to be disappointed in this instance. Nor were more tangible and more immediate evidences of the serial's success lacking. According to Percy Fitzgerald, publishing *The Woman in White* was 'one of [Dickens's] greatest *coups*' as an editor: it 'did wonders for the magazine, and the weekly portions were read— "devoured" almost—with an absorbing interest'.[19] The novel not only had a healthy effect on the circulation of the already flourishing magazine, but was a best-seller when it appeared in England and the USA in 1860. When Sampson Low inserted a pre-publication advertisement in the *Publishers' Circular* on 1 August 1860, they advised the trade 'to provide against disappointment in obtaining a supply of this work on the day of publication', and their optimism was justified. In London the first impression was sold out on the day of publication, and six subsequent impressions were called for during the next six months. Including it in its regular list of 'Books of the Quarter Suitable for Reading-Societies' in October, the *National Review* noted that it was 'probably the most popular novel of the year'. Public enthusiasm was manifested in '*Woman in White* perfume, *Woman in White* cloaks and bonnets, and . . . *Woman in White* waltzes and quadrilles',[20] as well as through more conventional channels. Not surprisingly, success bred imitations, and as early as 8 September 1860 *John Bull* commented, in a review of Terence Doyle's *The Two Households*, that it 'appears to have been in some measure suggested by Mr Wilkie Collins's popular title of "The Woman in White"'. Among Collins's more distinguished readers, the Prince Consort sent a copy to Baron Stockmar, and Mr Gladstone noted in his diary on 18 October 1860:[21]

I did not get to the play last night from finding *The Woman in White* so very interesting. It has no dull parts, and is far better sustained than *Adam Bede*, though I do not know if it rises quite so high. The characterization is excellent.

Thackeray was to read it 'from morning till sunset', and Edward FitzGerald to re-read it repeatedly (Nos 35 and 37).

Hall Caine describes in his memoirs Collins's reactions to the immediate reception of his novel, in which the letters from readers, brimming over with eulogy, were in marked contrast to the published reviews, 'nearly all as bad as it was possible for the good critics to make them'. This is not, however, quite a fair account of the book's reception, though a discrepancy between common readers and critics was by no means rare in Collins's case. 'The end of it was', Caine comments, 'that Collins lost all faith in review articles, and went the length of grievously underestimating their effect on public opinion.'[22] If his account is accepted as authentic, however, Collins's disgust was somewhat premature, for in the event the reviewers were far from being unanimously hostile. Favourable judgments eventually came from, among others, Mrs Oliphant, the young Henry James, and the anonymous reviewer in *The Times* (Nos 34, 36 and 30), though it may be noted in passing that Victorian book-reviews, especially in the monthlies and quarterlies, were sometimes an unconscionable time in appearing: Mrs Oliphant's *Blackwood's* review, for instance, did not appear until twenty months after the novel's publication. It must be added, too, that Collins had not only anticipated but perhaps to some extent provoked unfavourable reactions from some of his critics in his preface, in which he insists on the primacy of story-telling over other elements in the kind of fiction he has set himself to practise—a challenge to which reviewers with a taste for literary theory were hardly likely to fail to respond.

The same preface also refers to 'the warm welcome which my story has met with, in its periodical form, among English and American readers'; and the edition of 1861, which incorporates revisions prompted by the long review in *The Times* (see headnote to No. 30), again refers to the 'very kind reception' of the novel 'by a very large circle of readers', observations which may perhaps be interpreted as murmurs of defiance to the critics to do their worst.

The reviewing of a novel by *The Times* at this period constituted in itself something of an accolade, since its reviews of fiction were relatively infrequent. It was soon to return to *The Woman in White*, moreover: in reviewing *Great Expectations* on 17 October 1861, E. S. Dallas refers to the 'decided success' of Collins's novel with the public, but repeats the familiar complaint that its emphasis is almost entirely on plot, and such a plot as is 'not merely improbable' but 'impossible'. A few weeks earlier the *Sixpenny Magazine* (September 1861) had made the interesting comment that, as regards 'the artistic development of the story', Dickens's novel was 'almost equal to Wilkie Collins's extremely clever romance, which we regard as the greatest success in sensation writing, with the single exception of Mrs Stowe's deservedly popular work [presumably *Uncle Tom's Cabin* (1852)], produced within our memory'. The view represented by Dallas did not go unchallenged: in a long review in *Blackwood's* (No. 34) Mrs Oliphant recognized Collins's superiority to the sensation school in general, praising his naturalness and plausibility; and the *Spectator* attacked the notion that he was a mere fabricator of puzzles, and insisted on the imaginative and emotional qualities of the book (No. 29). The latter review is clearly a rejoinder to that which appeared two weeks earlier in the *Saturday Review* (No. 26). As these examples show, one of the main critical questions raised in discussions of *The Woman in White* concerns Collins's relative skills as a weaver of plots and a creator of characters—and, by implication, the Aristotelian problem of the relative importance of these elements in fiction. The depreciators saw him as offering plot and nothing more: 'Take that away,' as the *Dublin University Magazine* observed tartly, 'and there is nothing left to examine' (No. 31). His supporters, on the other hand, urged the vitality and originality of such creations as Count Fosco and Marian Halcombe—names often invoked in this context during the next hundred years. The more technical question was also raised of Collins's narrative method, and this too came under attack from the *Dublin University Magazine* in a long and consistently hostile review.[23] The use of a whole team of narrators, it complained, made for long-windedness and served no purpose. More good-humouredly, the *Critic* (No. 25) recognized the 'perfectly wonderful' elasticity of the narrative. The *Revue critique des livres nouveaux*, reviewing Forgues's translation of the novel in December 1861, noted the forensic influence on its narrative method: while questioning the wisdom of this technique, and observing that the book contained material equivalent to three or four full-length criminal trials, it acknowledged the author's skill in construction. Curiously enough, the *Athenaeum*, generally attentive to Collins's productions, did not review this novel, merely noting its appearance in a 'List of New Books' on 11 August 1860. One of the side-effects of the success of *The Woman in White* was the reissuing of some of Collins's earlier work.

Like its predecessor, *No Name* was serialized in *All the Year Round*; both there, and when published in volume form at the end of 1862, it achieved a considerable success. The first edition of 4,000 copies was nearly sold out on the day of publication,[24] and the financial rewards to the author were substantial. According to Edward Marston, at this time his publisher, Collins was a shrewd businessman who stood in no need of a literary agent to manage his affairs. The success of *The Woman in*

White had placed him in the agreeable position of having rival publishers compete for the privilege of paying him large sums of money for his copyrights, and for *No Name* he received £3,000 from Sampson Low, Son, and Marston. As Marston put it many years later in his reminiscences:[25]

This heavy payment was for a novel far inferior to *The Woman in White*, but following as it did so closely in the wake of that wonderful novel, it had a very considerable sale, and we came off without loss. It was a great risk forced upon us by very vigorous competition.

Once again, however, not all the reviewers were prepared to endorse the enthusiasm shown by Collins's public: the novel's central theme of illegitimacy inevitably encouraged those for whom 'wholesomeness' was a prerequisite of acceptable fiction to permit their literary judgment to be coloured by their moral disapprobation. *Blackwood's* (No. 44) referred in indignant terms to the 'pollution' of the heroine, and the *Quarterly* commented more coolly on the inconsistencies of the novelist's ethical position. But others, more concerned with literary quality, found much to commend: the *Athenaeum* (No. 39) praised Collins's 'creative and constructive powers', and the *Saturday Review* (No. 41) made a lengthy comparison between *No Name* and another recent novel in order to show, at the expense of the latter, Collins's excellence as 'an artist in the construction of fiction'. The review is in fact a sturdy defence of the importance of good plotting, and a comment on its rarity in contemporary fiction. A thoughtful review in the *Reader* (No. 40) makes the interesting suggestion that the English sensation novelist, unlike his French counterpart, was hamstrung by the requirement that his heroine should remain chaste. One of the novel's private readers, George Henry Lewes, confessed to finding it 'rather dreary': 'Perhaps because we have to read it aloud,' he wrote, 'the enjoyment is mitigated.'[26] What is interesting, however, is that such an arch-intellectual should have been reading a novel by Collins at all. In France, the *Revue critique des livres nouveaux* (June 1863) found it, in Forgues's translation, excessively melodramatic, but still a remarkable work which exhibited imaginative powers of a high order.

It was at this time that the term 'sensation novel' became current, thus identifying and drawing attention to a development in fiction that had been proceeding steadily for some time. The *Oxford English Dictionary* finds the earliest example of the label in the *Edinburgh Review* in 1864 ('sensation drama' had been used at least three years earlier); but

Professor Kathleen Tillotson has traced an instance in the *Sixpenny Magazine* for September 1861, where it is applied to, *inter alia*, *The Woman in White* and *Great Expectations*,[27] and certainly by 1863 reviewers were using the phrase as if it were already well established. (In an article on 'Sensation Pictures' in May of that year, the *New Review* comments that 'in an adjective form, the word "sensation" has come to us but recently from America'; the reviewer goes on to use the phrases 'sensation novel' and 'sensation play'.) It was at this time, too, that the sensation novel in general, and Collins in particular, began to receive the passing tribute of parody. *Punch* published in 1863 a five-part serial titled 'Mokeanna, or the White Witness', the contents of which imply an audience sufficiently familiar with the kind of material satirized to enjoy the joke. Later examples include Bret Harte's composite Collins parody 'No Title' (No. 52), the Rev. Francis Paget's *Lucretia, or the Heroine of the Nineteenth Century: a Correspondence, Sensational and Sentimental* (1868), and W. S. Gilbert's operetta *A Sensation Novel*, produced in 1871.

Collins had done well out of *No Name*: 'the amount reaches Four thousand, six hundred,' he wrote to his mother with pardonable elation; 'Not so bad for story-telling!'[28] Even more substantial recognition of his success soon followed. George Smith offered him £5,000 for a novel for his monthly, the *Cornhill*, and Collins wrote jubilantly (and probably accurately) to Charles Ward that 'No living novelist (except Dickens) has had such an offer as this for one book'.[29] The result was *Armadale*, in which Collins turned from the weekly to the monthly serial; it appeared in the *Cornhill* from the end of 1864 to the middle of 1866, and in the USA, in *Harper's Monthly*, at approximately the same time. The latter magazine had been suffering a serious drop in circulation, but *Armadale*, assisted by *Our Mutual Friend*, set it on its feet again: 'from the very first instalment [of *Armadale*] the old popularity began to flow back', and, before the end, 'the magazine had reached its former circulation'.[30] In May 1866 it was published in two volumes; this too was a notable success in the USA (an American biographer of Collins has claimed that 'it importantly influenced the course of American literature'[31]), but at home there was the now familiar contrast between its reception by the public and its treatment by certain reviewers, and yet again Collins himself helped to provoke the attacks by his preface, which contains a forestalling onslaught on the Grundy-ites. Distinguishing between his two audiences, the 'readers in general' and 'readers in particular', he predicted all too accurately that the latter would be offended by his boldness, and went on to insist: 'Estimated by the clap-trap morality of the present day, this may be a very daring book. Judged by the Christian morality which is of all times, it is only a book that is daring enough to speak the truth.' His prediction was no doubt self-fulfilling, and more than one reviewer took specific exception to the sentences quoted. The *Saturday Review* (No. 49) and the *Spectator* (No. 48), for instance, quote and reply to this challenge in their reviews of the novel; the latter journal's attack upon its morality and plausibility is distinctly acrimonious. The *Westminster Review* (No. 51) criticized the book and the school of fiction it was taken as representing more good-humouredly, ridiculing its improbabilities and concluding that 'sensationalism must be left to be dealt with by time, and the improvement of the public taste'. The Methodist *London Quarterly* (No. 50) was more seriously concerned about the effect on public morality of presenting in fiction such monsters as Miss Gwilt—'a portrait drawn with masterly art, but one from which every rightly constituted mind turns with loathing'. One presumes either that the reviewer had never read *Othello* or *Clarissa*, or that what was sauce for the classical goose was forbidden to the modern gander; and indeed this obscuring of literary qualities by issues related to moral education is characteristic of one kind of mid-Victorian approach to fiction. Chorley's criticism in the *Athenaeum* (No. 47) is on similar lines, but in much more vehement terms. The modern reader's interest in Miss Gwilt as a study in abnormal psychology comparable with Miss Wade in *Little Dorrit*, and as a type of femininity refreshingly different from the general run of Victorian fictional womanhood, is unlikely to be diminished by such considerations, but they were unquestionably of overriding importance for some at least of Collins's reviewers. Not all, of course, were troubled by these anxieties: as the *Saturday Review* sensibly observed, 'the real objection to *Armadale* is not that Miss Gwilt is too sinful to be drawn. The question is whether it is worth while drawing her, and what the picture comes to when it is painted.' One of the novel's most distinguished private readers, Bishop Thirlwall, was unimpressed, but evidently found himself compelled to read on to the end (No. 46).

Collins had made a start on *The Moonstone*, his fourth novel of the 1860s, by the middle of 1867, as Dickens's letter of 30 June (No. 53) makes clear. With it he returned to the weekly serial and to Dickens's editorship. William Tinsley, who eventually published it in volume form, later gave a vivid account of its success as a serial in *All the Year Round*: he wrote that *The Moonstone*[32] perhaps did more for it than any other novel that was printed in it as a serial before or since, not excepting *Great Expectations* by the famous editor himself. During the run of *The Moonstone* as a serial there were scenes in Wellington Street that doubtless did the author's and publisher's hearts good. And especially when the serial was nearing its ending, on publishing days there would be quite a crowd of anxious readers waiting for the new number.... Even the porters and boys were interested in the story, and read the new number in sly corners, and often with their packs on their backs....

That final vignette reminds us that Collins, like Dickens, succeeded in appealing to a highly diversified public composed of 'porters and boys' as well as intellectuals and public figures such as Matthew Arnold, Edward FitzGerald, Lord Macaulay and Mr Gladstone. His popularity was of an order that justified *The Times* in later observing (24 September 1889) of *The Woman in White* that 'everybody has read it'. Certainly by the time *The Moonstone* was published he was one of the most widely-read novelists of his day, whose books were to be found (in the words of a recent historian of Victorian publishing) in every drawing-room in the country, as well as in every back-kitchen.[33] (The anecdote, recounted by W. P. Frith, of the dinner-party at which 'a rude guest' said to Collins, 'Why, your novels are read in every back-kitchen in England', no doubt enshrines an insult that Collins was prepared to receive as an unintended compliment.[34])

In volume form *The Moonstone* sold well in both Britain and the USA. One of its earliest readers was the seventeen-year-old Robert Louis Stevenson, who wrote to his mother: '*The Moonstone* is frightfully interesting: isn't the detective prime? Don't say anything about the plot; for I have only read on to the end of Betteredge's narrative, so don't know anything about it yet' (5 September 1868). In the twentieth century it has earned high praise from, among others, T. S. Eliot, Dorothy Sayers and Alexander Woollcott, and has received more attention from recent critics than any of Collins's other novels. Its success with unprofessional readers has been no smaller, if one is to judge from its continuing appearance over the years in a multiplicity of editions and reprints. Contemporary reviewers were generally enthusiastic, though the *Spectator* (No. 55) and, in the USA, the *Nation* (No. 56) found nothing to praise, and the *Pall Mall Gazette* (17 July 1868), evidently irritated by Collins's claims in his preface to be taken seriously as a literary artist, launched an attack on the novel in a long review, comparing him to a mere 'conjuror at a country fair' whose appeal was to 'the vacuous curiosity of the schoolboy or the scullery-maid', and concluding fervently: 'as a creator of character, a depicter of the mutual play of character and circumstances, as a humorist, may heaven defend us from him!' On the other side of the account, tributes were paid by the *Athenaeum* (No. 54), *The Times*, which in a long and detailed review (No. 57) acknowledges Collins as the leader of 'the sensational school in novels', and the Philadelphia magazine *Lippincott's* (No. 59), which hailed *The Moonstone* as 'a perfect work of art'. Swinburne was later to blaze a trail for modern critics by pronouncing it the best of the novels (No. 83).

IV

THE LATER NOVELS

One might suggest, with truth if not with gratitude, that if Collins, like Dickens, had died in 1870, his reputation today would be in no significant respect different from what it is. In a study of his reception and contemporary reputation, however, 1870 will certainly not do as a terminal date. As it was, he outlived his friend by nearly twenty years—years of steadily continuing literary activity. He was never to repeat, or even approach, the breathtaking success of *The Woman in White*; but neither was he, as has sometimes been suggested, to witness the death and burial of his own fame as a novelist. At the opening of the new decade, indeed, his success showed little sign of waning, and in *Blackwood's* Mrs Oliphant opened her review of his next novel, *Man and Wife*, with the comment that it 'has probably by this time been read by most readers of fiction' (No. 62). Earlier it had appeared as a serial in *Cassell's Magazine* during the first nine months of 1870, and had 'pushed up the sales ... to well over 70,000'.[35] Like so many of the novels which were to follow, *Man and Wife* offered itself for evaluation on two separate counts—as a work of fiction, and as a piece of social propaganda; and inevitably its author was not always judged to have succeeded equally in both directions. 'As an indictment a failure,' announced a reviewer in *Harper's New Monthly Magazine* (September 1870), 'as a romance "Man and Wife" is pre-eminently superior to any fiction of the year.' Others agreed that Collins's hand as a story-teller had lost none of its cunning—a phrase that was to be revived on more than one occasion in subsequent years. Mrs Oliphant found the story 'full of power', and a writer in the *Saturday Review* (No. 60) confessed to having read it at a sitting, though both criticized the part played by

Geoffrey Delamayn and the author's attack on athleticism. The New York magazine *Putnam's* (No. 61), on the other hand, praised Delamayn as 'the finest study of character that [the author] has yet produced', but advised Collins to 'drop social abuses'—good advice to which he paid no attention. The Catholic weekly review the *Tablet* (1 October 1870), while admitting that 'the last two hundred pages are written with a power and a vigour which equal anything the writer has yet attempted', found much to deplore: 'The morality of the story is bad. It is unfortunately too much the fashion of the present day to slur over great sins and call them by soft names . . .'; and added severely that the novel had been discussed in its pages not on account of its literary merits but in order to draw attention to the state of the marriage laws.

In *Poor Miss Finch*, also serialized by *Cassell's*, the author's highly individual manner, with its peculiar combination of strengths and limitations, was again recognized. Due acknowledgment was made to his supreme ingenuity as a weaver of plots and his capacity for stimulating and sustaining the reader's interest; yet the *Athenaeum*'s concession that 'his cleverness is beyond all question' (No. 63) is accompanied by a damaging criticism—that whilst he is unquestionably a first-class entertainer, he does not really begin to represent life as it is, and that he is, in short, 'a very clever mechanist and a very inferior novelist'. Across the Atlantic, the *Nation* (No. 65) made a similar point: 'Whatever may be said against the vanity of existence, it is not all a combination of missing trains, listening behind doors, and mysterious meetings. That is all that Mr. Collins sees in it, and therein lies his weakness.' And for the *Dublin Review*, comparing Collins unfavourably to Trollope in October 1872, this latest novel represented a marked diminution of his powers: 'What a falling off is *Poor Miss Finch* from *The Woman in White*, or even its greatly inferior successor *No Name*!' Ruskin was later to attack it as an example of the unhealthy trend towards extravagance and morbidity in fiction: his 'Fiction, Fair and Foul' contains a contemptuous reference to 'novels like *Poor Miss Finch*, in which the heroine is blind, the hero epileptic, and the obnoxious brother is found dead with his hands dropped off, in the Arctic regions'.[36] The most positive reception of the novel I have found was provided by the *Spectator* in a review probably written by its editor, Richard Holt Hutton.[37] Although he begins in an unpromisingly familiar vein ('There is really wonderful ingenuity and originality in the plot of *Poor Miss Finch*, and when we have said thus much, we have said all we can for it'), and goes on to describe the heroine as 'one of the least attractive characters in modern fiction', he recognizes the skill and originality with which Collins has handled the scientific background of the story:

When we pass beyond the moral psychology of the plot to its optical psychology, it is far easier to speak with praise. No machinery more original and ingenious has been devised in our day, and though there are points on which we strongly believe that Mr. Wilkie Collins is mistaken, it is obvious he has very carefully studied the optical psychology of blindness, and the optical phenomena accompanying the first restoration of the blind to sight.

The reviewer concludes by affirming 'the very great merit of Mr Wilkie Collins's most ingenious and striking plot'.

Two additional outlets into which Collins's abundant energies were diverted may receive brief mention at this point. The preface to *Basil* had stated his theory that 'the Novel and the Play are twin-sisters in the family of Fiction:... the one is a drama narrated, as the other is a drama acted'; and his direct interest in the theatre found its expression in a considerable number of plays—both adaptations of his novels (*Miss Gwilt, No Name, Armadale*) and original dramas such as *The Red Vial*, which later became the basis of the novel *Jezebel's Daughter*, and *The Frozen Deep*, in which Dickens's performance of the leading role no doubt furnished him with the idea for Sydney Carton's self-sacrifice. Their success was very varied: among the adaptations, for example, *Armadale* and *No Name* were never produced, but *No Thoroughfare* (1867), written in collaboration with Dickens, ran for over 200 performances. A different kind of contact with the footlights was provided by Collins's public readings from his own work on his North American tour of 1873-4. A trial reading, based on the short story 'A Terribly Strange Bed', was given at the Olympic Theatre on 28 June 1873 as part of an entertainment which also included a lady reciting 'The Charge of the Light Brigade'. One member of the audience set down his recollections of the occasion many years later:[38]

He had little or no voice, and scarcely attempted to raise it. He seemed to think that the word '*bed*stead' was full of tragic meaning, and we heard again this '*bedstead*' repeated till it became almost comic. ... He was destitute of every qualification for his task.

Fitzgerald's portrait of Collins is, however, generally unsympathetic, and his memory may have deceived him in this instance, for *The Times* (30 June 1873) reported on Collins's experiment in much more favourable terms:[39]

Mr. Collins does not *act* to so great an extent as the late Mr. Dickens, but the manner in which he represented an old soldier shows that he is fully equal to the delineation of character, and his narration, quietly delivered, riveted the attention of the audience. His success was complete.

Collins can hardly have been daunted by the outcome of this trial reading, for he crossed the Atlantic and appeared before audiences in New York, Boston, Philadelphia, Chicago and elsewhere; but he obviously lacked Dickens's phenomenal histrionic gifts, and the American readings were, according to one of his friends, 'not so successful as he anticipated'.[40] That they should ever have been undertaken, however, is evidence of his considerable transatlantic reputation at this period—evidence confirmed by the serialization of many of his novels in American periodicals simultaneously with their appearance in Britain, and by their subsequent publication in volume-form and discussion by American reviewers. F. L. Mott, the historian of American periodical literature, mentions Collins together with Dickens, George Eliot and Victor Hugo as novelists who enjoyed 'immense popularity' in the USA in the 1870s, notes that his books were 'eagerly reprinted by competing periodicals', and quotes the New York *Citizen and Round Table* for 13 November 1869 as declaring that 'after Dickens, there is no living novelist who enjoys a popularity which even approaches that of Wilkie Collins'.[41] Nor was his American popularity short-lived: fifteen years later, the *Pall Mall Gazette* (4 September 1884), basing its report on the experience of 'a large wholesale and retail bookseller in New York', was to observe that 'Wilkie Collins has a host of admirers'.

More than a dozen novels were to appear during the last seventeen years of Collins's life, and about the decline in the quality of his work— variously attributed to ill-health, massive drug-taking, and over-productivity—there can be little disagreement. The view that he slipped into obscurity, forgotten by readers and critics alike, is quite unacceptable, however: there is no shortage of evidence that he enjoyed a continuing popularity during the 1870s and 1880s. Nevertheless, the legend was to grow up which presented a pathetic picture of the ageing novelist, lonely and forgotten, compulsively scribbling tenth-rate stories which no one cared to read. Perhaps the cautionary tale of Collins's descent into oblivion, *sans* readers or critics, owed something to Harry Quilter's statement, in an essay (No. 80) published in the year before the novelist's death, that, although still very widely read in Europe and America, his name was 'but rarely . . . mentioned in

England nowadays'. It is hard to see on what such an impression could have been based; possibly, like many another writer of an 'appreciation', Quilter was anxious to justify his own attention to the subject by exaggerating its neglect at the hands of others. In any case, the legend grew vigorously: in the last period of Collins's life, wrote Michael Sadleir in 1922, 'he suffered severe eclipse', and the melancholy metaphor was only slightly varied by a writer in *The Times Literary Supplement* nearly thirty years later who observed that by the mid-1880s 'Collins's sun had . . . long set'. For Sadleir this 'eclipse' completed an elegant but probably unjustified antithesis: 'Few novelists have enjoyed greater glory than did Wilkie Collins at the height of his fame; to few did loss of popularity in later years come more bitterly.' In the same decade Hugh Walpole claimed that 'by 1870 [Collins] had reached that sad decline into contemporary neglect that clouded all his later years'.[42] This fate may be no more than Collins's later novels deserved—but it hardly seems to fit the facts of what actually happened, and several pieces of evidence from the last years of his life point unmistakably in the opposite direction. In 1882 *Punch* published a cartoon of 'Wilkie Collins as the Man in White doing Ink-and-Penance for having written *The Black Robe*': he is shown surrounded by copies of some of his earlier books, clearly titled, and it is obvious that the reader's familiarity with Collins's name, and with his earlier and most recent productions, is taken for granted. As late as 1886, *The Evil Genius* was serialized in a large number of publications in many parts of the English-speaking world, as well as in several European countries, earning its author a larger sum of money than any other of his works; in the following year *The Guilty River* sold 20,000 copies in a week.[43] It was in 1887, too, that W. P. Frith declared in his autobiography: 'When I speak of Wilkie Collins . . . I shall meet with no contradiction when I say he is one of the most popular novelists of the present day.'[44] In the year of Collins's death, William Sharp, reviewing *The Legacy of Cain* in the *Academy*, spoke of him as a 'delightful story-teller whose best novels are still read with avidity or remembered with pleasure'. *The Times*'s obituary of Collins (24 September 1889), while acknowledging the artistic weakness of the later novels, affirms that they were read 'by multitudes of people'; and in the same week the *Athenaeum* (No. 81) observed that 'when his *Blind Love*, now appearing in the *Illustrated London News*, is concluded, modern novel-readers will be conscious of an unwelcome gap, which comes somewhat prematurely'—a striking tribute to a man who had died in his mid-60s after forty years of authorship! If this is 'eclipse' and 'neglect', it is surely a fate that many writers would gratefully embrace.

Collins had not lost his readers, then; moreover, as the later extracts in this volume make clear, the reviewers had certainly not forgotten him. As already noted, the *Athenaeum*, the *Spectator*, and other leading arbiters of taste continued to discuss his books at length throughout these decades and right to the end of his life. The novels of this final period are represented only very selectively and relatively briefly in the present collection, partly because their literary value is slight in comparison with the masterpieces of the 1860s, and partly because there are some inevitable but tedious repetitions in the comments of reviewers as novel quickly followed novel. Similarly, in this Introduction, the novels from *The New Magdalen* (1873) to *Blind Love* (1890) need be dealt with only summarily. Before beginning the roll-call of largely forgotten titles, however, two areas of recurrent critical attention may be indicated. His pre-eminence as a story-teller, a master of narrative structure and suspense, continued to be recognized, and reviewers were still ready to congratulate him on holding the reader's interest throughout a long novel. Thus the *Spectator* (No. 76) found *The Evil Genius* an 'extremely clever' story which 'commands the reader's attention throughout', and the *Athenaeum* (19 July 1879) could even detect a similar merit in *The Fallen Leaves*, whilst in the author of *Jezebel's Daughter* the same journal recognized 'the gift, which hardly any of his contemporaries possess in any degree, of inventing plots which are fascinating apart from personal interest in the characters' (20 March 1880). Reviewing *The Law and the Lady* in the *Academy* (3 July 1875), Walter Macleane described Collins, in a phrase which characteristically combines praise for his skill with devaluation of his achievement, as 'the most ingenious carpenter in the trade'. For some critics, though, this talent for plot-carpentry was a sterile and mechanical affair: the plots were found to be preposterous in their complexities and improbabilities, and the thinness of the characterization was judged a grave weakness. The *Saturday Review*, for instance, admitted in its assessment of *The Law and the Lady* (13 March 1875) that he had retained his narrative skill, but declared uncompromisingly, 'Characters he cannot draw, and manners he cannot sketch'; and in considering *The Fallen Leaves* (No. 69) it found story and characters alike improbable and absurd.[45] The *Spectator* (No. 71) had a similar complaint concerning *The Black Robe*, pronouncing 'unnaturalness' to be Collins's besetting sin and concluding that the novel 'lacks human nature'.

The other favourite theme of these later reviews concerns the degree of success with which Collins had sought to make an alliance between the sensation novel and the propaganda novel, grafting his convictions and prejudices about such diverse topics as prostitution, vivisection and the influence of the Jesuits on to the well-established stock of the melodramatic suspense story. The operation was not always found to be successful: of *Heart and Science*, for instance, the *Athenaeum* (No. 73) commented that the writer had 'hampered himself by trying to write with a purpose'—charitably adding, however, that 'he is so much more an artist than an advocate that, on the whole, his novel is good enough to make one almost fail to notice that it was written against vivisection'. Reviewing *The Legacy of Cain*, the *Spectator* (No. 77) came to a similar conclusion: 'Mr. Wilkie Collins may occasionally have a theory to illustrate, but he always has a story to tell, and the story is of more importance both to him and his readers than the theory.' Other critics were more severe in their treatment of his claims to be a novelist with a purpose: with heavy-handed irony the *Spectator* (No. 70) stated the case as follows in reviewing *Jezebel's Daughter*.

Is Mr. Collins, in fact as he declares himself to be in purpose, a moral reformer, or is he merely an ingenious story-teller? . . . Do his puppets exist solely for the sake of the dance, or is the dance contrived to elucidate the mechanism of the puppets?

Collins published eleven novels, as well as novelettes and stories, during the last sixteen years of his life; it is not surprising, therefore, that excessive facility was one of the charges levelled against him, though his fecundity was by no means remarkable by Victorian standards— Trollope, for example, and many less distinguished figures, wrote more books in a comparable career-span. Further critical reactions to this body of fiction may be quite briefly indicated. *The New Magdalen* seems to have been originally conceived as a play, and a dramatic version was written alongside the novel version. The former waited for production until February 1873, when it was well received and ran for nineteen weeks in London; the latter had meanwhile been serialized in *Temple Bar* in 1872 and appeared as a three-decker in 1873. *The Law and the Lady* was issued in 1875 by Chatto & Windus, who were to publish nearly all of Collins's subsequent novels. It was unfavourably received: the *Athenaeum* (20 February 1875), recalling its praise of his earlier work, and incidentally describing *No Name* as 'the best of sensation novels', observed that he had now perpetrated 'an outrageous burlesque upon himself'. The *Academy* (3 July 1875) also accused him of self-parody: 'he has played such fantastic tricks with his former works as must have made Mr. Mudie weep.' The *Saturday Review* (No. 67) took the opportunity of attacking the limitations of Collins's talents, and went on to dismiss his next novel, *The Two Destinies*, in even more uncompromising terms—but nevertheless examined it at length and in detail (No. 68). Collins's failures seemed capable of securing attention almost as readily as other writers' successes. The *Academy* (14 October 1876) criticized the 'wild improbability' of the story, and expressed a sense of disappointment: 'the reader feels wronged that when he has been expecting a really thrilling ghost-story from Mr. Wilkie Collins, and has given himself up to be startled, he gets only the somewhat monotonous hallucinations of two people of apparently weak intellect.' The *Athenaeum* (9 September 1876) and the *Spectator* (16 September 1876) were more moderate in their criticism, and *Harper's Monthly* (December 1876) even found something to praise, commenting that the author 'has used the supernatural with his usual skill'.

But it is *The Fallen Leaves* (1879) which enjoys the distinction of general recognition as Collins's worst novel—a judgment endorsed by Swinburne (who found it 'ludicrously loathsome') and Sadleir, as well as by most of the contemporary reviewers. Collins's claim in his preface that a 'scrupulous delicacy of treatment' had been exercised naturally succeeded in provoking the heavy guns of the *Saturday Review* (No. 69), who found it 'as unpleasant as a story can well be'. The condemnation was not unanimous, however: the *Athenaeum* (19 July 1879) printed a brief but laudatory notice, and the Congregationalist and Baptist *British Quarterly Review* (October 1879) praised the 'delicacy' with which a difficult topic, that of prostitution, had been handled, and concluded, with more generosity than discrimination, 'Everywhere we recognize the hand of the master in fiction'. It was at this time that Stevenson, in a letter to W. E. Henley (October 1879), frankly describing one of his own stories as a piece of 'carpentry', asked: 'who else can carpenter in England, now that Wilkie Collins is played out?' Something of the critical reaction to the provocative preface of *Jezebel's Daughter* has already been indicated; again the *Saturday Review* (20 March 1880) adopted a tone of dismissive ridicule, but the *Spectator* (No. 70), in a witty and fair-minded review, found the novel 'capital entertainment', provided that its moralistic claims were not taken too seriously. Repeatedly, indeed, one finds the censure of one review offset by the praise of another; and the conclusion must be that any account of

Collins's later work as having suffered a uniformly hostile reception has been based on a very partial acquaintance with the evidence.

The propaganda element in these late novels was at times a serious obstacle to critical approval. Thus the attack on the Jesuits in *The Black Robe* was deplored by the *Spectator* (No. 71), which found the novel 'rubbish ... but light and readable rubbish, [which] keeps up the interest throughout'. The verdict of the *Athenaeum* (30 April 1881) was more favourable, though it queried the accuracy of some of the legal details. The *Saturday Review* (28 May 1881) found occasion to criticize Collins's experiments in narrative technique, complaining that 'he cannot be content with the ordinary modes of writing a novel', but 'passes from one narrator to another as it pleases him; and, in utter defiance of all probability, makes any person that suits his convenience keep a diary or write letters at great length'. Even if it be granted that Collins overworks these conventions, his technique of story-telling is genuinely brilliant and original, and the strictures of critics who find merit only in 'the ordinary modes of writing a novel' fall somewhat oddly on modern ears.

Of *Heart and Science*, the *Spectator* (No. 74) expressed a generally held opinion, in an otherwise favourable review, in suggesting that 'the announcement that [it] has been written partly as a contribution to the literature of the Anti-vivisection movement' was an error of authorial judgment: Collins's attraction for the reader resides not in his powers as a social critic but in his 'simple skill in the art of narration', in relation to which the novel is 'most fascinating'. Many reviews of the period anticipate Swinburne's famous couplet (see No. 83):

> What brought good Wilkie's genius nigh perdition?
> Some demon whispered—'Wilkie! have a mission.'

and the later and no less effective jibe that Collins sold his novelistic birthright for 'a pot of message'. For these reviewers he was still, it seems, an Ancient Mariner (the *Academy* on one occasion, indeed (1 May 1880), made the inevitable allusion) who was capable of holding their attention so long as he confined himself to story-telling; but his moralizing and propagandizing was at best an irksome superfluity and at worst an offence against public morality.

The last four novels show unmistakable signs of fatigue, yet Collins's technical skill did not fail him even when his imagination ran dry. Of '*I Say No*' the *Athenaeum* (25 October 1884) commented that 'It is impossible not to trace the practised hand in the way in which Mr.

Collins has made a readable story out of most flimsy materials'; and the *Saturday Review* (No. 75), even while insisting that 'No one but the inexperienced reader ... could be deluded by the sundry false scents which the novelist trails across the true and obvious track', praised the plot as a 'genuine construction, a matter to be gratefully acknowledged in these days', and found the story 'eminently readable'. *The Evil Genius* was praised by both the *Athenaeum* (18 September 1886), which found in it 'many strong points', the *Spectator* (No. 76), which pronounced it 'extremely clever', and the *Academy* (2 October 1886), which improved the occasion by paying tribute to Collins as 'the greatest living master of narrative, pure and simple'. But the *Spectator's* verdict on *The Legacy of Cain* (No. 77) is more typical of the general attitude towards these final novels: 'we regard [it] as a comparative failure. We say comparative, because to a writer with such a wonderful gift of narration as that possessed by Mr. Wilkie Collins, absolute failure is all but impossible.' The *Academy* (12 January 1889) made the same point in observing that 'it would be impossible for Mr. Wilkie Collins to write a dull story'. The posthumously-published *Blind Love* earned little praise, the *Athenaeum* (1 February 1890) finding it 'not specially characteristic of its dead author', and the *Academy* also recording that it was 'disappointing and unsatisfactory', with none of the 'singular fascination' of its predecessors.

Before this time, Harry Quilter had contributed to the *Contemporary Review* the first overall survey of Collins's work (No. 80). Published more than a year before the novelist's death, it nevertheless has something of the flavour of an obituary article, frankly announcing itself as a 'eulogium' and an attempt to retrieve Collins from an undeserved obscurity—a claim that, as already suggested, may well be regarded with scepticism. Quilter finds the culmination of Collins's achievement in *Armadale*; he seriously underestimates *The Moonstone* and, more forgivably, ignores the later novels entirely; but his enthusiasm for the earlier books is genuine, and some of his detailed criticism of points of technique was in advance of his day.

Collins's death in 1889 was the occasion for a number of other general surveys, ranging from brief obituary notices in *The Times* (24 September), the *Athenaeum* (No. 81) and elsewhere to substantial and important critical essays by Swinburne in the *Fortnightly Review* and Andrew Lang in the *Contemporary Review* (Nos 83 and 84). Swinburne acclaims him as 'a genuine artist' who stands in the company of such novelists as Trollope and Reade in relation to a major genius of the order of Dickens rather as the minor Elizabethan dramatists stood in relation to Shakespeare—a judgment which still seems just. He pronounces *The Woman in White* and *The Moonstone* the best of the novels, and deplores the flirtations with the propaganda novel in Collins's later career. His conclusion praises the 'French' qualities of 'lucidity' and 'order' to be found in Collins's work—an interesting if unconscious turning of the tables on those reviewers who, more than a generation earlier, had noted the influence of French fiction with regret and alarm. Lang draws attention, fairly enough, to Collins's unevenness—the 'intermittent brilliance' which may be explained, in part at least, by biographical factors. He nominates *The Woman in White*, *No Name* and *The Moonstone* as the best of the novels, but does not share Swinburne's enthusiasm for *Armadale*. His final verdict is that Collins is a good second-class novelist, not to be compared with the highest practitioners of fiction because 'the *genre* of novel to which [he] devoted himself was lower than theirs'. Both critics give Collins the highest marks for 'construction' and narrative power; under this heading, Swinburne's comments on the 'shapeless' quality of *Little Dorrit*, in comparison with Collins's work, are striking.

One further obituary episode is worth mentioning. Shortly after Collins's death, Harry Quilter, who had championed him in the essay already referred to, wrote a letter to *The Times* (3 October 1889) urging that 'a suitable memorial' should be erected 'in Westminster Abbey or St Paul's', and inviting subscriptions. He refers to Collins's worldwide fame, and suggests that, in the development of fiction towards the status of a serious literary genre during the nineteenth century, 'five writers bore a chief part—Thackeray, Dickens, George Eliot, Charles Reade, and Wilkie Collins. Each of these possessed a unique gift. . . .' A subsequent note in *The Times* reported that a committee had been formed for this purpose, its members including Meredith and Hardy. In a leading article, however, the *Daily Telegraph* (5 October 1889) found Quilter's suggestion 'an ill-judged proposal' which called for 'resistance': while conceding that 'few Englishmen or Englishwomen of our generation have not been at some time or other under the spell of [Collins's] remarkable narrative power', it deemed his permanent literary value not such as to entitle him to a place among the nation's greatest. It may well be that the literary question was not unaffected by moral considerations, since the unconventionality of Collins's private life had been an open secret; but certainly the memorial never materialized.

V

AFTERWARDS

It is with a selection of these obituary assessments that the present collection of documents virtually comes to an end. For the next thirty years Collins received little serious critical attention—a fate shared, it must be said, with many other Victorian novelists and to some extent the effect of an inevitable reaction against the high Victorian achievement in the novel. It is true that his name makes an appearance in many books of memoirs and reminiscences,[46] but such references, though often adulatory, are in the main quite uncritical. He was omitted from the 'English Men of Letters' series, edited by John Morley, and received only a brief mention in most of the literary histories of the period: George Saintsbury, for instance, writing in 1913, praises his 'coarse vigour', but finds it sufficient to dispose of him in a single paragraph. On the other hand, the article by Thomas Seccombe in the 1901 Supplement to the *Dictionary of National Biography* is comprehensive and generally fair. His work was not forgotten by the reading public, however: since the complete works and separate titles were issued and reissued in Britain and America during these years, one must conclude that there was a steady demand for his books from old and new readers.[47] By the 1920s there were signs of a revival of interest at a scholarly and critical level. Sadleir, writing in 1922, although making no secret of his personal estimate of Collins as 'a writer for tired minds', admitted that his name was 'more familiar to the world' than that of Trollope.[48] T. S. Eliot published essays on Collins in 1927 and 1928,[49] in which he considers his relationship to Dickens and asserts his interest for the twentieth-century reader. Eliot's claims for Collins are generous without being excessive, and endorse the judgment of those Victorian reviewers who praised him as supremely endowed with the gift of holding the reader's interest: he has, says Eliot, 'the immense . . . merit of never being dull', and 'there is no contemporary novelist who could not learn something from Collins in the art of interesting and exciting the reader'.[50] One seems to detect in Eliot's remarks signs of his generation's increasingly sophisticated interest in fictional technique—an interest to which such experiments in narrative as *The Moonstone* were obviously relevant. A little earlier, no less austere a man of letters than A. E. Housman had confessed to a partiality for Collins: in a letter written to Eliot in 1926, he said that he would 'like to see him revived as they are reviving Anthony Trollope, whose merit, whatever may be thought of their comparative value, was of a much less singular and original sort'.[51] To the same period belong essays by Hugh Walpole and Walter de la Mare, as well as two more academic studies which include extensive discussions of Collins: Walter Phillips's *Dickens, Reade and Collins: Sensation Novelists* (New York, 1919) and S. M. Ellis's *Wilkie Collins, Le Fanu and Others* (1931). But it is from 1939 that the pace of scholarly interest begins to quicken, and the next decade sees a crop of articles in the learned journals and three American dissertations. At last, in the 1950s, a century after his appearance as a novelist, Collins's status was recognized by three full-length studies. Kenneth Robinson's *Wilkie Collins: A Biography* (1951) is a sound account of the life and work which draws on the surviving but still uncollected letters; it was widely reviewed, and earned for itself, and for Collins, the distinction of a long front-page article in *The Times Literary Supplement* (30 November 1951). Robert Ashley's *Wilkie Collins* (1952) is a short study written for an American series of introductions to standard authors; it represents a considerable feat of condensation and draws on Ashley's own extensive researches for his Harvard dissertation; but it lacks detail and documentation, and is no substitute for the more ambitious book that he was obviously qualified to write. Another American study, N. P. Davis's *The Life of Wilkie Collins* (Urbana, 1956), is lively and detailed, but takes excessive liberties in drawing biographical conclusions from Collins's fiction. The same decade saw half-a-dozen important articles on Collins in *Nineteenth Century Fiction* and the *Dickensian*. At the moment of writing, Collins's place in general critical esteem is perhaps sufficiently firmly established without inflated claims being made for him of a kind which inevitably produce an eventual reaction. Moreover—what would probably have given him greater satisfaction than the approval of academic critics and the attention of thesis-writers—his masterpieces still find no shortage of readers. *The Woman in White* and *The Moonstone* are included in most of the standard series, and new editions of both are at the moment in preparation; several other titles have been reissued in recent years; and indeed virtually all his fiction is now in print, a reprint firm having recently (1970) reissued the 1900 New York edition of his *Works* in thirty volumes. Radio and television adaptations have also proved popular. All in all it seems that his boast to be writing for 'the great audience of the English people' has proved neither hollow nor shortlived.

Victorian reviewers were not always quick to acknowledge that the house of fiction has many mansions; and their critical inflexibility sometimes led them to underrate Collins through judging him by largely irrelevant standards—the standards of a kind of fiction he never aspired to write. *The Times* was, indeed, perceptive above the average in remarking, in its review of *The Moonstone* (No. 57), that we must not 'murmur at Mr. Wilkie Collins because his primary aims are not those of Miss Austen or even Mr. Anthony Trollope'. But if he was not in the mainstream of the English novel, he was consciously and unashamedly one of the pioneers of the type of novel which contrives to enjoy a wide popular appeal at all levels while retaining the claim to be more than merely ephemeral. This makes him a figure of some importance in the history of literary taste in England—of literature seen, that is, at least as much from the point of view of its readers as from that of its writers.[52] A full assessment of his influence would need to take into account not only literature, serious and popular, but the art of the cinema—for example, in the work of Alfred Hitchcock and other masters of the 'psychological thriller', in which Collinsian plot-situations and character-types have a habit of recurring. (Enthusiasts of the genre will, for instance, recognize in the Mr Gutman of John Huston's *The Maltese Falcon* a latter-day Count Fosco.) 'Melodrama is perennial', wrote T. S. Eliot, 'and the craving for it is perennial and must be satisfied.'[53] The best of Collins has been satisfying that craving for more than a hundred years; and his modern readers are likely to be prepared to endorse the praises of his earliest critics without necessarily going all the way with their censures. In the words of one of his earliest posthumous critics, 'If his novels do not represent the highest possible development of fiction, he did an excellent thing in a better way than anyone else, and on that must rest his title to fame.'[54]

NOTES

1 J. D. Jump, 'Weekly reviewing in the eighteen-sixties', *Review of English Studies*, n.s. iii (1952), 244.
2 According to M. M. Bevington, 'Wilkie Collins was clever enough to get the grudging admiration of the *Saturday Review*, and not profound enough to earn its respect' (*The Saturday Review 1855–1868* (New York, 1941), 193). Not all the examples in this collection bear out Bevington's verdict, however.
3 G. H. Ford, *Dickens and his Readers* (Princeton, 1955), 26.

4 *Spectator*, xxv (1852), 349.

5 M. Wolff, 'Victorian reviewers and cultural responsibility', in *1859: Entering an Age of Crisis*, ed. P. Appleman *et al.* (Bloomington, 1959), 286.

6 Quoted by G. L. Griest, *Mudie's Circulating Library and the Victorian Novel* (Bloomington, 1970), 104–5.

7 W. Holman Hunt, *Pre-Raphaelitism and the Pre-Raphaelite Brotherhood* (1905), ii, 185–6.

8 K. Robinson, *Wilkie Collins: a Biography* (1951), 47.

9 Quoted by R. Ashley, *Wilkie Collins* (1952), 29.

10 Quoted by M. L. Parrish and E. V. Miller, *Wilkie Collins and Charles Reade* (1940), 4.

11 P. Fitzgerald, *Memories of Charles Dickens* (1913), 260. The book utilizes material which had earlier appeared in Fitzgerald's *Memoirs of an Author* (1894).

12 J. Forster, *Life of Charles Dickens* (1966), ii, 73.

13 *The Letters of Charles Dickens*, ed. G. Hogarth and M. Dickens (1893), 263; J. W. T. Ley, *The Dickens Circle* (1918), 286. See also Ley's 'Wilkie Collins' Influence upon Dickens', *Dickensian*, xx (1924), 65–9; A. A. Adrian, 'A note on the Dickens-Collins friendship', *Huntington Library Quarterly*, xvi (1952–3), 211–13; R. P. Ashley, 'Wilkie Collins and the Dickensians', *Dickensian*, xlix (1953), 59–64; K. J. Fielding, 'Dickens and Wilkie Collins: a reply', *ibid.*, 130–6.

14 *E. Yates: his Recollections and Experiences* (1884), ii, 93.

15 Fielding, *op. cit.*; P. Collins, *Dickens and Crime* (1964), 352. For dissenting views, see Ashley's article cited in note 13, and M. Allott, *Novelists on the Novel* (1959), 179.

16 T. S. Eliot, *Selected Essays* (1951), 461. Cf. also Eliot's 1928 Introduction to the 'World's Classics' edition of *The Moonstone*: 'the work of Dickens after 1850 would not be what it is but for the reciprocal influence of Collins' (v).

17 N. P. Davis, *The Life of Wilkie Collins* (Urbana, 1956), 181.

18 Reliable circulation figures for Dickens's magazines are very hard to obtain. Figures sometimes suggested for *Household Words* (such as W. E. Buckler's of 950,000 at one point) are almost certainly grossly exaggerated; Edgar Johnson's estimate of 40,000 is likely to be nearer the truth, and Professor Robert L. Patten, basing his calculations on profits, has arrived at an average sales figure somewhat below 39,000. *All the Year Round*, therefore, may have started in the region of 120,000, and seems to have approached the impressive figure of 300,000 at its peak. (See Buckler, 'Dickens's success with *Household Words*', *Dickensian*, xlvi (1950), 198–9; Johnson, *Charles Dickens: his Tragedy and Triumph* (1952), 946–7.)

19 Fitzgerald, *op. cit.*, 203, 221–2.

20 Robinson, *op. cit.*, 149.

21 Quoted by A. Cruse, *The Victorians and their Books* (1935), 322.

22 Hall Caine, *My Story* (New York, 1909), 329–30.

23 The journal thus showed a striking shift of attitude towards Collins since its review of *Basil* (No. 8).

24 Robinson, *op. cit.*, 168.

25 E. Marston, *After Work: Fragments from the Workshop of an Old Publisher* (1904), 86.

26 Letter of 10 May 1862, in *The George Eliot Letters*, ed. G. Haight (New Haven, 1954), iii, 203.

27 Preface to the 'Riverside' edition of *The Woman in White* (Boston, 1969), xii.

28 Robinson, *op. cit.*, 169.

29 *Ibid.*, 178.

30 J. H. Harper, *The House of Harper* (New York, 1912), 233.

31 Davis, *op. cit.*, 246.

32 W. Tinsley, *Random Recollections of an Old Publisher* (1900), i, 114–15.

33 S. Nowell-Smith, *The House of Cassell 1848–1958* (1958), 122.

34 W. P. Frith, *My Autobiography and Reminiscences* (1887), ii, 334.

35 Robinson, *op. cit.*, 236.

36 'Fiction, fair and foul' was originally published in the *Nineteenth Century* (June 1880–October 1881); it is reprinted in *The Works of John Ruskin*, ed. E. T. Cook and A. Wedderburn (1908), xxxiv (see pp. 227–8 for the passage cited).

37 Attributed to Hutton on internal evidence by Professor Robert Tener (private communication). The review appeared on 2 March 1872.

38 Fitzgerald, *op. cit.*, 261.

39 *The Times* (30 June 1873), 10.

40 W. Reeve, 'Recollections of Wilkie Collins', *Chambers' Journal*, ix (1905–6), 461. See also C. K. Hyder, *Wilkie Collins in America* (Kansas, 1940).

41 F. L. Mott, *A History of American Magazines 1865–1885* (Cambridge, Mass., 1938), 223, 251.

42 M. Sadleir, *Excursions in Victorian Bibliography* (1922), 129; *The Times Literary Supplement* (30 November 1951), 757; H. Walpole, 'Novelists of the seventies', in *The Eighteen-Seventies*, ed. H. Granville-Barker (Cambridge, 1929), 30.

43 Reeve, *op. cit.* Robinson notes (*op. cit.*, p. 311) that Collins at this period 'was still able to earn large sums with every book he wrote'. A few years earlier Collins himself had written, not untruthfully, in a letter to Frances Power Cobbe (23 June 1882), 'I am writing to a very large public both at home and abroad . . .' (*The Life of Frances Power Cobbe as Told by Herself* (1904), 559).

44 Frith, *op. cit.*, ii, 333.

45 See note 2 above.

46 For a useful list of minor material, see L. Stevenson, ed., *Victorian Fiction: a Guide to Research* (Cambridge, Mass., 1964), 282–3 (the section on Collins is by R. P. Ashley).

47 Ashley, in his unpublished Harvard dissertation (1948), concludes from an examination of British and American lists of books in print for the period

that there is no foundation for the view that Collins was forgotten by readers for a generation after his death. In his later survey of Collins scholarship (see note 46 above), he states that 'the complete works were apparently kept in print until 1925, with separate titles available after that date'.

48 Sadleir, *op. cit.*, 129.

49 T. S. Eliot, 'Wilkie Collins and Dickens', *The Times Literary Supplement* (4 August 1927), 525–6, reprinted in *Selected Essays* (1951), 460–70; Introduction to the 'World's Classics' edition of *The Moonstone* (1928). These two essays, though containing some duplication of material, are by no means identical—a fact apparently not always recognized by bibliographers of Eliot and Collins.

50 T. S. Eliot, *Selected Essays*, 468–9.

51 *The Letters of A. E. Housman*, ed. H. Maas (1971), 235. In another letter to Eliot (p. 262) Housman comments briefly on several of Collins's novels.

52 'A full knowledge of [Collins's] work is essential to a full understanding of the literary tastes of the mid-nineteenth-century reading public', according to an anonymous reviewer of N. P. Davis's book, *Notes & Queries*, ccii (1957), 183.

53 T. S. Eliot, *Selected Essays*, 460.

54 H. Chartres, 'Wilkie Collins', *London Society*, lvi (November 1889), 523.

Note on the Text

The documents in this collection are reproduced as they originally appeared, except that a few obvious misprints have been silently corrected and the punctuation has been regularized on the rare occasions when it might otherwise be confusing or distracting to the modern reader. Texts are given in their entirety unless omissions are indicated; where necessary a brief summary of the omitted sections has been provided. Where a reviewer quotes at length from one of Collins's novels, a simple reference to the passage in question by chapter-number and opening and closing words has been substituted. Footnotes by the present editor are numbered and those in the original are marked with an asterisk. In all references to published works the place of publication is London unless otherwise stated.

ANTONINA

Published in three volumes by Richard Bentley on 27 February 1850. It appeared in the USA in the same year.

1. From an unsigned review, *Spectator*

11 March 1850, xxiii, 257

Mr. Collins has succeeded better in his romance of the fifth century than might have been expected from his previous training as a biographical writer, or the choice of a theme so remote from our own experience, and an age of whose manners few pictures have been preserved. Indeed, this latter difficulty is rather evaded by the style of composition than overcome. Mr. Collins is a follower of the school of Chateaubriand and Bulwer; possessing many of their merits, but with the inherent defects of the rhetorical style. Everything is pictured in too high a key. . . . For a brief space this artificial manner is striking, but for a long spell the reader desires the repose, the congruity, the variety of nature. In the rhetorical school, the narrative stalks on stilts; the descriptions have too much of the glare and mannerism of the scene-painter; the motives and emotions of the characters partake too much of 'King Cambyses' vein'; and the dialogue itself has too unvarying a strain of grandiloquence. Nature and the subject are both made subservient to the composition of the writer: usually there is not the thing but the rhetorician's exaggeration. There is, too, a tendency to stop the story for reflections, with a disposition to resort to startling contrast, strong effects, and glitter; not only 'o'erstepping the modesty of Nature', but tricking her out for the claptrap of the stage. When freshly taken, or only read by sections, all this, as we have just observed, is very striking; but it palls in continuance: to which the uniform and artificial character of the style contribute. The reader is tired, not so much by writing, as by 'composition'.

From the inherent defects of his school Mr. Collins is not free, especially from the last fault we have mentioned: but *Antonina* is an able, a skilful, and a powerful romance. The author has a painter's eye for description, much eloquence of a florid kind, clever 'treatment' and invention in the incidents, with some tenderness if not pathos. He has studied his subjects so as to be possessed with distinct historical ideas of the age. He comprehends the classes, costumes, and qualities of the period, if he has not caught its living manners. . . .

2. H. F. Chorley, unsigned review, *Athenaeum*

16 March 1850, 285

Henry Fothergill Chorley (1808–72) was on the staff of the *Athenaeum* from 1833, and was its most prolific reviewer for more than thirty years. (See L. A. Marchand, *The Athenaeum: A Mirror of Victorian Culture* (Chapel Hill, 1941), 181–93; H. G. Hewlett, *Henry Fothergill Chorley: Autobiography, Memoir and Letters* (1873).) As well as reviewing a wide range of literature, he wrote much music criticism and a series of uniformly unsuccessful novels, plays and poems. 'As years grew upon him,' wrote Richard Garnett in the *Dictionary of National Biography*, 'his criticism became more and more tinctured with acerbity': for his review of *Armadale* sixteen years after *Antonina*, see No. 47. See also the headnotes to Nos 6 and 18 on the question of erroneous attributions to Chorley.

The indifference with which the average reader—disconsolate in the recollection of many failures—may naturally regard a new classical romance, will not long 'serve his turn' when *Antonina* is opened. It is a richly-coloured impassioned story, busy with life, importunately strong in its appeals to our sympathy—one which claims rank not far behind the antique fictions of Lockhart, Croly, Bulwer and Ward. Mr. Collins is possibly less deeply scholastic, less precisely antiquarian than many of his predecessors; but his dramatic instinct makes up for want of elaborate training. Goth and Roman, Christian and Pagan are contrasted by him with a power which no closet study can give. In their vitality we have a glimmer of that burning breathing life which the Warwickshire deer-stealer could throw into his *Cleopatra*, and *Cressida*, and *Coriolanus*, and *Brutus*. This, as we have a thousand times said, commands, and will win, the crown. The subject selected by Mr. Collins is one tempting an inventor to details which shock the sense. The revenge of the Gothic woman Goisvintha, made frantic by the murder of her children at the siege of Acquileia—the famine in the City of the Caesars,—the hideous death-banquet of the Patrician Vetranio, (sad imitation of the last revel of Sardanapalus)—the sacrifice of the idol-worshipper in his temple—all fall naturally within the scope of a legend of 'The Fall of Rome.' All are incidents and catastrophes in painting or in penning which the waiting-gentlewoman's palette and crow-quill as implements would become offensive by reason of their unbefitting feebleness. Still, we must warn Mr. Collins against the vices of the French school,—against the needless accumulation of revolting details,—against catering for a prurient taste by dwelling on such incidental portions of the subject as, being morbid, ought to be treated incidentally. Need we remind a painter's son how much Terror and Power are enhanced by Beauty? There is possibly no more rivetting picture in the world than Da Vinci's *Medusa* in the Florence Gallery,—yet how calm it is as compared with many a *Mater dolorosa* by inferior hands.—This caution given, we have little to do but repeat our commendations. The extent and complexity of Mr. Collins's pictures prevent our extracting any scene which could afford a fair idea of his manner;—but we have little fear that any romance-reader who takes up this book on our warrant will accuse us of exaggerated praise.

3. From an unsigned review, *Bentley's Miscellany*

April 1850, xxvii, 375–8

The passage given is the final paragraph of a long article which is less a review of Collins's novel than an essay on ancient Rome.

But the work is not more remarkable for its admirable delineation of the characters it brings out, than for the learning and perfect acquaintance of the habits and feelings of the times it alludes to; everything is truthful about it; it represents Rome as it was, and the Romans as they were, with all their insolence and recklessness, their idleness and improvidence. What we know through their poets and historians of the manners and daily life of the inhabitants of imperial Rome, even so, in every tittle, do we find our knowledge confirmed by these volumes, and, therefore, as an historical work, we can very highly recommend it. Its fiction even is founded upon truth, and perhaps no historical romance was ever published that is so entirely free from misrepresentation of facts, or that so entirely agreed with the assertions of history. The author, in his first work, has stepped into the first rank of romance writers.

4. From an unsigned review, *Gentleman's Magazine*

April 1850, n.s. xxxiii, 408–9

It is our intention shortly to offer some general remarks on the rather numerous historical romances which have been published within the last two or three months; but the one whose title we here give, which has come to us the last, is so remarkable a production that we will not wait for our proposed article on such romances in general before we recommend it to our readers. The first work of a new aspirant after fame in this class of literature, it is one sufficient in itself to entitle its author to a place in the foremost rank.

Mr. Collins has chosen for his theme a period of history with which people in general are but slightly acquainted, but which from the mystery in which most of its transactions are wrapped, and from their wild, fitful character, furnishes a rich mine of romantic materials. The mightiest empire that the world had ever seen, sunk into the feebleness and imbecility of old age; a people who had once excited astonishment by their masculine character, degenerated into the last stage of effeminacy; new people and young nations rising up around in the first rough, unfashioned grandeur of that strength which was soon to change the face of Europe,—all these afford in an extraordinary degree the bold scenes and contrasts necessary to give interest and character to such a work. Even the difficulty which appeared most formidable, that of making the modern reader interested in scenes and manners so far removed from those which he is accustomed to contemplate, has been encountered and overcome with skill; and yet Mr. Collins's *Antonina* presents no slight, superficial sketch of the history of the time, but shows a profound study of the history of Rome's latter days, and even presents us sometimes with deep philosophic views. It is, in fact, history as well as romance; to readers who seek the former, it offers a clear and distinct picture, such as perhaps they would find with difficulty elsewhere, of the causes of the final ruin of the Roman empire, and of the state of society which produced and accompanied it; while to the other it is a beautiful and touching story, full of incident and feeling. To realise this, is the chief and highest aim of historical romance. . . .

[High praise of Collins's descriptive powers follows: an episode is cited as 'one of the most powerfully-written chapters we have ever read'.]

These are some of the bolder characters in the romance of *Antonina*. As we shall have reason to speak of it again, we will only at present give it a recommendation as one of the most remarkable publications of the present season. Although scarcely any of its characters are historical personages, it possesses some of the most valuable characteristics of history, from the very circumstance that it is more easy to create a personage who embodies the whole character of his age than to find one; as a romance it is full of attractions of no ordinary character.

BASIL

Published in three volumes by Richard Bentley on 16 November 1852. A later edition in one volume (1862) incorporates minor revisions. It appeared in the USA under the title *The Crossed Path*.

5. From an unsigned review, *Bentley's Miscellany*

November 1852, xxxii, 576–86

A double review of *Basil* and Thackeray's *The History of Henry Esmond* (1852).

We have put these two books 'over against' each other, to use one of Mr. Thackeray's favourite Queen Anne-isms, because they have no kind of family resemblance. They are, indeed, as unlike each other as any two books can be. They constitute a kind of literary antithesis. Both have very striking merit—but their merits are of an adverse and conflicting character. There is the same difference between them as between a picture by Hogarth and a picture by Fuseli. We had well nigh named in the place of the former one of the great painters, whose names are borne by the author of *Basil*. But in truth the writer of that work ought to have been called Mr. Salvator Fuseli. There is nothing either of Wilkie or Collins about it.

Mr. Thackeray has written a work remarkable for its extreme quietude. There are no highly-wrought scenes from the beginning to the end of the drama. There is not anywhere a trace of exaggeration. The reader, indeed, is never excited into anything stronger than a gentle glow. But *Basil*—although a story of to-day, although all its

45

accidental environments are of the most ordinary character, although the scene is laid in a scarce-finished suburban square (say in Brompton or Camden Town), although some of the personages are nothing more romantic than London linen-drapers, although the whole action of the drama rises out of an every-day omnibus adventure—is a story remarkable for nothing so much as its intensity—for the powerful excitement which it must produce in every breast, not absolutely containing a mass of stone in place of a human heart. Both romances are admirable in their way, and both are likely to number readers by thousands.

[A long discussion of Thackeray's novel follows, concluding with praise of the style of *Esmond*: it is written 'in the manner of a complete gentleman of Queen Anne's time'.]

To write effectively of *Basil* we ought to have another vocabulary at command. It is a story of love and hatred—of passionate love and deep vindictive hatred. The *intense* everywhere predominates. It is of the Godwin school of fiction. A single grand idea runs through the whole. There is a striking unity of purpose and action in it. The interest is single—undivided. The fatality of the Greek tragedians broods over the drama. There is a Nemesis not to be escaped. The hero of the tale sees a pretty girl in an omnibus; and he—goes to his doom.

[An outline of the early stages of the story follows.]

Out of this state of things arises a tremendous tragedy, developed, in these volumes, with remarkable power. We shall say nothing to weaken the absorbing interest which the perusal of such a story must excite. It is something not to be forgotten. The novel-reader may devour scores of fictions afterwards; but they will not efface the recollection of this. . . .

The book is one that is sure to excite attention. It is not by any means a faultless work, but the faults are, for the most part, the faults of genius. We hesitate to pronounce anything improbable. There are many of us whose lives are so full of improbabilities, that a faithful chronicle of the incidents even of a seemingly uneventful career, would be received with incredulity by the majority of readers. That *Basil* will be pronounced 'improbable' we do not doubt. There is a startling antagonism between the intensity of the passion, the violent spasmodic action of the piece, and its smooth, common-place environments. The scenery, the *dramatis personæ*, the costumery, are all of the most familiar every-day type, belonging to an advanced stage of civilization; but there is something rude and barbarous, almost Titanic, about the incidents; they belong to a different state of society. But this very discrepancy enhances the terror of the drama; and there is something artist-like even in this apparent want of art.

6. D. O. Maddyn, unsigned review, *Athenaeum*

4 December 1852, 1322–3

This and some subsequent reviews of Collins's novels have been attributed to H. F. Chorley, whom N. P. Davis (312, n. 51) describes as 'the *Athenaeum* reviewer who pre-empted Wilkie's books as his special field'. The editorial records, however, identify the author of this piece as D. Owen Maddyn, who reviewed regularly for the *Athenaeum*; the 'we' of the fifth sentence is, therefore, presumably to be taken as referring to the collective voice of the journal rather than to that of any individual contributor.

The paucity of good novels amongst our recent fictions, and the merits of this writer's former production, made us turn with interest to his new work. That interest has been disappointed. *Basil* is a piece of romantic sensibility,—challenging success by its constant appeal to emotion, and by the rapid vehemence of its highly wrought rhetoric. We had hoped that the author would in his second publication have become more reflective,—and that he would have studied literary art in another school than that to which we fear he has irrevocably devoted himself. Amidst our praise of *Antonina*, we warned him against the exaggeration of the French school and 'its accumulated horrors.' [See p. 41 above.] He has prefaced his present work with an explanation of his views of Art in fiction, occupying a score of pages; and we must say that its crude criticism is practically refuted even by his own story.

Mr. Collins, as the son of an eminent painter, should know that the proper office of Art is to elevate and purify in pleasing. Without the element of pleasurable emotion, colour and design in painting, like eloquence and fancy in literature, will fail to gain our sympathies. 'Basil' is a tale of criminality, almost revolting from its domestic horrors. The vicious atmosphere in which the drama of the tale is enveloped, weighs on us like a nightmare. The jail, the gibbet, and the madhouse are the accessories of the story:—the adultery of a wife, the jealous torture of the injured husband, the ferocious thirst for revenge of the detected paramour, are its themes!

Our readers may ask, on what has the author relied to make us adopt his aesthetics of the Old Bailey? To that we answer, that the main resource on which he instinctively leans is, his vivid and impassioned eloquence. The style of *Basil* is as eloquent and graceful as its subject is faulty and unwholesome. There is a gushing force in his words, a natural outpouring of his sensibility, a harmony, tone, and *verve* in his language that still give us hopes of his one day achieving some work far superior to his present painful and unpleasant tale. *Basil* reads like the production of a rose-water Maturin or Eugène Suë 'Bowdlerized.'[1]—A statement of the plot will carry its condemnation. . . .

[The reviewer summarizes the story and quotes two examples of Collins's descriptive powers.]

Again, we will repeat a hope that a writer of so much promise will produce some fiction calculated to obtain a wider appreciation than he can ever secure in the unwholesome literary school in which he has apparently enrolled himself.

[1] C. R. Maturin (1782–1824), Irish writer of the 'novel of terror'; Eugène Suë (1804–57), French writer of mystery novels.

7. Charles Dickens, letter to Collins

20 December 1852

This is the first of a series of extracts from letters written by Dickens to Collins and others in which Collins's novels and stories, read in manuscript or print, are discussed. On the relationship between the two writers, see Introduction, pp. 9–11. According to Percy Fitzgerald, *Basil* was a favourite book of Dickens's (*Memories of Charles Dickens* (1913), 90).

The text of this and subsequent letters is taken from the 'Nonesuch' edition (*The Letters of Charles Dickens*, ed. W. Dexter (1938)).

If I did not know that you are likely to have a forbearing remembrance of my occupation, I should be full of remorse for not having sooner thanked you for *Basil*.

Not to play the sage or the critic (neither of which parts, I hope, is at all in my line), but to say what is the friendly truth, I may assure you that I have read the book with very great interest, and with a very thorough conviction that you have a call to this same art of fiction. I think the probabilities here and there require a little more respect than you are disposed to show them, and I have no doubt that the prefatory letter would have been better away, on the ground that a book (of all things) should speak for and explain itself. But the story contains admirable writing, and many clear evidences of a very delicate discrimination of character. It is delightful to find throughout that you have taken great pains with it besides, and have 'gone at it' with a perfect knowledge of the jolter-headedness of the conceited idiots who suppose that volumes are to be tossed off like pancakes, and that any writing can be done without the utmost application, the greatest patience, and the steadiest energy of which the writer is capable.

For all these reasons I have made *Basil*'s acquaintance with great gratification, and entertain a high respect for him. And I hope that I shall become intimate with many worthy descendants of his, who are yet in the limbo of creatures waiting to be born.

8. Unsigned review, *Dublin University Magazine*

January 1853, xli, 77–9

Under the title 'A Trio of Novels', the reviewer considers *Basil*, Thackeray's *The History of Henry Esmond* and M. W. Savage's *Reuben Medlicot*.

The abundant promise of future excellence contained in the former writings of Mr Collins led us to anticipate a brilliant success when he should again make his appearance in the lists. That he has not yet achieved it is less owing to any want of imaginative excellence, than to an unfortunate selection of material. The writing by which *Basil* is distinguished, eloquent and graceful as it is, affords another proof that the author is qualified to take a high place among his contemporaries. It is beside our purpose to enter into a discussion as to the limitations and restrictions which bound the province of fiction. The taste of the age has settled the point, that its proper office is to elevate and purify, as well as to amuse; and unless the writer keep this object constantly before him, he can never hope to win a lasting popularity.

[The reviewer offers a partial plot-summary, but finds himself compelled to 'drop a veil' over certain elements.]

The author in his preface has stated that the incident is one which actually occurred in real life; and we believe him. But much occurs daily—as any one may see who reads the police reports in the *Times*—about which the less that is said the better; and we must confess, that we would rather some catastrophe less startling had been selected as the turning-point of a story, so full of carefully finished pictures and beautiful imagery. With this drawback, the novel is not only carefully considered, but very brilliantly written. . . .

In point of artistic merit this book is an advance upon its predecessors, and gives us the very highest opinion of the author's powers. If the

copy nature as he sees it, and then the spectator has a pleasure propor-
tioned to the beauty of the scene copied. He may give a noble spirit-
stirring scene, and he will raise high thoughts and great aspirations in
those who contemplate it. He may take a higher moral ground, and
move to compassion by showing undeserved suffering, or, like Hogarth,
read a lesson to the idle and the dissipated. He may also paint scenes of
cruelty and sensuality so gross that his picture will be turned to the wall
by those who do not choose to have their imagination defiled.

The novelist has a high and holy mission, for his words frequently
reach ears which will hear no others, and may convey a lesson to them
which the preacher would enforce in vain; . . .

Published in three volumes by Richard Bentley on 6 June 1854.
The 1861 edition in one volume incorporates revisions, introduces
a changed ending, and adds a preface.

---

10. From an unsigned review, *Spectator*

17 June 1854, xxvii, 645

Mr. Wilkie Collins succeeds better in fiction with the distant than the
near. No one in an historical subject selects low or common life for a
theme; probably because the Muse of History has not troubled herself
about any classes below the highest, so that there is a want of data; and
though there are many authors who cannot rise to the heights of a great
argument, Mr. Collins can at least mount the stilts of rhetoric. Another
reason for his greater success in his first novel, *Antonina*, was that his
tendency to over-description was less felt as an obstruction. The reader
took minute particulars about the degenerate Romans, and the rough
vigorous barbarians, for information; but long word-pictures of the
suburbs of London, their interiors, and similar things, are wearisome,
because they are mere repetitions of familiar common objects.

Hide and Seek, however, is a great improvement upon Mr. Collins's
novel of *Basil*. There is less offence in the main drift of the story; the
characters have more vigour, variety, and purpose; and though it
cannot be said that the book is very natural, it is not so unnatural as its
immediate predecessor. . . .

Middle and humble or perhaps low life are the classes of society
depicted in this novel, and with much distinctness and force, but hardly
with thorough truthfulness. We see them not exactly as they are, but as
they appear after passing through the author's mind. This, no doubt, is
inseparable from all representation in art; but some artists, while they

hold their mastery over the nature they are about to depict, sympathize with it, retaining the higher qualities, but rejecting or subduing what is common. Mr. Collins too often lets the common predominate; and thus gives a species of lowness or vulgarity to his scenes and persons. Or he derives his 'good feeling' and humour too much from the theatre or theatrical novelists. In all cases he is too literal.

With a good deal that is questionable in taste, or of an effect below the labour bestowed upon it, there are passages of power and feeling. . . .

[After a lengthy quotation, the review concludes with praise of the characters of Valentine Blyth and Mrs Peckover.]

11. Geraldine Jewsbury, unsigned review, *Athenaeum*

24 June 1854, 775

Geraldine Jewsbury (1812–80) was a minor novelist and a friend of the Carlyles. (See an unsigned article by Virginia Woolf in *The Times Literary Supplement* for 28 February 1929, 149–50, and the subsequent correspondence.)

In *Antonina* and *Basil* Mr. Collins showed himself possessed of gifts of genius; but in those works his strength was like the strength of fever, and his knowledge of human nature resembled a demonstration in morbid anatomy. Over both those works there hung a close, stifling, unwholesome odour: if fascinating, they were not wholesome; if powerful, they were not pleasant. In his present work, *Hide and Seek*, he has ceased walking the moral hospital to which he has hitherto confined his excursions. Here we have health and strength together. The plot of the story is very simple, but it is skilfully and artfully worked out; there is not a single scene, or character, or incident, however trivial, that does not in some way tend to carry on the story and to bring on the *dénoûment*; there is nothing useless or extraneous introduced, and yet the foliage of the story grows in the most careless and accidental luxuriance. The pages abound in proofs that Mr. Collins has a genuine healthy sense of fun, and a humour of his own, bright, delicate and yet playful. The root from which the story grows is a deep and most pitiful tragedy,—'to make men tremble who never weep;'— but it is almost free from exaggeration and false sentiment. The pity that is roused for Madonna's mother is skilfully kept from becoming too painful by the introduction of human incidents, as true to nature as they are well managed,—and when, at the end of the story, that woman's betrayer is revealed, the reader's pity and forgiveness are secured for him also. A knowledge of human nature is displayed in the course of this sad story which will appeal to all who read in arrest of harsh judgment when they have closed the book and gone back to their own business. Valentine Blyth, the artist, with his bad pictures, which are charming, and his sunny disposition, his child-like integrity and common sense, has all the effect of genius; poor dear tormented Zach, who begins by being a naughty boy at church over a sermon two hours long,—goes through the book one of the most fascinating young scamps who was ever mismanaged and 'misunderstood' by his family;— Mrs. Peckover, Mrs. Blyth, in her sweet cheerful patience,—Madonna, the adopted daughter, are all charming in their way. Mathew Grice, the backwoodsman, the brother of Madonna's mother,—the patient vindictive pursuer of her betrayer, is a most powerful character, and looks like a study from real life. We will not spoil the reader's interest in the book by developing the story,—and it is useless to extract passages from a work which every one should read.

12. Unsigned review, *Leader*

24 June 1854, v, 591–3

The *Leader*, a Radical weekly founded in 1850, was at this time owned and edited by Edward Pigott, who became a friend of Collins.

We had many and serious objections to raise against Wilkie Collins's former novel, *Basil*, in balance of our praise; *en revanche*,[1] we have very hearty plaudits to bestow on this one, with only just enough criticism to serve as ballast and to 'trim the boat'. In the first place, there is praise loud enough and rare enough in the fact that we read the three volumes through page by page, hurried on by the story, yet never 'skipping', *reading* the book, and not running as we read. There are few novels which can hope for such a compliment. . . . There are no lofty conversations swelling out the volumes while the author takes breath and thinks of how to prepare the next incident. There are no redundant platitudes sprawling over the fatigued pages. There are no 'How often do we finds,' no 'So true it is that man,' &c. No sermons. The dialogue is dramatic—put there either to carry on the story or fetch out the traits of character. The writing is bright, clear, nervous, often felicitous, occasionally extravagant, but never slip-slop.

Then the story, without being new in itself or in the leading incidents, has a certain complicated clearness with enough of mystery and expectation to keep attention alive, although it wants climax, and leaves an indefinite, unsatisfied feeling remaining in the reader's mind. In fact, there seems to have been another volume requisite to work out all the drama suggested here. In his preface, the author says that he has endeavoured to combine interest of story and development of characters in nearly equal proportions—a good endeavour, but one in which he has not quite succeeded; and the reason of that non-success we take to be his substituting portrait-painting for development. The characters in

[1] On the contrary.

this book are well conceived, well drawn, but they are *described*; they do not move through the story, revealing themselves in it.

[The reviewer cites three characters in the novel—Mr Thorpe, Valentine Blyth and Madonna—as instances of this deficiency.]

Mat is the best specimen in the book of the other mode of character-drawing. No description is given of him. But he makes himself known to us vividly enough. Let the author, in future, throw his efforts in that direction, and he will find the combination of incident with character far more effective for both.

[The review concludes with several substantial quotations from the novel.]

13. Unsigned review, *Bentley's Miscellany*

July 1854, xxxvi, 97–8

The passage forms part of an omnibus review, 'Short Notes on Recent Novels'.

Novels continue to be written, and the luxurious world still looks for its ordinary amusement, although taxes increase, the war lingers, and the Emperor of Russia is not yet beaten to his knees.[1] *Hide and Seek*, the first that presents itself on our well-replenished table, is from the pen of an author who has previously won favour with the public by *Antonina* and *Basil*. Both his former works have been liberally praised, but we consider this, by several degrees, the best of the three. It has more power of conception, greater distinctness, and a sustained purpose, wrought out with superior effect. The opening chapter, descriptive of the childhood and early training of young Zachariah Thorpe, reminds us of Dickens, whom Mr. Wilkie Collins emulates rather than imitates, and

1 See Introduction, p. 8.

with good success. Mrs. Peckover, the spouse of the strolling clown, Valentine Blyth, the eccentric, but kind-hearted painter, his invalid wife, and their adopted Madonna, or Mary, the little deaf and dumb heroine, are well-drawn portraits. The idea of the latter is conceived with skill, and has several traits of originality, though she cannot play a very prominent part, from her position and physical deficiencies. The account of her infancy, childhood, and the accident which occasioned her loss of hearing and consequent inability to speak, is the most touching and attractive portion of the book. Few characters are introduced, whether principal or subordinate; but they are ingeniously contrasted, and each seems necessary to the progress of the story. Mr. Mathew Marksman (or rather, Grice), reminds us of some old acquaintances, with his features and dress considerably changed. He is not altogether agreeable, and, from the nature of his life and adventures, his perceptions of moral propriety are neither very rigid nor delicate, but he acts an important part throughout, and makes his final exit in perfect keeping. 'Zach,' the hero of the tale, is a high-spirited youth, wilful from a mistaken plan of education, and driven into irregularities by the obstinate, ill-planned discipline of the paternal roof; not viciously inclined, but easily led astray, and yielding to impulse from lack of judgment rather than absence of principle. There is a want of refinement in his thoughts and actions, perfectly natural under the circumstances in which he is placed, and suited to the scenes in which he is engaged. The story might have been more condensed, and is somewhat elaborated towards the end, but the interest and mystery are well preserved, and we are really grateful to Mr. Collins for sparing us the usual wind-up of a happy marriage. This he renders impossible, as the hero and heroine are discovered at last to be brother and sister, and no other parties are introduced with whom they can be respectively joined in the bands of holy wedlock. Thorpe senior, the bad man of the tale, and the originator of all the mischief, is treated more indulgently than he deserves, allowed to die in the course of nature, with time for penitence, and an affectionate wife to attend him in his seclusion from the world. Zach returns home from travelling in the wilds of America (on hearing of his father's death), a wiser and steadier man than he was when he departed, and the curtain drops on the family group, re-united in the painter's drawing-room. These scenes and incidents which are confined to every-day life and homely position, are rendered extremely exciting by the artistic skill of the author, who borders on romance without sacrificing probability.

14. W. M. Rossetti, unsigned review, *Morning Post*

13 July 1854, 3

William Michael Rossetti (1829–1919), brother of Christina and Dante Gabriel, was a versatile scholar and man of letters and published much criticism of literature and art.

[After praising *Antonina* as a 'grand historical romance' and *Basil* as belonging to 'the romantic school of composition, and to the highest order in that school', the reviewer continues:]

Hide and Seek is a modern novel, of the Dickens and Thackeray class, and not inferior, in our judgment, to any of the productions of those popular writers. It combines the narrative and descriptive felicity of the one with the satirical humour of the other. . . . It is the matured work of a master mind. . . .

[The character of Madonna, the deaf-mute, for which Collins had acknowledged his indebtedness to the medical writings of a Dr Kitto, is singled out for praise:]

No reader can fail to admire the delicacy and skill with which these materials have been employed by Mr. Collins. . . . [The reader's] interest is kept sensitively alive to the last. There is, indeed, no tameness of any sort about *Hide and Seek*, but alike in plot and character, freshness, and originality, and power. We have no misgivings as to its success. . . .

15. Charles Dickens, letter to Georgina Hogarth

22 July 1854

Text from 'Nonesuch' edition, II, 570.

Neither you nor Catherine [Dickens's wife] did justice to Collins's book. I think it far away the cleverest novel I have ever seen written by a new hand. It is much beyond Mrs. Gaskell, and is in some respects masterly. Valentine Blyth is as original and as well done as anything can be. The scene where he shows his pictures, is full of an admirable humour. Nor do I really recognize much imitation of myself. Old Mat is the thing in which I observe myself to be most reflected, but he is admirably done. In short, I call it a very remarkable book, and have been very much surprised by its great merit. . . .

16. Performance and promise: a French estimate

November 1855

Émile Forgues, 'William Wilkie Collins', *Revue des deux mondes*, 15 November 1855, xii, 815–48.

Émile Forgues (1813–83) contributed many articles on English writers to the *Revue*, of which he was editor at the time his long essay on Collins appeared, and to other French journals. The present essay was one of a series of 'Studies in the English Novel'; he turned to the sensation novel again in an article (June 1863) which discusses two novels by Miss Braddon. Forgues also translated several of Collins's novels, including *The Dead Secret* and *The Woman in White*. *The Queen of Hearts* is dedicated to him: on Collins's appreciation of the present essay, see Introduction, p. 12.

Much of the original article, which fills thirty-four pages of the *Revue*, consists of plot-analyses and quotations; it has here been drastically abridged. After a brief consideration of the *Memoirs*, Forgues examines the first three novels in turn.

Antonina, the young author's first significant production, though characterized by the kind of boldness which often overshoots the mark, and bedecked with those affectations of style which fall so readily from the pen of the professional author, was nonetheless one of the outstanding books of its season. For all its faults, nothing in it is merely commonplace. The composition is unsatisfactory, but the weakness of the overall design is offset by the handling of the individual elements. The priest of the false gods, who in France would have the grave weakness of too vividly recalling the well-known character of Quasimodo, the terrible bell-ringer in *Notre-Dame de Paris*, doubtless had for many English readers a certain merit of novelty. The classical tastes of many others were flattered by the accuracy with which the historical portions of the story are presented. The requirements of the most prudish readers were satisfied by the immaculate purity of the heroine. . . . The favourable treatment accorded to this first book by the critics might have been the ruin of the author who was its happy recipient: he might well have followed a false trail and have prepared for himself some rude shocks. If one concedes that this kind of fiction is capable of satisfying the demands of contemporary taste, it must be recognized that success in this vein requires more maturity than Mr Wilkie Collins had yet displayed, as well as less preoccupation with a purely dramatic interest. . . .

The preface to Mr Collins' second novel tells us that he hesitated, on the threshold of his second literary enterprise (so much more perilous than the first), between a subject drawn from history, but this time from modern history, and a narrative based on contemporary life (*Basil:* Letter of Dedication to Charles James Ward). Without attempting to predict what would have happened if the young novelist had chosen the first of these alternatives, we may take it that he has reason for self-congratulation on his decision: his second novel has, up to the present time, enjoyed a greater success than any of his other books.

Basil is a very simple and very moving story: we would have wished to have seen removed from it only a few unnecessary details and a few excessive complications of plot for it to have been, if not a work of the first order, at any rate one of the most successful studies of manners to have appeared for a long time. It is a book which invites comparison with *Jane Eyre* and *Mary Barton*, with a somewhat more manly touch than they display, the imprint of a better and more comprehensive education, and an openmindedness more in harmony with the general tendency of our country and our century. We must dwell a little longer on this last point, so as to be more clearly understood. The two ladies, both remarkably talented, to whose novels we have just referred—Miss Brontë and Mrs. Gaskell—both possess to a somewhat greater degree than is ideal the hallmarks of their origin and their education. Without venturing to reproach them with this—for everyone must remain free in his opinions and beliefs—we wish simply to observe that their novels, on account of their strong elements of protestant preaching and demands for social reform, lack that serene and placid impartiality (sometimes, alas, *too* serene and placid!) which characterizes the philosophy of the present age. Mr Wilkie Collins, who is pre-eminently an artist, is of a different temperament. His opinions, manifested in places without being ostentatiously displayed, are truly liberal, the sworn enemy of hypocrisy and prejudice and of those materialistic tendencies which are the characteristic vices of present-day England. It is evident that he detests the whining cant and the petty restrictions of a false puritanism; he weighs aristocratic vanity in the balance, accepting it when it is the source of generous actions and attacking it without mercy when it consists only of empty pretensions. And he has only irony and scorn for the mercenary mentality of the counting-house.... Nevertheless, these antipathies of his do not partake of the nature of passions, and do not turn him into a preacher....

[A long analysis and discussion of *Basil* follows.]

We believe that the esteem in which we hold Mr Collins should not allow us to lay stress on the closing pages of a novel which is, up to that point, so striking and truthful. They remind us, regrettably, of a host of second-rate works and of methods too often abused by hack-writers for a genuine author to stoop to their use....

The defects of the novel are to be found in the structure of its narrative, its excellences in the brilliant and glowing colours with which this structure is covered.... The characters are more convincing than the story....

After the success of his second novel, Mr Wilkie Collins would have been ill-advised to attempt another experiment in historical fiction; and his third work, *Hide and Seek*, is again a novel of intrigue and a portrait of contemporary manners. We do not rate it as high as *Basil*, even though Mr Collins once more shows himself to be a pleasant story-teller and a penetrating observer: the book is too feeble in conception and too hackneyed in its situations to stimulate any very lively interest.

[The novel is briefly summarized.]

Such as it is, this most recent book still remains superior to many English novels of the present time. This superiority is derived not from the nature of the story—itself quite commonplace and naïve—but from the narrative skill which the writer consistently manifests....

[A long discussion of the characters follows.]

Regarding the conception of the character of Valentine Blyth [the painter in *Hide and Seek*], we are not entirely certain that the author can be given full marks for originality. He could have found the idea for this character in a story by M. de Balzac entitled *Pierre Grassou*, which depicts the effect upon an essentially bourgeois nature of the perilous profession of the artist. If we compare the English with the French specimen, we find the former much less searching in its analysis, which is conducted with less patient curiosity and application. On the other hand, thanks to the generosity of spirit and the essentially philanthropic nature which, as we have said, belong to Mr Collins, Valentine Blyth provides a quite different kind of interest from Pierre Grassou; and the slightly patronizing (though sincere and cordial) compassion which the reader accords to the former in no way resembles the bitter scorn he feels for the latter and the intolerant ostracism to which he would be tempted to condemn him and his like. Generally speaking, this is the great defect of M. de Balzac, the immense gap in his talent—he lacks humanity and charity. . . . Mr Collins suffers rather from the opposite fault, which seems to us indeed to be the lesser evil. He belongs to the class of portraitists who flatter, not by calculation, but by instinct and genuine kindliness. If, like any other novelist, he found himself obliged to create a profoundly wicked character, he would suffer, one suspects, a certain discomfort and regret. . . .

It is hardly surprising that a nature of this order, sufficiently rare among professional authors, should evoke a sympathetic response from a large audience of readers. Such has been the happy fortune of Mr Wilkie Collins. The steep slopes of fame have levelled out before him; hardened reviewers have benignly granted him a place among eminent writers without waiting for the young recruit to complete the arduous task of winning his spurs. . . .

[Forgues turns next to the unpublished play *The Lighthouse*, privately produced by Dickens at his home, Tavistock House, in June 1855.]

This little drama is the latest production of the youthful talent which we have attempted to study and describe from its earliest appearances. We believe in his future, . . . we recognize in him the major qualities of the novelist, above all, skill in the art of narrative and delicacy of observation; but if he has the virtues of his age, he also too often shares its defects. The confident optimism which is one of the hallmarks of his talent, a talent still at the stage of growth, seems to extend itself to his manner of writing. He allows himself to be captivated, and too readily contented, by an ingenious notion. His characterization needs more precision and clarity of outline: he is too quickly satisfied by a felicitous sketch which lacks emphasis and detail. In our time the novel, which has enlarged its frontiers to a remarkable degree, cannot be fashioned with so little effort. It calls for more patiently conducted analysis, more

fastidious dissection of character, more refined and complex interrela-
tionships. . . .

We would not be seeking to raise obstacles in the path of the young
writer if we did not believe that he is capable of surmounting them. Mr
Wilkie Collins, with the abundant resources provided by a quite
unusual kind of education, has the necessary powers to tackle the problems that lie before him. Who is better qualified than he, for example,
to depict for us the life of the artist in England and in our period? . . . It
is not enough to aim at success by the servile imitation of works which
have already won favour. What he must strive for above all, if he
wishes decisively to attain the rank as a novelist which he has shown to
be within his capabilities, is originality in the basic conception of a
story. To reach this level, it is not quite enough to have found readers
for *Antonina, Basil* and *Hide and Seek* among the same public which has
enjoyed *The Caxtons*,[1] *David Copperfield* and *Vanity Fair*. One further
step remains, and we like to hope that, with the maturing of his art
through experience, and by concentrating his energies towards a more
clearly-defined goal, Mr Wilkie Collins will take this decisive step. He
will thus justify the affectionate interest which is already felt in him, and
to which we have attempted to add our voice.

[1] Bulwer-Lytton's novel was published in 1849.

17. An unequalled story-teller

June 1857

Edmund Yates, 'W. Wilkie Collins', *Train*, June 1857, iii, 352–7.

This early appreciation of Collins appeared as the second in a series of articles on 'Men of Mark' in the short-lived *Train*, edited by Yates and G. A. Sala. Yates (1831–94), novelist and journalist, subsequently founded the *World*, edited *Temple Bar* and was one of Dickens's contributors to *All the Year Round*. For his later estimate of Collins, see No. 85 below.

[Yates begins by castigating the amateurishness of nearly all writers of fiction of the day: to write a good novel calls not only for natural gifts but for the devoting of 'time, patience and reflection to their proper employment'.]

Mr. Wilkie Collins, a short sketch of whose career I propose to write, is without doubt the most conscientious novelist of the present day. No barrister or physician ever worked harder at his profession, devoted more time, or thought, or trouble to it, was prouder of it, or pursued it with more zeal and earnestness than Mr. Collins has done with regard to literature. By Mr. Thackeray's own confession in the preface to *Pendennis*, we learn that his plot was not clearly defined beforehand, but was liable to alteration and modification,—for does he not tell us, that until the very morning on which the 'copy' was to be delivered to the printer, he was uncertain whether or not to kill Amory by a fall from the window? Writing on this present eighteenth day of May, I am in strong doubt whether the author of *Little Dorrit* has even yet made up his mind how to dispose of some of his *dramatis personæ*; but, after long and careful observation of Mr. Collins's writings, I am perfectly certain that he never enters upon a story until the plot, in all its ramifications and bearings, has been thoroughly weighed and digested in his own mind; and also, that when once he has set to work, his original intention is never departed from. All his honesty of purpose, all this labour, this artistic preparation would, however, be useless had he not the power to carry out his intentions; but this power he has. Placing him in my own estimation as the fourth in rank among the British novelists of the present day (and among those prior to him I have classed that wondrous woman whose biography has so recently been given to us), I contend that as a story-teller he has no equal; that he possesses the *art de conter* above all living writers. Inferior to Dickens in pathos and humour, inferior to Thackeray in the knowledge of the secret workings of the human heart, and in the popular exposition of a cynical philosophy, inferior to Miss Brontë in his grasp of persons and places, his power of description, and in the quaint uttering of startling and original doctrines, —he yet possesses a considerable amount of the qualifications of all these authors; while in the talent with which the foundations of his story are laid, and the edifice afterwards raised to completion, he far surpasses them.

[An outline of Collins's life and literary career to date follows, with a brief examination of individual books. The section on *Basil* is given as a sample.]

[1852] saw the production of *Basil*, the most original, striking and thoughtful of his novels. Many and various as have been the opinions about this book, I have yet found no critic able to deny that it carries out the intention so well described in the author's prefatory letter, viz., that it shows the careful preliminary training to which the writer had subjected himself, and—what is not described in the prefatory letter— that it is the work of a master of his art. The policy of fixing the reader's interest, exciting his suspense, occupying his feelings, and stirring his thoughts by appealing to sources beyond the general experience, may be questioned; but the manner in which all this has been done can but call for admiration. The main incident of the story may appear objectionable to many, on grounds particularly English, and not particularly defensible. The concluding portion may be condemned as too highly coloured, too melodramatic and unnatural; but so admirably is the plot worked out, so forcible is the language, and so powerful the delineation of character (I speak more especially, perhaps, of the characters of the hero's father and brother), that I defy the reader to withhold his interest, or not to follow the author page by page.

[The article concludes by recommending Forgues's essay (No. 16), which 'contains a longer and abler dissertation on his talents, but which could not express greater admiration of them than is felt by the writer of this slight sketch'.]

THE DEAD SECRET

Serialized in *Household Words* from 3 January to 13 June 1857; published in two volumes by Bradbury & Evans in June. On its reception, see Introduction, p. 11.

18. Horace St John, from an unsigned review, *Athenaeum*

20 June 1857, 788–9

Horace St John (1832–88) was a journalist who for many years wrote leaders for the *Daily Telegraph*. (N. P. Davis attributes this review to Chorley: see headnote to No. 6.)

No injustice will be done to Mr. Collins if we trace the outline of his story before estimating its qualities as a work of art. *The Dead Secret* is no secret to a numerous class of readers. . . .

[Observing that 'the tale . . . appeals simply to one element in the imagination—*curiosity*', the reviewer proceeds to summarize the story at length.]

The resurrection of the Secret, after all, brings no terrible consequences. In fact, too much is made of too little mystery. Now, this story, although an exaggeration of melo-drama, is cleverly told: the writing is keen, spirited, graced occasionally with happy allusion, and equal to the exigencies of the slowly-moving incidents. But the slow movement we allude to is a signal defect in Mr. Collins's method. There is an abundance of pale Dutch painting bestowed upon trivial objects: we detect continually where touches have been elaborately multiplied to deepen the pathos, to intensify the mystery, to finish the dramatic parts. So much patient manipulation has been devoted to every chapter, that it is with unaffected regret we confess the result to be not commensurate with the author's ambition. After reading and re-reading an entire novel by so proficient a writer as Mr. Collins, we are disappointed to find that no character has left an impression upon us, and that not a single epigrammatic saying has been added to our memory. What we do recollect and admire is the power of certain dramatic passages, which, if the action were more rapid, would make the blood tingle as the narrator proceeded with his story: the construction is everywhere excellent, although upon too large a scale. Now and then, when the artist seems inspired by his own creation, some real and noble tenderness suffuses a scene of love, and penitence, and sorrow. . . .

[A long quotation from Book VI, ch. 4 follows: from 'The western clouds . . .' to '. . . rested at last'. The review ends with the verdict that, despite all its merits, *The Dead Secret* is 'only a moderately-successful work of fiction'.]

19. Unsigned review, *Saturday Review*

22 August 1857, iv, 188

Mr. Wilkie Collins possesses the art of writing plays and stories so as to awaken and sustain the interest of the reader. He can create and work out a plot. It is true that the subject-matter of the plot is generally rather trivial, the characters commonplace, and the whole tone and cast of the work conventional and insignificant. But the story, such as it is, has the merit of being neatly and pleasantly told. The author has set himself assiduously to inquire how the materials which he has been able to collect should be strung together, what proportion the several parts should bear to each other, and how the end of the story may be constantly anticipated by introductory hints without its precise character being divulged. The result of this painstaking industry is that the reader is carried gently on, and is forced to take an interest in the web of circumstance which is spun for his benefit. Few writers give themselves so much trouble. If they have anything to say, they are ordinarily wrapt up in saying it, and trust to the guidance of their own genius to give it expression. If they have nothing to say, they are generally so happily constituted as not to perceive their own defects. It is, therefore, rare to find an author who, without originality, or great powers of any sort, has the gift of seeing how much arrangement and contrivance may do to enhance the value of the little he has to offer. This gift has been sufficient to ensure Mr. Collins a very considerable success, and his novels have been welcomed by the public, which always relishes the treat of small ingenuities, and likes any species of unambitious, intelligible entertainment. Besides, to have the art of narration implies the possession of many good literary qualities. It indicates that sort of good sense and good taste which rejects the superfluous, the incongruous, and the extravagant. It involves the power of putting a mass of detached minute facts into a decisive and appreciable shape. It makes us sure that the writer will keep tolerably clear of all that could annoy, weary, or offend us. We find these qualities displayed in Mr. Collins's stories, though less conspicuously in some than in others. The *Dead Secret*, now reprinted from *Household Words*, does not seem to us a very favourable specimen. Perhaps it has lost by its several parts having first appeared in a detached form. However this may be, we think it scarcely equal to its predecessors. In spite of a portion of the story being skilfully told, the general effect is certainly flat; and the poverty of conception and incident, and the triviality of the principal characters, are scantily disguised by the arts of mechanical contrivance. . . .

[A plot-summary follows.]

As the secret is plainly discernible in the very opening of the book, the interest of the story hangs not upon the nature of the secret, but upon the mode in which it is discovered. The ingenuity of the author is shown in devising a great many plausible incidents, by which the searchers shall be alternately brought a step nearer to the discovery, and then removed a step from it. The portion of the tale which describes the occurrences happening between the arrival of Rosamond at Porthgenna and her taking the paper out of the drawer is very well told. The story constantly moves forward, and we feel at the end of each chapter that we are one step nearer the end of the search, and yet the movement is so slow that it seems as if the paper would never be found. This sort of contrivance is not a very high style of art, but it requires much skill and patience to work it out. By dint of sheer cleverness of management the discovery of the secret is made to last a hundred pages, and yet it seems quite natural that it should last so long. This is certainly a considerable effort of narrative power, and we cannot speak slightingly of a book that contains it. But, apart from this display of ingenuity, nothing could be more tame and poor than the story. The subordinate characters are especially conventional and unmeaning. There is the old established miser and recluse, who at the end of the tale draws a cheque for 40,000*l.* and sends it to Rosamond with his blessing—there is the familiar, pompous, timorous steward, echoing the opinions of the housekeeper, whom he affects to guide—there is the amiable young man, with a pride of birth 'that is perhaps excessive.' Such personages of romance are sufficiently commonplace; but the amount of what is commonplace which it contains is not the only fault of the book. In order to bring it up to the level of *Household Words* edification, it is sprinkled with the outpourings of a melo-dramatic sentimentalism. Of these its concluding passage is perhaps a fair specimen. Our readers will easily recognize who is the Gamaliel at whose feet Mr. Collins must have sat. . . .

[Quotes the concluding paragraphs of the novel: from 'At the gate . . .' to ' ". . . LOVE and TRUTH" '.]

THE QUEEN OF HEARTS

Published in three volumes by Hurst & Blackett in the spring of 1859. On the contents of this collection of ten linked stories, see Introduction, p. 9.

20. Charles Dickens, letter to Collins

13 July 1856

Dickens had evidently read the story eventually titled 'The Diary of Anne Rodway' in manuscript; he published it in *Household Words* in two parts on 19 and 26 July, and Collins included it in *The Queen of Hearts*. In another letter, written to Miss Coutts two days after the one quoted, he urges her to read the story, saying that it 'possesses very remarkable merit—especially the close of it'. Text of the two letters in 'Nonesuch' edition, II, 791–3.

I cannot tell you what a high opinion I have of 'Anne Rodway'. I took 'Extracts' out of the title because it conveyed to the many-headed an idea of incompleteness—of something unfinished—and is likely to stall some readers off. I read the first part at the office with strong admiration, and read the second on the railway coming back here, being in town just after you had started on your cruise. My behaviour before my fellow-passengers was weak in the extreme, for I cried as much as you could possibly desire. Apart from the genuine force and beauty of the little narrative, and the admirable personation of the girl's identity and point of view, it is done with an amount of honest pains and devotion to the work which few men have better reason to appreciate than I, and which no man can have a more profound respect for. I think it excellent, feel a personal pride and pleasure in it which is a delightful sensation, and know no one else who could have done it.

21. Unsigned review, *Saturday Review*

22 October 1859, viii, 487–8

Both in his preface and in the body of his work, Mr. Collins invites the reader to observe what is the object which the author has set before him in composing the series of tales collected under the name of the *Queen of Hearts*. What Mr. Collins aims at is being a story-teller. He wishes to construct a narrative the effect of which shall be to awake, sustain, and satisfy the interest of the reader. There are plenty of novels written in these days to unfold the philosophy or to instil the instruction which finds favour with the writer. There are novels in which the author attempts to elaborate character, and to show how certain vices or virtues are revealed or fostered by the circumstances in which the actors of the fiction are placed. There are, again, novels intended to describe states of society which have passed away, or ways of life unfamiliar to the English public, or scenery, customs, and institutions foreign to our usual habits of thought. Mr. Collins considers that all these attempts are divergencies from the proper duty of a novelist. A story-teller should have a story to tell, and should tell it. It is his business not to improve or to instruct mankind, but to amuse. Common life is full of strange incidents. If these are related disjointedly and unmethodically, the attention of a reader or hearer is only momentarily arrested. But here lies the field for a novelist's skill. He can so arrange the story that the interest shall be prolonged. He can devise a number of minute incidents, all converging in a central point. He can bring constantly home to the conviction of his reader that this central point exists, and yet can conceal what it is. He can manage that, when this central point is revealed, all that before seemed obscure shall seem clear, and every main incident shall appear to have occurred independently and naturally, though conducing to the evolution of the final mystery. A story thus becomes a well-managed puzzle. First of all, the narrator has to find the right sort of puzzle to set. It must be something nearly connected with common life, or the final explication will appear forced. At the same time, it must be something removed from every-day experience, or the theatre of action will seem too mean or obscure. Then, when the right species of puzzle has been hit on, the storyteller must set it in the right way, using none but legitimate contrivances, and coming to an end when the facts of which he makes use naturally lead him to do so. Mr. Collins asks his readers and critics to observe that this is by no means an easy thing to do, and he claims that he shall have due credit for any success he may have achieved in carrying out his conception of his art.

There are ten stories in the three volumes which bear the title of the *Queen of Hearts*. They are held together by a device which is at least as good as such devices generally are. A young lady comes to stay with three old brothers in a lonely Welsh valley, and the son of one of these brothers is in love with her. The lover is away from home, and in order to detain her till he comes, the old men agree to read a story in the evenings. These separate stories are exceedingly well told. They are possible, interesting, and natural, and have the great merit that they stop when it is probable in real life they would have stopped. We may take as a specimen a story called 'The Dead Hand.' A young man going to Doncaster in the race week is obliged to sleep in a double-bedded room, and finds that the occupant of the other bed is a corpse. He strikes a light in the middle of the night, and to his horror sees that the hand of the corpse has moved. He awakens the house; medical aid is obtained, and the dead man is restored from his trance to life. The young stranger does not learn who the person is whom he has resuscitated, but the doctor, who is acquainted with the family, discovers that the supposed dead man is an illegitimate brother of the young man. Some years afterwards, a stranger arrives at the doctor's surgery, and bringing a recommendation with him applies, under an assumed name, to be the doctor's assistant. He is received on this footing, and stays with the doctor several years. The doctor strongly suspects that the stranger is the man who had been laid out as dead, but he never can make himself quite sure. Here the story ends, and it is slight enough to make its chief interest centre in the manner of its treatment. The moving of the limbs of a supposed corpse is one of those incidents which we know to be possible, for evidence is abundant that the circumstance has often happened, but it is uncommon, and horrible enough to thrill the nerves of readers. Of course, the art of the story chiefly consists in the manner in which we are prepared for the moving of the hand. We are told how the young man came to hire the room—how he was persuaded to stay in the room when he found that he had a dead man beside him—and how the thought of his room-fellow fascinated him, until he could not avoid watching the dead body closely. But although our interest is thus worked up, it is worked up in a legitimate manner. This young man is not represented as a peculiarly nervous or fanciful person. He does not undergo the excitement which might befall a mind of unusual timidity or strength of imagination. He feels merely what an ordinary young man would feel. After the dead man is recovered, the interest is sustained by the suggestion that the two are brothers; but the complication of circumstances is not more curious or more wonderfully unravelled than is customary in real life, and at the end of the story we are left in uncertainty whether the dead man revisited the doctor or not. This is evidently a contrivance of the artist to bring us to the level of the uncertainties of daily experience, for it might be objected that the point could scarcely be left in doubt between persons who were for years in constant intercourse. Mr. Collins is willing to run the risk of this being considered slightly improbable in order that he may finish without any excessive wonder of a catastrophe. There can be no doubt that the contrivance succeeds, and an air of reality is thus imparted to the narrative.

Occasionally, however, we have to complain of incidents in these stories which are too poor and thin for the occasion. . . .

We notice, too, in all the stories a very great similarity of talking, thinking, and acting. Everybody, whatever may be his or her sex, age, or education, uses precisely the same language and entertains precisely the same views of right and wrong, of what is expedient, customary, and practical. The whole group of stories, therefore, seems worse than any one does when taken by itself.

Still, the stories are well written and very cleverly contrived. According to Mr. Collins' views of a story-teller's duty, his success has been great. It requires much thought, much patient elaboration, great practice, and considerable native power to tell a tale as he tells it. Very few people could tell a story founded on the incidents selected by Mr. Collins, so well as he does. But we cannot agree with him that this art of setting and solving a puzzle is anything like the ideal of a novelist. It is an ingenious trick, and produces a very good marketable novel. But it is by no means a great performance. If we compare the work of a great master with these stories of Mr. Collins, we perceive at once how very small a thing it is to keep the interest of the reader alive in the same way, although in a higher degree, as it is sustained by a newspaper anecdote. The story of the *Bride of Lammermoor* is exactly the story which Mr. Collins would like to tell. But the *Bride of Lammermoor* is a masterpiece, not because it leads us naturally to a fearful catastrophe, but because in doing so it unfolds to us the characters of Lucy Ashton, Caleb Balder-

stone, and the Master of Ravenswood. We read on without the sense of
an ingenious puzzle, and yet at the end the story seems almost painfully real. Mr. Collins constructs his machinery well, but he never rises
above a machinist. He avoids entirely drawing character. There is no
more interest about the people of whom he tells us in themselves than
there is about the sufferer when we read in a newspaper that a farmer
was robbed, a lady knocked down, or a clergyman assaulted. There is
some interest in the fact that persons of this description sustained the
calamities mentioned, but the interest is in the fact, not in the individual.
If Mr. Collins were to tell the story of the Bride of Lammermoor, he
would, on his principle of setting us a puzzling plot, merely have to tell
us that Lucy Ashton was a young Scotch lady. We need scarcely go into
the reasons which have long ago decided great artists to believe that
it is in the combination of characters which appeal to our feelings, with
a good machinery, that the ideal of fiction lies. As compared with the
host of foolish novels that are written every year, Mr. Collins' stories
are good—for the ordinary novel has no character and no plot. But
although, by careful attention to his machinery, Mr. Collins achieves a
definite success, this success is a small one.

THE WOMAN IN WHITE

Serialized in *All the Year Round* (26 November 1859–25 August 1860) and simultaneously in the American *Harper's Weekly* (26 November 1859–4 August 1860); published in three volumes in both countries in August 1860. The 'new edition' of the following year, in one volume, incorporates revisions prompted by *The Times*'s review reprinted below (No. 30) and substitutes a new preface.

The Woman in White: a drama in three acts was produced at the Theatre Royal, Leicester, on 26 August 1870, and was subsequently revised and published as *The Woman in White: a Drama in Prologue and Four Acts* in 1871. The latter was favourably reviewed when it was staged at the Olympic Theatre, London, on 9 October 1871.

On the background of the novel, see C. K. Hyder, 'Wilkie Collins and the woman in white', *PMLA*, 54 (1939), 297–303. Dickens's own 'woman in white', Miss Havisham in *Great Expectations* (serialized in *All the Year Round* from 1 December 1860), perhaps owes something to Collins's example: see M. Meisel, 'Miss Havisham brought to book', *PMLA*, 81 (1966), 278–85.

22. George Meredith in his letters

January 1860

Meredith (1828–1909), novelist and poet, was at work on *Evan Harrington* (serialized during 1860) when he read the early portions of *The Woman in White* and wrote the letters quoted from. Only six instalments of Collins's novel had appeared at this time. Text from *The Letters of George Meredith*, ed. C. L. Cline (1970), I, 51–2.

To invent probabilities in modern daily life is difficult; you can't work up the excitement of melodrama and *Women in White*—at least till you are in full career.

(?3 January 1860)

I send a chapter [of *Evan Harrington*] . . . I stress small incidents; but they best exhibit character: and remember (or such is my view) serial reading demands excitement enough to lead on, but, more and better, amusement of a quiet kind. The tension of the *W[oman] in W[hite]* is not exactly pleasant, though cleverly produced. One wearies of it. . . .

(?5 January 1860)

23. Charles Dickens, letters to Collins

January–July 1860

Text from 'Nonesuch' edition, III, 145, 169.

I have read this book with great care and attention. There cannot be a doubt that it is a very great advance on all your former writing, and most especially in respect of tenderness. In character it is excellent. Mr. Fairlie as good as the lawyer, and the lawyer as good as he. Mr. Vesey and Miss Halcombe, in their different ways, equally meritorious. Sir Percival, also, is most skilfully shown, though I doubt (you see what small points I come to) whether any man ever showed uneasiness by hand or foot without being forced by nature to show it in his face too. The story is very interesting, and the writing of it admirable.

I seem to have noticed, here and there, that the great pains you take express themselves a trifle too much, and you know that I always contest your disposition to give an audience credit for nothing, which necessarily involves the forcing of points on their attention, and which I have always observed them to resent when they find it out—as they always will and do. But on turning to the book again, I find it difficult to take out an instance of this. It rather belongs to your habit of thought and manner of going about the work. Perhaps I express my meaning best when I say that the three people who write the narratives in these proofs have a DISSECTIVE property in common, which is essentially not theirs but yours; and that my own effort would be to strike more of what is got *that way* out of them by collision with one another, and by the working of the story.

You know what an interest I have felt in your powers from the beginning of our friendship, and how very high I rate them? *I* know that this is an admirable book, and that it grips the difficulties of the weekly portion and throws them in a masterly style. No one else could do it half so well. I have stopped in every chapter to notice some instance of ingenuity, or some happy turn of writing; and I am absolutely certain that you never did half so well yourself. . . .

(7 January 1860)

Let me send you my heartiest congratulations on your having come to
the end of your (as yet) last labor, and having triumphantly finished
your best book. . . .

(29 July 1860)

24. Unsigned review, *Morning Advertiser*

20 August 1860, 3

[Noting that, as a serial in *All the Year Round*, *The Woman in White* had
'attracted, weekly, a very large and deeply-interested class of readers',
the reviewer goes on to predict that, in three-volume form] in the circulating libraries it will have what is technically called a 'run'. It is written
in a light and pleasing style. It always keeps up the interest, and is full of
striking situations, while the plot is wrought out with great ability. In
fact, it is, by common consent, Mr Collins's best work. . . . There is one
feature of novelty about the work, which is, that the different characters
are made to tell their own stories. This feature is successfully carried out,
the differences of style being not only natural but exceedingly well
sustained.

[The reviewer concludes by conceding the reasonableness of Collins's
request that the plot should not be divulged, and acts accordingly.]

25. Unsigned review, *Critic*

25 August 1860, xxi, 233–4

The *Critic*, at this time a weekly, 'clearly aimed at a less educated public than the *Athenaeum*' and sought to 'provide a guide for the choice of Book Clubs and Libraries' (Ellegård, 23).

Mr Wilkie Collins takes the critics by the forelock; he warns them in his preface to keep their hands off his property [and not reveal the plot of the novel]. We may be allowed, perhaps, to observe that the plot is in point of intricacy a masterpiece, and to defy Oedipus himself, after reading two volumes, to predict the end of Sir Percival Glyde. We may also say without offence that the story is one of 'thrilling interest;' its elasticity is perfectly wonderful, and the elongation it suffers without much detriment is a caution even to indiarubber.

[The reviewer goes on to discuss the characters, praising Mrs Catherick as 'the paragon of she-devils' but finding Count Fosco 'preposterously unnatural'.]

This is not a novel which evokes the better feelings of human nature; it does not go home to you; you acknowledge its artistic construction, but you feel the want of nature; it rouses your curiosity, it thrills your nerves, it fills you with admiration, contempt, indignation, hatred, but your softer feelings are seldom played upon.... That there is an inclination of over-minuteness we cannot deny, but pre-Raffaelitism is in the ascendant. We were more struck by the general tendency of the book to sacrifice everything to intensity of excitement.

26. Unsigned review, *Saturday Review*

25 August 1860, x, 249–50

See headnote to No. 29.

Mr. Wilkie Collins is an admirable story-teller, though he is not a great novelist. His plots are framed with artistic ingenuity—he unfolds them bit by bit, clearly, and with great care—and each chapter is a most skilful sequel to the chapter before. He does not attempt to paint character or passion. He is not in the least imaginative. He is not by any means a master of pathos. The fascination which he exercises over the mind of his reader consists in this—that he is a good constructor. Each of his stories is a puzzle, the key to which is not handed to us till the third volume. Each part is elaborated only so far as is consistent with its due subordination to the whole. He allows nothing to distract our attention from the narrative, or to induce us to forget that what he is putting before us is a riddle, and has its answer. The great object of the author—the one man who is behind the scenes—is to say what he has got to say so well as to make us follow up the thread he gives us right on to the very end. At the end comes the explanation. The secret spring is touched—the lock flies open—the novel is done. Mr. Wilkie Collins is content to accept from us the kind of homage that a skilful talker extorts from his audience. We have heard him with eager curiosity to the close. We have spent some exciting hours over the charade, and have been at last obliged to come to him in despair for the solution.

With him, accordingly, character, passion, and pathos are mere accessory colouring which he employs to set off the central situation in his narrative. All the architecture of his plot tapers to one point, and is to be interpreted by one idea. Men and women he draws, not for the sake of illustrating human nature and life's varied phases, or exercising his own powers of creation, but simply and solely with reference to the part it is necessary they should play in tangling or disentangling his argument. None of his characters are to be seen looking about them.

They are not occupied in by-play. They are not staring at the spectators, or, if they are, they are staring listlessly and vacantly, like witnesses who are waiting to be called before the court, and have nothing to do until their turn arrives. There they stand, most of them, like ourselves, in rapt attention, on the stretch to take their share in the action of the central group—their eyes bent in one direction—their movement converging upon one centre—half-painted, sketchy figures, grouped with sole relation to the unknown mystery in the middle. The link of interest that binds them is that they are all interested in the great secret. By the time the secret is disclosed, the bond of unity will have been broken—the action of the drama in which they figure will have been finished—and they will go their own ways in twos and threes, and never meet again.

To use a long but expressive word, there is nothing architectonic about the mind of Mr. Wilkie Collins. He is, as we have said, a very ingenious constructor; but ingenious construction is not high art, just as cabinet-making and joining is not high art. Mechanical talent is what every great artist ought to possess. Mechanical talent, however, is not enough to entitle a man to rank as a great artist. When we have said that Mr. Wilkie Collins succeeds in keeping up our excitement by the happy way in which he interweaves with mystery incident just sufficiently probable not to be extravagant, and that he is an adept at administering continual stimulants to our attention, we have said all. Nobody ever leaves one of his tales unfinished. This is a great compliment to his skill. But then very few feel at all inclined to read them a second time. Our curiosity once satisfied, the charm is gone. All that is left us is to admire the art with which the curiosity was excited. Probably he himself would hardly expect us to use his books as we use really great books—for companions of our solitude. His are works not so much for the library as for the circulating library. We should prefer hiring them out as we hire out a Chinese conjuror—for the night. As soon as we have found out the secret of his tricks, and admired the clever way in which he does them, we send him home again. Just so it is necessary to the enjoyment of Mr. Wilkie Collins's writings that we should not have read them before, or should have forgotten all about them since the first perusal.

The *Woman in White* is a longer and more sustained story than we are in the habit of receiving from his pen. In other respects, it is pretty nearly of the same stamp with his earlier creations. In this, as in the rest, we are much less interested in the people than in what happens to the people. Like the women in Pope, most of Mr. Wilkie Collins's characters have no character at all. There is one exception, or rather what looks like an exception, in the *Woman in White*. Count Fosco, the Italian villain of the piece, is a clever conception, though we are not prepared to say that it is altogether as original a conception as Mr. Wilkie Collins appears to imagine. This character is drawn with much more life and animation than the rest. It is clear that the author has an interest in him beyond what he feels for him as a mere instrument in the plot. But then, half of the reason that he is better drawn is that he is easier to draw, both because he is a foreigner, and because he is eccentric in his figure and conversation. The other half of the reason is, that he is what Mr. Wilkie Collins is so fond of—a puzzle. Subtract from him his eccentricities, his Italianisms, and his corpulency—what is left? Simply this, that he is a very undecipherable villain. The author has put him together, just as he puts together his mysterious plots. The only difference is that Mr. Wilkie Collins gives us the key to the plot, and cannot, or does not, give us any key to the villain. So far he is right. Circumstances are an enigma which it is the task of the storyteller artfully to solve. Human nature is an enigma which the truest painter will leave unsolved and unattempted.

The other personages in the book seem to be an exact illustration of the above remarks. They have characteristics, but not character. They might all be summed up in as many sentences as there are personages. One is a silly hypochondriac. There is merit, but not much merit, in making him talk like one. Another is a good-natured family lawyer of the old school. A third is a brave and determined lady. A fourth, who is a quiet little Italian music-master, in point of value comes next to the Italian villain. The reason is, that a good narrator like Mr. Wilkie Collins finds it easier to sketch a music-master than a man who is nobody in particular, and easiest of all to sketch a music-master who has this additional peculiarity that he is an Italian. Far the most interesting part about any of Mr. Collins' characters is the manner or degree in which he or she adds to the complication of the story. Remove all that there is of rather improbable incident in the *Woman in White*, and you might burn what remains without depriving the world of any imaginative creation, any delineation of character, or portrait of human nature worth preserving. Mr. Wilkie Collins would perhaps reply that he is not to be judged except on his own ground—that he is not to be condemned for failing where he has not attempted to succeed. This we cannot allow. It is the duty of those who wish to criticize honestly and fairly to state explicitly the position which a book in their opinion occupies, weighed in the balance with what is first-rate. Estimated by the standard of great novels, the *Woman in White* is nowhere. It certainly is not pure gold. It is not even gold with an alloy. It is an inferior metal altogether, though good and valuable of its kind.

The story of the *Woman in White* is related in a way at once pleasing, novel, and ingenious. Each actor in the scene contributes his quota of evidence, narrates what he has seen and done, so far as his sayings or doings bear upon the issue of the whole transaction, and then makes way for a succeeding witness and narrator. It is scarcely necessary to point out the advantage which the constructor of a tale of mystery thus gains. First of all, the great secret never can be revealed, and the author guards himself from revealing it, prematurely—for the actors are as much in the dark as the reader on the subject, and the author, in *propriâ persona*, does not trust himself to speak. Secondly, the description is thus made lifelike and spirited—just as *veni, vidi, vici* is more spirited than *venit, vidit, vicit*. Lastly, by such means, the action of the tale is presented to us semidramatically from various points of view, and recounted in a manner which, in the case of the *Woman in White*, either is, or at least is supposed by Mr. Wilkie Collins to be, congenial to, and characteristic of the various actors. Indeed, Mr. Wilkie Collins neglects none of those little artifices which are easily seen through, but which, on the whole, have a certain kind of influence on the casual reader, in lending a spurious air of reality to what he reads. Asterisks, cleverly inserted in a letter, afford the novelist an opportunity for remarking in a note that they represent passages which he has thought it expedient to omit. This, for a single moment, gives him the air of a veracious historian, and excuses him at the same time from drawing on his constructive powers for more than is absolutely requisite to his general purpose. The device of painting oneself as unwilling to transcribe and print what in reality never has been composed, is very neat, and has the advantage, at the same time, of calling attention to one's capabilities of reticence. Then, again, Mr. Wilkie Collins (and again in a foot-note) feels it his duty upon conscientious grounds to decline giving the name of an awful Society whose existence he has gratuitously invented in the text. So we call it the Brotherhood, by his directions—an expedient which will no doubt prevent much bloodshed in Leicester-square. This is also tremendously lifelike, adds to the sum total of the air of mystery, and makes the female reader shudder. In reality, it is a puerile and unworthy trick, and one that shows that Mr. Wilkie Collins mistakes the object of true art, which is certainly not to deceive. In spite of this little weakness, whatever the machinery of Mr. Collins be worth, he works it on the whole well. The last twenty or thirty pages in the second volume are a capital specimen of his best mechanical mannerism. Nor is there less talent in the way in which the author, at the close of each diary or piece of evidence, leaves us with expectations actually increased, and eager for the next revelation. We are reminded of an oratorical artifice which is said to have been the creation of the lively mind of the late Dr. Wolff. That great man, whenever he was describing his personal experiences of the King of Bokhara, or some other savage chieftain of the kind, and had arrived in his narrative at the part where he himself had just been sewn up alive in the stomach of an ox for roasting, used to pause, and close his discourse. 'How it pleased Almighty God,' he would conclude, 'to deliver me from the stomach of the ox, I will relate in my next lecture.'

The *Woman in White* has already appeared in numbers in the columns of Mr. Dickens's serial. On the present occasion it would be unnecessary, and perhaps unfair to the story, considering its nature, to analyze it in detail. Before quitting the subject, there is one remark we feel bound to make. We have often suggested that every novelist should keep a professional adviser. It would be a source of pecuniary profit to the legal profession, and of much peace of mind to imaginative authors. Mr. Wilkie Collins, in particular, on the subject of life estates, is either more obscure in his expressions, or else less sound in his law, than we could wish. As the case at present stands, we cannot help thinking that half the crime and folly in the tale has been committed in consequence of a misconception. If Mr. Collins is not unjustifiably unintelligible, the titled villains of the story must have been unjustifiably stupid. Before the second edition appears, we trust the author will either explain himself better, or else get his property tied up by a professional man.

27. Unsigned review, *Observer*

27 August 1860, 7

Having acknowledged that the story is 'more or less known to many readers', the reviewer proceeds to offer 'a brief abstract of the fable' which in fact takes up five-sixths of his space and, in spite of Collins's prefatory plea, gives away the plot in considerable detail.

The author puts forward the theory on which his novel is based, which, he says, has never hitherto been tried in fiction—namely, that 'the story of the book is told throughout by the characters of the book'—in other words, . . . it is based upon the proceedings at a criminal trial. He seems, however, . . . either to have read very little fiction except his own, or to have unaccountably forgotten that several of the best novels in the English language are written in the epistolary form, which, in fact, is making 'the characters of the book tell the story of the book', or it is nothing. Nor can the plan of a criminal trial be considered as the best for a novel, even if it was never 'hitherto tried in fiction'—at least as it is developed in these pages; for the author has so overlaid his story with minute details, which are wholly irrelevant to the issue, that the reader ceases to feel any interest in that result before the work is half concluded. . . .

28. Unsigned review, *Guardian*

29 August 1860, xv, 780–1

The *Guardian*, founded in 1846, was a widely-circulating religious weekly.

How many of our readers are readers also of *All the Year Round*? It is an important question to us, for upon the answer to it depends the answer to another question—Must we introduce the *Woman in White* to them with the ceremonious politeness due to a perfect stranger, or shall we discuss her with the easy familiarity of old acquaintance? To those who have hung upon her course from week to week, and waited for each new chapter with an intenser interest than has, perhaps, ever before been given to periodical fiction, and who have at last mastered the mystery and the *dénouement* of its elaborate plot, it will be aggravating to find that plot handled as if it were still a mystery to them; while to betray the plot to those who are yet ignorant of it would be to take the edge from their enjoyment and rob the riddle of the charm of conjecture. In the absence of any possibility of answering our first question, we must decide between these two alternatives; and in the inevitable dilemma, we fix on the former horn. Indeed, we are scarcely free agents in the matter. Mr. Collins makes a direct appeal to his reviewers, which we admit to be entirely just and reasonable, to abstain from telling his story for him at second hand. There is no harm in doing this in the case of the great majority of novels, where the plot is obvious and the incidents loosely strung together; and where the reader can easily guess the last volume from the first, and omit any given number of pages without seriously injuring the connection of events. But Mr. Collins's plot is an elaborate work of art. The reader is long kept in a real state of uncertainty—first, as to what the mystery is; and secondly, how it is to be cleared up: it is never possible to see more than a very few pages ahead; while all the time the attention is kept alert by suggestive hints, which show you that the writer himself never loses sight of his plan.

Such a story, in which the gradual involving and unrolling of events constitutes the chief interest, would be obviously spoiled by the previous knowledge of a meagre outline: and we forbear to give it.

But are we, therefore, to abdicate the critic's function, and abstain from pointing out the faults that seem to us partially to disfigure what we acknowledge to be on the whole a very skilful and successful piece of work? It does not seem necessary. We are guilty of no breach of confidence, for instance, in pointing to the extreme inconsistency of Sir Percival Glyde's deportment before and after marriage, which seems to us to exceed the bounds of probability. There are limits within which a false part may be successfully acted, but the mask of delicate and refined feeling is beyond the reach of vulgar brutality, and rude, uncontrolled passion. The Sir Percival of the latter half of the book would have been quite unable to personate the Sir Percival of the former. It would have needed all the mental power, the self-mastery, and the versatility of his friend Fosco to have done it. Again, it is difficult to understand how a great country-house in Hampshire (by no means a wild or depopulated county), the seat of a man of the first social rank, one who had stood contested elections, should be secluded from the neighbourhood in such complete isolation as to allow of the doings recorded to have taken place therein, without at once drawing down upon it the attentive watchfulness of a thousand eager eyes. One requires a castle in the Alps, or at least a manor-house in the district of Currer Bell, to harmonise with the moral landscape. And a shrewd lawyer, like Mr. Gilmore, with such a warm interest as his in Laura's welfare, and so much misgiving about her future husband, would assuredly have made inquiries on the spot, which would have revealed enough of Sir Percival's singular antecedents and early acquaintances to give good reason for deferring the marriage till things were made a little clearer about Anne Catherick. Perhaps it is hard to say that Count Fosco could not have been so soft-hearted as to restore so dangerous a weapon as Marian's diary when he once had it in his possession; and it is almost a compliment to point out a slip in vol. iii., where an important entry in a register, assigned in p. 149 to September, is given in p. 203 to April, for such a blunder could only be worth noticing in a very highly finished and accurate work. Some places moreover occur in which it seems to us that the writer, careful as he is, has not wholly escaped the vice of periodical writing, and has allowed himself to be tempted to alter the plot as he proceeded, and so produce an occasional want of harmony between passages taken from different parts of the story. The conversation in the boat-house, in vol. ii., p. 60, and the incident which terminates it, must, we think, have been written when Mr. Collins had a different intention about Sir Percival's secret; and we cannot help supposing that Count Fosco's share in Marian's illness was meant to be more direct than it was found convenient to make it afterwards. At least, if this is not the case, the incidents to which we allude must be regarded as purposeless excrescences. But we have got to the end of our catalogue of blemishes. Mr. Collins will not be offended at the minute criticism which has elicited them; for he will recognize a just tribute to the excellence of his work in the careful reading implied in their detection. Whatever deduction may be made on their account, the main fact remains undisputed, that, in these days of loose and easy writing, Mr. Collins has constructed an original plot of rare intricacy, and has unwound the skein which he had knotted up with a lightness of touch and a patient industry, of which the modern novel furnishes us with very few examples.

Nor is it only the plot which deserves praise. Mr. Collins possesses the talent of the drawing-master who is his hero. He paints his scenes with a fulness and an accuracy which produces the effect of a stereograph. Mr. Fairlie's room at Limmeridge Hall, the gloomy lake and the library front of the house at Blackwater, are instances of them. They stand out before the eye like known and familiar scenes. And this is true of the persons also. Each one is very clearly and distinctly, almost visibly, drawn.

[The characters of Mr Fairlie and, inevitably, Count Fosco are singled out for commendation. Collins's narrative technique is also praised: he 'has devised this ingenious method by means of which an external and objective aspect is given to the whole history, while, nevertheless, it is presented from the different points of view in which it appears to several actors in it'.]

29. Unsigned review, *Spectator*

8 September 1860, xxxiii, 864

Evidently a rejoinder to the unfavourable verdict of the *Saturday Review* (No. 26) two weeks earlier. Collins's novel shares the review with Emily Eden's *The Semi-Attached Couple* (1860) but is given two-thirds of the space.

The *Woman in White* is the latest, and by many degrees the best work of an author who had already written so many singularly good ones. That mastery in the art of construction for which Mr. Wilkie Collins has long been pre-eminent among living writers of fiction is here exhibited upon the largest, and proportionately, the most difficult scale he has yet attempted. To keep the reader's attention fairly and equably on the alert throughout a continuous story that fills three volumes of the ordinary novel form, is no common feat; but the author of the *Woman in White* has done much more than this. Every two of his thousand and odd pages contain as much printed matter as three or four of those to which the majority of Mr. Mudie's subscribers are most accustomed, and from his first page to his last the interest is progressive, cumulative, and absorbing. If this be true—and it appears to be universally admitted—what becomes of the assertion made by some critics, that it is an interest of mere curiosity which holds the reader so fast and holds him so long? The thing is palpably absurd. Curiosity can do much, but it cannot singly accomplish all that is imputed to it by this theory, for it is impossible that its intensity should be sustained without intermission through so long a flight. If *The Woman in White* were indeed a protracted puzzle and nothing more, the reader's attention would often grow languid over its pages; he would be free from the importunate desire that now possesses him to go through every line of it continuously; he would be content to take it up and lay it down at uncertain intervals, or be strongly tempted to skip to the end and find out the secret at once, without more tedious hunting through labyrinths devised only to retard his search, and not worth exploring for their own sake. But he yields to no such temptation, for the secret which is so wonderfully well kept to the end of the third volume is not the be-all and end-all of his interest in the story. Even Mr. Wilkie Collins himself, with all his constructive skill, would be at fault if he attempted to build an elaborate story on so narrow a basis—witness his tale of *The Dead Secret*, which is in some degree chargeable with this defect of construction, and therefore with a corresponding measure of prolixity. The strength and symmetry of the tale before us are marred by no such organic defect. Here the secret underlies, indeed, the whole tenour of the story, and its vital connexion with it is often more or less strongly surmised; but it is only at intervals that it is brought prominently into notice, and that direct efforts for its discovery become the sole business of the moment. Meanwhile there is other matter in hand sufficiently copious and exciting to keep the reader's mind perpetually occupied with a flow of varying emotions.

It is not true then, it is not even a half truth, that this story owes its extraordinary fascination only to its power of awakening and sustaining curiosity, and that 'our curiosity once satisfied, the charm is gone;' neither do we give an unqualified assent to the proposition that 'it is necessary to the enjoyment of Mr. Wilkie Collins's writings that we should not have read them before, or should have forgotten all about them since the first perusal.' Our own experience, so far as it goes, contradicts the latter statement, and we still own the genuine enchantment of *The Woman in White* although we have been for some weeks in possession of her secret. The vivid and manifold emotions with which we read her story are still fresh in our memory, and we retain a lively sense of the personality of every actor in it from Marian and Laura down to the old parish clerk. Yet we are told that the author 'does not attempt to paint character or passion. He is not in the least imaginative!' Mashallah! he is then a more wonderful man than we took him to be, since he can do the work of the imagination so well without having any of the faculty. Presently we are assured by the same consistent authority that this wholly unimaginative artist, who does not attempt to paint character or passion, does actually draw men and women—and it is not said or insinuated that he draws them untruly; but the charge against him is that he subordinates the development of character to the exigencies of his narrative. Possibly he does; and we have a notion that every great artist has done the same thing upon occasion. There are undeveloped and partially developed characters in Shakespeare's plays, and it is notorious that the so-called heroes and heroines of many of Scott's novels—*Old Mortality*, for instance—were purposely left 'half-painted, sketchy figures.' Is a landscape-painter to be condemned as incapable of high art because the figures in his picture are not as large as life, and done after the manner of Raphael or Michael Angelo? Is Béranger a small poet because he wrote nothing but songs? Or is there, in fine, only one style of work worthy of high esteem in any given brand of art, whether painting, poetry, or literary fiction? To sneer at the best thing of its kind because it is not something else is a convenient mode of detraction, and, when done with assurance and a certain degree of literary tact, it may pass with the unwary for authoritative criticism; but it seems a pitiful thing after all when once the trick of it has been discovered.

30. Unsigned review, *The Times*

30 October 1860, 6

The Times waited more than two months before reviewing *The Woman in White*, by which time a third impression had already been called for. The revelation, in the final paragraph of the review, of Collins's error over chronology was promptly acted on: he wrote to his publisher, Edward Marston,

If any fresh impression of *The Woman in White* is likely to be wanted immediately, stop the press till I come back. The critic in *The Times* is (between ourselves) right about the mistake in time. Shakespeare has made worse mistakes—that is one comfort, and readers are not critics who test an emotional book by the base rules of arithmetic, which is a second consolation. Nevertheless we will set it right at the first opportunity.

His corrections were incorporated in subsequent editions; the different readings are recorded in the 'Riverside' edition of the novel, ed. Anthea Trodd (Boston, 1969), which also reprints the 1860 and 1861 prefaces—the former slightly longer and more aggressively directed towards 'the Critics' than the latter, which admits to 'certain technical errors which had escaped me while I was writing the book' but adds the claim that it has received 'careful correction and revision'.

The Woman in White is a novel of the rare old sort which must be finished at a sitting. No chance of laying it down until the last page of the last volume is turned. We have lately got into the habit—strange for these fast days—of reading our novels very leisurely. They are constructed on the principle of monthly instalments, and we read a chapter on the 1st of every month, quietly sauntering to the end of the story in about a couple of years. Even the novels which are published complete in three volumes are for the most part built on the same model. It is possible to open the volume at any page and to read right on without embarrassment. These works of fiction profess to be natural, and therefore avoid the intricacies of a too elaborate plot. The authors take life as they find it, and spend their strength rather in the elucidation of character than in the unravelling of a subtle intrigue. In so doing they are apt to underrate the advantages of a good plot, and to despise the talent that is required for its construction. The greatest of all dramatists borrowed his plots unblushingly from the Italian novelists, and was so careless in the arrangement of his stories that in one of his masterpieces— the tragedy of *Othello*—it is impossible to say whether the action represented occurs within a few days or is spread over weeks. Why, then, should not lesser men be equally unmindful of the plot, and give their whole attention to what is at once the most interesting and the most difficult of all studies—human character? A character is a character under all circumstances, and is equally true to itself whether there is or is not a story to be unfolded. The story, therefore, is in danger of being neglected—because it is not necessary; and there are critical formulas which even go further, and would establish the dogma that it is impossible for a novel in which character has full play to be a good story. We shall not afflict our readers by dwelling on the fashionable German jargon as to the relations of the subjective and the objective in fiction—as to the doctrine of freewill, or the victory of man over circumstance, implied in a feeble plot; and as to the doctrine of necessity, or the conquest of man by circumstance, implied in a good plot. We must be content to ask, in the name of common sense, why great characters should not be mixed up with romantic incidents and complicated events. There is really no incompatibility between good characters and good plots, though, as a matter of fact, it must be admitted that we do not often see the two in conjunction. Certainly we do not see the combination of both excellencies in the present novel of Mr. Wilkie Collins. But neither do we see why the story should not be as clever as it is, and should not at the same time delineate character better than it does.

Meaning to praise the cunning with which Mr. Wilkie Collins has laid his plot, we find ourselves of a sudden pulled up, and at a loss how to proceed. The author warns his critics not to reveal the story, and not to diminish by word or sign the interest of the reader's curiosity, or the excitement of his surprise. But the story is so constructed as to be a continual series of surprises and a sustained appeal to curiosity. It is so artfully put together that if we say a word about anything we shall reveal some important link, and anticipate some projected surprise. On the whole, Mr. Wilkie Collins is right in protesting against the ordinary method of reviewing novels, the greater part of the review being devoted to an abridgment of the story. Nobody cares for the abridgment; and, if the story is a good one, the abridgment may be unjust both to author and reader, yet not so much as Mr. Wilkie Collins supposes. It is a pity that any part of the reader's pleasure should be anticipated; it is hard that what an author has carefully elaborated with many subtle threads of interest, all leading the reader unconsciously to one grand result, should be submitted to a process not unlike that which the great conqueror applied to the knot upon the chariot of the Phrygian King. But in general the interest of the novel is not more forestalled than the interest of a remarkable trial is by the revelations of the previous inquest. We know that the masses who are already acquainted with the story of a man's guilt, and who have read all the evidence adduced at the coroner's inquest or at the trial previous to committal, will devour with unabated interest whole pages of the same evidence when it is reproduced before the jury. The great pleasure which the public take in such a trial as that of Palmer[1] is not in the expectation of new facts, but in the purely intellectual study of the evidence already known, worked up as it is by logical minds into a demonstration. It is not often that much new matter comes to light at these jury trials, and it is rather the manner than the matter that occupies the public attention, which is heightened, no doubt, by suspense as to the verdict. It is much the same with the displays of a romance-writer. The framework of the story is of comparatively small interest. A critic might, in nine cases out of ten, give the leading points without sensibly affecting the pleasure which a reader takes in the more detailed account of the novelist, who, either by filling up his page with the record of human passion and the exhibition of human character, or by appealing to our curiosity, letting out a little piece of information here and a little bit farther on, continually making us feel our ignorance, and throwing us at the proper moment a few crumbs of comfort, gives a charm to the plot of which in itself it is destitute. We therefore think that so good a story-teller as Mr. Collins might have been a little less peremptory in forbidding us to handle his tale. We might ask in return, has he so little faith in his own powers as to imagine that if the secret is once out his novel will lose its fascination, and have nothing else to recommend it to the reader? In a more savage mood, which no one will be inclined to indulge towards an author who has contributed so much to our amusement, we might put the question differently, and ask—if we are not to touch the story, what else is there to touch? Where is the vivid portraiture of character on which we are

[1] Dr William Palmer, the celebrated Staffordshire poisoner, executed 14 June 1856.

to dwell? Where is the life-like description of manners? Where is the suggestion of thought or the display of passion which is to engage our minds? Nay, if such qualities as these were to be found in the story before us, we should find some difficulty in speaking of them, because they must necessarily be connected with incidents about which we are commanded to be silent, lest we should let the cat out of the bag. The cat out of the bag! There are in this novel about a hundred cats contained in a hundred bags, all screaming and mewing to be let out. Every new chapter contains a new cat. When we come to the end of it out goes the animal, and there is a new bag put into our hands which it is the object of the subsequent chapter to open. We are very willing to stroke some of these numerous cats, but it is not possible to do it without letting them out. How can we talk of what happened to Sir Percival Glyde—how can we criticize the leading incident with which Lady Glyde is connected—without a betrayal of some important fact? We forbear as much as we can. We must humour an author who has told such an impressive tale. But, surely, never before have critics been warned by an author not to say a word about the most important thing in his book.

Mr. Collins follows up an unprecedented request by laying claim to an unprecedented method of telling his story. His claim is, to the best of our knowledge, a just one. The story is told by a number of persons, all of whom, taking a more or less active part in the incidents of the tale, are eyewitnesses and earwitnesses of what they report. Practically there may not be much difference between this mode of relating a history and that which was once so common—the epistolary method. The epistolary method was more natural, but it had the disadvantage of leading to many digressions and endless repetitions, and of spinning out novels, like those of Richardson, to a prodigious number of volumes. In the method of story-telling devised by Mr. Wilkie Collins the narrators are like the witnesses at a trial. Each one speaks according to his or her knowledge; the succeeding witness adds a few touches to the evidence of the previous one, and so the story moves forward bit by bit, until at last the mosaic of evidence is complete and every hole is filled up. The advantage of this new method is, that the story moves forward without interruption, and that the reader's curiosity is continually teased by a sense of mystery. The witness, relating only what he knows, piques our curiosity by his ignorance even more than he satisfies it by his disclosure. The disadvantage of the method is, that it is unnatural, and we pay Mr. Wilkie Collins a compliment when we advise all future novelists to beware of his example, for where he, who has studied so carefully the art of story-telling, has failed it is not likely that they will succeed. The art of telling a story in a series of letters was exploded about the end of last century, because it was felt to be an affectation. An author had to tell a story, and he wished to avoid the appearance of doing so; he would conceal his art; he would be natural; he would make the heroes and heroines tell their own stories in their private letters. This was all very well when it was done once or twice, but people soon got tired of the trick, and insisted upon the author relating the story, if he had one, in a straightforward way. In starting a new style the object of Mr. Wilkie Collins is not so legitimate as that of Richardson. The elder novelist was simply trying to appear natural—the younger is trying to appear ignorant. The affectation of ignorance in almost every page is a prime necessity of his novel, and this ignorance he works up into a stimulant of curiosity. He has perfectly succeeded in doing so, but it is at no small sacrifice of truth and nature. Is it natural to suppose that a number of persons, some of them at daggers drawn, others with a horrible aversion to writing, should conspire together to compose a novel, of which the several parts dovetail into each other with astonishing precision? Mr. Hartright and Miss Halcombe are brother-in-law and sister-in-law—devoted to each other. But Miss Halcombe is not permitted to see Mr. Hartright's narrative, and Mr. Hartright may not look into Miss Halcombe's diary, because each speaks of the other in terms they do not like to confess. Yet, by a miracle of art, Miss Halcombe's diary exactly fits into all the little gaps of Mr. Hartright's narrative. If this be wonderful enough when the writers are so intimate, what shall we say when they are hostile? Count Fosco is the villain of the tale. It is requisite that at the end of the story he should clear up a certain mystery. He is compelled to do so under pain of death. All that it is necessary for him to say in his peculiar position might be compressed into a single page. But the Count is generous, and, though he has only a few hours in which to pack up and get ready for the Continent under terror of his life, he devotes the greater number of these to the concoction of a capital narrative, which takes up all the threads of interest that have been left loose in the previous record, gives much pleasant but perfectly unnecessary information as to his private habits, and brings the novel to a satisfactory conclusion. So with Mr. Frederick Fairlie. This gentleman is a hypochondriac who carefully avoids trouble. On occasions of the greatest moment he has been begged and implored to make a very slight exertion in order to avert from his relatives a very great calamity. He is not to be moved. He refuses doggedly.

This selfish and nerveless vegetable, who refuses to interest himself in the affairs of his relatives when every consideration of duty and palpable necessity would prompt, is induced when there is no necessity, when there is no duty, and when he has at last ceased to be on speaking terms with these relatives, to interest himself so far on their behalf as to take the, to him, enormous trouble of writing a long narrative which supplies certain missing links in the chain of evidence. It is into such palpable violations of probability as these that a writer so able as Mr. Wilkie Collins is driven by his peculiar new scheme of writing a tale in the words of a dozen different narrators, each of whom confines his testimony to the series of facts of which he has personal knowledge. We have said that the object of this method of storytelling is to make play with our ignorance. Sometimes, however, the author cannot even in this way get ignorance enough, and he has to invent more of it. For example, the principal complication of the story depends upon the loss of a date. Recover that date, and, everything being cleared up, the story must come to an untimely end. The date might be very easily recovered if the author chose—but he doesn't choose, and he insists, against all probabilities, upon everybody forgetting it. The person who would be most likely to remember it is the housekeeper at Blackwater-park, who pretends to some education, who is the widow of a clergyman, and who writes a pretty long narrative, in which she contrives to remember with wonderful accuracy a great number of minute facts in the precise order of their occurrence. On the day in question her mistress leaves Blackwater-park, she herself resigns her situation as housekeeper, and during the day several very remarkable incidents occur, the whole being wound up by the master of the house leaving it in a fury at night. The lady who has such a wonderful memory for everything else cannot remember this day of days—what day of the month, or what day of the week it was. 'I can only remember now that it was towards the latter part of July,' she says. 'We all know the difficulty, after a lapse of time, of fixing precisely on a past date, unless it has been previously written down,' she adds in her own defence. But the lapse of time after which the date was lost was a very short one—only a few months. And her mistress had not left Blackwater-park more than a day or two, when there came news of what occurred to her, which would have fixed indelibly on the mind of any housekeeper the date of her departure— not to speak of the all-important fact to a housekeeper that on the same day she resigned her place. In addition to all this, Miss Halcombe, too, forgets the date. She knew of her sister Lady Glyde's departure from

Blackwater the day after it took place, knew where she had gone to, understood all that was implied in the journey, and in one or two days afterwards heard of the astounding result. Nothing could have erased the dates from her mind but the dire necessity of the novelist to invent ignorance which could not exist.

Great in the art of mystification, Mr. Wilkie Collins delights in a mystified character, and in the present novel has expended all his power in the setting forth of an enigmatical personage—the Count Fosco. Count Fosco is the great character of the novel. As Satan is the hero of Milton's poem, the Count may be said to be Mr. Collins's hero. Everybody else in the tale is a sketch. Count Fosco is something more than a sketch. He is very vividly portrayed, and is the one interesting character of the work. We cannot, indeed, say that he is the original creation of Mr. Collins. On the contrary, we are well acquainted with the Count under a different name. Who does not remember Mr. Harold Skimpole?[1] Harold Skimpole, with his airy manner and simple good-nature, was one of Mr. Dickens's most vivid and successful portraitures. It will be remembered that as the story in which he played a part proceeded from month to month, the question was continually suggested, Is he a villain, or is he a child? Can all this infantile impulse be real? Or is it the elaborate disguise of a sharper? As it turns out, Mr. Harold Skimpole is not a villain or a sharper; he is simply a selfish fellow, full of impulses, vain of these impulses, and, in the desire to gratify every whim of the moment, utterly regardless of the feelings of others. He would light his cigar with a widow's pension. Mr. Wilkie Collins has quite unconsciously taken the same character, and endowed it with a strong will and the power of sustained action. He has accepted that alternative which all who studied Harold Skimpole saw as the possible solution of his character; he has rendered him a knave. Here he is with his childlike tastes, with his love of tart and cream, with his fondness for birds and mice, with his affection for sugar and water, with his horror of blood, but also with a contempt for human suffering, with a disregard for the laws of property, with a determination to gain his own ends, and with the knowledge that under his childlike tastes and impulsive ways he can easily conceal the most nefarious designs. With all the innocent gaiety of Harold Skimpole, he has all the cunning of Iago, and becomes by his craft the most important personage in the story. It is wonderful what he can do. He is irresistible. Everything goes wrong, and everybody is powerless in his hands. He detects every

[1] In Dickens's *Bleak House* (1853).

design; he forestalls every plan; he is always prepared. Everybody else fails at the proper moment, like straws in the wind. He alone is firm and carries his point, equal to every emergency, and victorious on every encounter, until at last fate turns against him. At the beginning of the third volume all the luck falls to Mr. Walter Hartright. It is destined that he should foil the Italian Count, and so by the most extraordinary insight he discovers things at the right moment, or by the most extraordinary good fortune he obtains information hitherto undreamt of by those most likely to know it. There is no reason for all this but the will of the author, who usurps a somewhat tyrannical sway over both characters and incidents, insomuch that the novel will not bear a very close inspection. It is rather to be devoured whole, as a boa constrictor bolts a rabbit, than to be criticized in detail, and we gladly bear witness that it is successful, before the reader has had time to examine it, in producing an over-mastering excitement. Let no one accuse us of contradiction in cordially lauding a book in which at the same time we discover serious faults. The contradiction is easily explained. There are many illusions which astound us for a time and which we take to pieces afterwards. The rustic who is frightened by bogie in the night laughs in the morning to find that it was only the stump of a tree. We defy anybody to read Mr. Wilkie Collins's tale for the first time without admitting it to be one of the most thrilling stories he has ever perused; but when the excitement is over, though not till then, he will be disposed to treat the whole thing as a joke—to ask whether that thunder was real, to complain that the moon was a paper lantern which occasionally went out, and to insist upon the impossibility of his being so enthralled again. It is only men of real talent, however, that can play such jokes, and Mr. Collins has every reason to be satisfied with the extraordinary fascination which he exerted over an immense number of readers when his tale appeared week by week in the pages of Mr. Dickens's periodical, and which he still exerts now that his work, having reached a third edition, can be read in a complete form.

Perhaps the following fact will give a better idea of the character of the novel than any epithets which it would be possible to invent, and, in justification of the foregoing remarks, we will endeavour to state this fact without divulging the important incidents connected with it. The question of a date is the pivot upon which the novel turns. The whole of the third volume is devoted to the ascertaining of this date. Everything depends upon it. But it is lost in the most marvellous obscurity—it is lost even to Mr. Wilkie Collins, who is a whole fortnight out of his reckoning. If we dare trespass upon details after the author's solemn injunction, we could easily show that Lady Glyde could not have left Blackwater-park before the 9th or 10th of August. Anybody who reads the story, and who counts the days from the conclusion of Miss Halcombe's diary, can verify the calculation for himself. He will find that the London physician did not pay his visit till the 31st of July, that Dawson was not dismissed till the 3rd of August, and that the servants were not dismissed till the following day. The significance of these dates will be clear to all who have read the story. They render the last volume a mockery, a delusion, and a snare; and all the incidents in it are not merely improbable—they are absolutely impossible. Nor is this the only impossibility of the tale; we could point out a dozen scarcely less glaring. But if here we have evidence of Mr. Collins's weakness, we have also convincing proof of his great ability. What must that novel be which can survive such a blunder? Remember that it is not now published for the first time. It was read from week to week by eager thousands in the pages of *All the Year Round*. In those pages a blunder which renders the whole of the last volume, the climax of the tale, nugatory, escaped the practised eye of Mr. Dickens and his co-adjutors, who were blinded, as well they might be, by the strong assertions and earnest style of the narrator. A plot that is worked out of impossibilities, like that of robbing the almanack of a fortnight, may be treated as a jest; but we vote three cheers for the author who is able to practise such a jest with impunity. He will not have a reader the less, and all who read will be deceived and delighted.

31. Unsigned review, *Dublin University Magazine*

February 1861, lvii, 200–203

This attack on Collins's novel follows a discussion of George Eliot's *The Mill on the Floss* in an article titled 'Recent Popular Novels'.

With all her faults, however, a writer like George Eliot may look down from a very far height on such a dweller in the plains as he who wrote *The Woman in White*. In this novel, which claims a passing notice from the marked disproportion of its actual merits to its seeming popularity, the spirit of modern realism has woven a tissue of scenes more wildly improbable than the fancy of an average idealist would have ventured to inflict on readers beyond their teens. Mr. W. Collins has for some years been favourably known to the general reader as a painstaking manufacturer of stories, short or long, whose chief merit lies in the skilful elaboration of a startling mystery traceable to some natural cause, but baffling all attempts to solve it until the author himself has given us the right clue. Some praise is also due to him for the care with which these literary puzzles are set off by a correct if not very natural style, a pleasing purity of moral tone, and a certain knack of hitting the more superficial traits of character. When we have said all we can for him, we have said nothing that would entitle him to a higher place among English novelists, than the compiler of an average school-history would enjoy among English historians. But to a higher place he seems ambitious to rise, if his readers would only estimate his last performance as highly as he does himself. At any rate, he has tried his best to make the world a partner in his own illusions. *The Woman in White* opens with a grand flourish on the author's own trumpet, and echoes of the same sweet music greet us ever and anon throughout the work. That many have thus been lured to take him at his own valuing, is likely and natural enough; and the pleasure that comes to most of us in reading a story full of movement and strange surprises, will often be enhanced by contrast with the surfeiting effects of certain other tales wherewith the genius of a great living novelist has made us too familiar. But to us it seemed as if all this self-approval rendered us the more alive to the author's weakness, even in those very points where he had hitherto come out best. If he has never yet succeeded in writing a noteworthy novel, he has signally failed for once in that field of mechanical excellence which redeemed his former essays from utter neglect.

Mr. Collins ends his preface with an implied request that his critics will contrive to praise or blame him 'without telling his story at second-hand.' Whether the story, involved and intricate as it is, would repay the trouble of abridging, we shall not try to ascertain by our own experience; but we appeal to that of others against the notion that such a process would certainly lessen to future readers the charm derived from suspended curiosity or sustained surprise. A good story with any life in it will lose nothing by our previous knowledge of the plot. . . .

A novel that cannot bear a slight rehearsal must either be wholly unreadable, or, at best, belong to a low type of literary art whose whole merit lies in the production of clever puzzles and startling metamorphoses. To which of these classes *The Woman in White* may be assigned we shall leave others to settle for themselves, only asking, for our own part, how it is possible to criticize a book of this sort without a continual reference to the plot. Take that away, and there is nothing left to examine. There is not one lifelike character: not one natural dialogue in the whole book. Both hero and heroine are wooden, commonplace, uninteresting in any way apart from the story itself. Even Mr. Tulliver, drawn as he is by a woman's hand, has far more of living flesh and blood in him than the drawing-master who runs off to America because his steps are dogged for a while by the paid spies of a secret enemy. Laura Fairlie fails to inspire us even with the gentler sort of interest we feel for Mrs. Osborne or Miss Dombey. Mr. Fairlie is a feeble caricature, and the Countess Fosco a convenient dummy. Sir Percival Glyde is made up of, at least, two utterly different beings: a two-fronted mask on the top of a stage-cloak. 'The Woman in White' herself is a useful shadow, and her mother an impossibility. On Marian Halcombe and Count Fosco the author has spent a great deal of meritorious pains; to what purpose, any student of Scott, Thackeray, or Currer Bell may easily guess. The former of these two is, however, the most human personage in the book; while the latter may, at least, be hailed by the minor theatres as a new and striking sample of accomplished ruffianism, turned out by a process peculiar to Mr. Collins, and embodying all the latest discoveries in science, morals, and general charlatanry.

What character his personages have, the author prides himself on bringing out in a way which other novelists will do well not to imitate. If they neither say nor do aught characteristic on their own account, yet in connexion with the story most of them have a good deal to write about themselves or about each other. This, indeed, forms the main peculiarity of the book. To be new and striking in many ways is clearly the author's grand aim; and if all high excellence lay therein, his triumph would be great indeed. Even the main incidents of the story are less strikingly new than the manner in which it is told. He will have nothing to say to that simple method which answered well enough in days when the story-teller was allowed to peep behind the scenes, and throw the light of occasional omniscience over the dark places of his tale. Even the later fashion of writing your own story, or helping out a narrative with scraps of letters and diaries, fails to satisfy his thirst for combining the new with the real. Undeterred by Miss Mulock's failure in the mechanism of her last novel, he has tried to better her teaching by a device more absurd and far-fetched than any. Instead of keeping up that seesaw between 'his diary' and 'her diary' which spoils the reading of *A Life for a Life*, he has achieved a literary feat wonderfully like to that of the gentleman at Astley's, who surpasses all rivals by straddling over six horses at once. 'The story of the book is told throughout by the characters of the book,' each of them in turn taking up the wondrous tale at the point where his or her shadow falls most invitingly across the scene. How many witnesses thus give their evidence we are afraid to reckon up; but any one who has ever floundered through all the particulars of an important trial for murder, or about a disputed will, can realize the bewildering effect of the same process carried out in the development of a three-volumed novel. The great difference against those who read the latter is, that in a court of justice witnesses are not allowed to ramble far from the point, while the judge conveniently sums up for the general behoof those results which a curious novel-reader is left to puzzle over for himself. Whatever some may think of the novelty of this arrangement, we are really at a loss to see how 'the substance of the book, as well as the form, has profited by it.' If abrupt changes in style and colouring, needless repetitions of facts already known, much interweaving of impertinent trifles, and many wearisome demands on our credulity, be, as we honestly declare, the mighty issue of this labouring mountain, the pretended profit must be far beyond our search. What movement the story has could have been imparted by much simpler means; and we would rather have seen the characters developed in the usual way, than by a process about as credible and straightforward as that employed by the spirits who are supposed to move our drawing-room tables, and play sweet music on accordions once attunable by mortal fingers alone. Do we get any further or more important light into the depths of Mr. Fairlie's small mind by perusing his statement of what befel himself at the time of Miss Halcombe's illness? Would a sickly, lazy, irritable gentleman, taking up the parable sorely against his own will, have extended a very short story over some thirty pages, even though it was all taken down from his dictation? How is it that the housekeeper at Blackwater Park, so stupid, forgetful, and unsuspecting, should have depicted her own experiences with regard to Fosco, Glyde, and others, in language strangely akin to that of Miss Halcombe's diary and Mr. Hartright's confessions? A longish statement by Mr. Fairlie's lawyer, besides going over some old ground, illustrates nothing but the kindly nature of a gentleman with whom we never meet again, and who allows his client's niece to fall too readily into the snare devised for her by her future husband. Some parts even of Marian's diary might have been cut away without leaving her less worthy to inspire her villainous Italian lover with that exceptional tenderness which insured his ultimate defeat.

Had the story been wrought out in the old-fashioned way it could have been told far more effectively and in less space. Much of the first and nearly half the second volume might have been easily condensed into two or three chapters. A story full of movement would not have kept us waiting so long beside Marian's sick bed, or among the art treasures of her silly and selfish uncle's sitting-room at Limmeridge. A few pages on the subject of Mrs. Michelson's narrative, and a few lines about the shorter depositions that follow, would have told us all that was needful regarding the plot laid for destroying the identity of Lady Glyde. Nor will it seem bootless to remind the author that incidents alone do not necessarily help the story forward, even if it be stuffed as full of them as an omnibus is with passengers on a rainy day. If some of those in the present novel are useful to mislead, others can only tend to weary the reader, without adding a perceptible link to the circumstantial chain.

But the attempt to combine newness of form and substance with reality of treatment has led to failure of a still more glaring kind. Throughout the book circumstances grotesque or improbable meet you at every turn. You are bidden to look at scenes of real modern life, described by the very persons who figured therein, and you find yourself, instead, wandering in a world as mythical as that portrayed on the boards of a penny theatre or in the pages of a nursery tale.

A novelist who aims at being natural, and writes seriously, should refrain from reminding us of so broad a farce as Shakespeare's *Comedy of Errors*.

[The rest of the review examines in detail the alleged absurdities of the plot, letting a good deal of it out of the bag in the process.]

32. From an unsigned review, *Sixpenny Magazine*

September 1861, i, 366–7

The magazine's regular 'Literature of the Month' article was on this occasion largely devoted to the sensation novel, and provides a very early example of the use of that term (see Introduction, p. 17).

There are three kinds of works of fiction, each with strongly marked characteristics—the first, in which acknowledged fidelity to nature is a marked feature; as examples we may instance the earlier works of Dickens, *The Caxtons* of Bulwer, and *Adam Bede*. The second, in which there is an evident element of exaggeration, treated with more or less artistic merit, such as the later works of Dickens, *Jane Eyre*, *John Halifax*, and the *Woman in White*. In the third, nature is entirely disregarded, and the author contents himself with repeating old forms of melodramatic narrative.

[In the discussion of specific novels, *Great Expectations* is judged inferior to *A Tale of Two Cities* in respect of 'the artistic development of the story':]

In this merit it is almost equal to Wilkie Collins's extremely clever romance, which we regard as the greatest success in sensation writing, with the single exception of Mrs Stowe's deservedly popular work [presumably *Uncle Tom's Cabin* (1852)], produced within our memory. . . .

33. From an unsigned review, *Spectator*

28 December 1861, xxxiv, 1428

The following are the opening sentences of a review of *The Castleford Case* by Frances Browne (1816–79), under the title 'The Enigma Novel'.

We are threatened with a new variety of the sensation novel, a host of cleverly complicated stories, the whole interest of which consists in the gradual unravelling of some carefully prepared enigma. Mr. Wilkie Collins set the fashion, and now every novel writer who can construct a plot, thinks if he only makes it a little more mysterious and unnatural, he may obtain a success rivalling that of the *Woman in White*. We beg to protest *in limine*[1] against any such waste of ingenuity. The *Woman in White* was endurable simply because the mystery to be unravelled was of its kind perfect, though we hold silently, nevertheless, that the delineation of Count Fosco was a far higher *artistic* effort than constructing the plot. A good detective might have prepared *that*, but he could not have conceived Count Fosco, or made him move if he had by the light of a special experience been able to conceive him. But there is not the slightest probability that the swarm of imitators will construct plots nearly so good, or achieve any result except that of wasting very considerable powers upon an utterly worthless end. . . .

[1] At the outset.

34. Mrs Oliphant, from an unsigned review, 'Sensation Novels', *Blackwood's Magazine*

May 1862, xci, 565–74

Mrs Margaret Oliphant published nearly 100 books and, between 1852 and her death, contributed more than 200 articles and stories to *Blackwood's*: her contributions are listed in *The Autobiography and Letters of Mrs. Oliphant*, ed. A. L. Coghill (1899). It has been suggested that her novel *Salem Chapel*, which was running serially in the magazine at the time this article was published, owes something to *The Woman in White* (see V. and R. A. Colby, *The Equivocal Virtue: Mrs. Oliphant and the Victorian Literary Market Place* (1966), 50–1). After the discussion quoted below, the reviewer turns to Dickens's *Great Expectations* as an example of 'sensation fiction', and finds it 'far from being one of his best works'.

Before the end of the year she had re-read Collins's novel, and wrote to William Blackwood: 'I must say I think the *Woman in White* a marvel of workmanship. I found it bear a second reading very well, and indeed it was having it thrown in my way for a second time which attracted so strongly my technical admiration . . .' (*Autobiography*, 186).

[The first part of the review is devoted to a short general discussion of the sensation novel.]

Shakespeare, even in the excitement of a new interpretation, has not crowded the waning playhouse, as has the sensation drama with its mock catastrophes; and Sir Walter himself never deprived his readers of their lawful rest to a greater extent with one novel than Mr Wilkie Collins has succeeded in doing with his *Woman in White*. We will not attempt to decide whether the distance between the two novelists is less than that which separates the skirts of Shakespeare's regal mantle from the loftiest stretch of Mr Boucicault. But it is a fact that the well-known old stories of readers sitting up all night over a novel had begun to grow faint in the public recollection. Domestic histories, however virtuous and charming, do not often attain that result—nor, indeed, would an occurrence so irregular and destructive of all domestic proprieties be at all a fitting homage to the virtuous chronicles which have lately furnished the larger part of our light literature. Now a new fashion has been set to English novel-writers. Whether it can be followed extensively, or whether it would be well if that were possible, are very distinct questions; but it cannot be denied that a most striking and original effort, sufficiently individual to be capable of originating a new school in fiction, has been made, and that the universal verdict has crowned it with success.

Mr Wilkie Collins is not the first man who has produced a sensation novel. By fierce expedients of crime and violence, by *diablerie* of divers kinds, and by the wild devices of a romance which smiled at probabilities, the thing has been done before now. The higher class of American fiction, as represented by Hawthorne, attempts little else. In that strange hybrid between French excitement and New England homeliness, we recognize the influence of a social system which has paralysed all the wholesome wonders and nobler mysteries of human existence. Hectic rebellion against nature—frantic attempts by any kind of black art or mad psychology to get some grandeur and sacredness restored to life—or if not sacredness and grandeur, at least horror and mystery, there being nothing better in earth or heaven; Mesmerism possibly for a make-shift, or Socialism, if perhaps it might be more worth while to turn ploughmen and milkmaids than ladies and gentlemen; or, if none of these would do, best to undermine life altogether, and find what creeping honours might be underground: here a Scarlet Letter and impish child of shame, there a snake-girl, horrible junction of reptile and woman. The result is no doubt a class of books abounding in sensation; but the effect is invariably attained by violent and illegitimate means, as fantastic in themselves as they are contradictory to actual life. The Master of English fiction, Sir E. B. Lytton, has accomplished the same end, by magic and supernaturalism, as in the wild and beautiful romance of *Zanoni*.[1] We will not attempt to discuss his last wonderful effort of this class, which is a species by itself, and to be judged only by special rules, which space debars us from considering. Of all the productions of the supernatural school, there is none more perfect in its power of sensation, or more entirely effective in its working out, than the short

[1] Bulwer-Lytton's *Zanoni* was published in 1842.

story of the 'Haunted House,' most thrilling of ghostly tales; but we cannot enter upon this school of fiction, which is distinct from our present subject. Mr Dickens rarely writes a book without an attempt at a similar effect by means of some utterly fantastic creation, set before his readers with all that detail of circumstance in which he is so successful. Amid all these predecessors in the field, Mr Wilkie Collins takes up an entirely original position. Not so much as a single occult agency is employed in the structure of his tale. Its power arises from no over-straining of nature:—the artist shows no love of mystery for mystery's sake; he wastes neither wickedness nor passion. His plot is astute and deeply-laid, but never weird or ghastly; he shows no desire to tinge the daylight with any morbid shadows. His effects are produced by common human acts, performed by recognizable human agents, whose motives are never inscrutable, and whose line of conduct is always more or less consistent. The moderation and reserve which he exhibits; his avoidance of extremes; his determination, in conducting the mysterious struggle, to trust to the reasonable resources of the combatants, who have con-sciously set all upon the stake for which they play, but whom he assists with no weapons save those of quick wit, craft, courage, patience, and villainy—tools common to all men—make the lights and shadows of the picture doubly effective. The more we perceive the perfectly legitimate nature of the means used to produce the sensation, the more striking does that sensation become. The machinery of miracle, on the contrary, is troublesome and expensive, and never satisfactory; a miraculous issue ought to come out of it to justify the miraculous means; and miraculous issues are at war with all the economy of nature, not to say that they are difficult of invention and hard to get credit for. A writer who boldly takes in hand the common mechanism of life, and by means of persons who might all be living in society for anything we can tell to the contrary, thrills us into wonder, terror, and breathless interest, with positive personal shocks of surprise and excitement, has accomplished a far greater success than he who effects the same result through super-natural agencies, or by means of the fantastic creations of lawless genius or violent horrors of crime. When we are to see a murder visibly done before our eyes, the performers must be feeble indeed if some shudder of natural feeling does not give force to their exertions; and the same thing is still more emphatically the case when the spiritual and invisible powers, to which we all more or less do secret and unwilling homage, are actors in the drama. The distinguishing feature of Mr Wilkie Collins' success is, that he ignores all these arbitrary sensations, and has boldly undertaken to produce effects as startling by the simplest expedients of life. It is this which gives to his book the qualities of a new beginning in fiction. There is neither murder, nor seduction, nor despair—neither startling eccentrics nor fantastic monsters in this remarkable story. A much more delicate and subtle power inspires its action. We cannot object to the means by which he startles and thrills his readers; everything is legitimate, natural, and possible; all the exaggerations of excitement are carefully eschewed, and there is almost as little that is objectionable in this highly-wrought sensation-novel, as if it had been a domestic history of the most gentle and unexciting kind.

Except, indeed, in one point. The sympathies of the reader on whom the *Woman in White* lays her spell, are, it is impossible to deny, devoted to the arch-villain of the story. The charm of the book, so far as character counts in its effect, is Fosco. He is a new type of the perennial enemy of goodness. But there is no resisting the charm of his good-nature, his wit, his foibles, his personal individuality. To put such a man so diabolically in the wrong seems a mistake somehow—though it is evident that an innocent man could never have been invested with such a combination of gifts. No villain of the century, so far as we are aware, comes within a hundred miles of him: he is more real, more genuine, more *Italian* even, in his fatness and size, in his love of pets and pastry, than the whole array of conventional Italian villains, elegant and subtle, whom we are accustomed to meet in literature. Fosco from his first entrance is master of the scene—his noiseless movements, his villainous bland philosophies, his enjoyment of life, his fine waistcoats—every detail about him is necessary to his perfection. Not Riccabocca himself, noble impersonation of national character as he is, is more complete or individual. The manner in which he despises and overawes and controls the violent and weak Sir Percival—the absolute but flattering sway he exercises over his wife, the way in which he pervades the whole surrounding atmosphere with his deep 'ringing voice,' his snatches of song, his caresses to his pets—is quite masterly. The reader shares in the unwilling liking to which, at his first appearance, he beguiles Marian Halcombe; but the reader, notwithstanding the fullest proof of Fosco's villainy, does not give him up, and take to hating him, as Marian does. The fact is, that he is by a very long way the most interesting personage in the book, and that it is with a certain sensation of sympathetic triumph that we watch him drive away in safety at last, after the final scene with Hartright, in which his own victorious force and cleverness turn discomfiture and confession into a brilliant climax of self-disclosure.

So far from any vindictive desire to punish his ill-doing, we cannot understand how Hartright, or any other man, finds it in his heart to execute justice upon so hearty, genial, and exhilarating a companion. In short, when it turns out that Laura is not dead, and that the woman in white was not assisted to die, Count Fosco becomes rather an ill-used personage than otherwise. He has not done a single superfluous bit of villainy—he has conducted himself throughout with a certain cheerful consideration for the feelings of his victims. He is so undaunted and undauntable save for a single moment—always master of the position, even when he retreats and gives in—that it is impossible to treat him as his crimes deserve. He is intended to be an impersonation of evil, a representative of every diabolical wile: but Fosco is not detestable; on the contrary, he is more interesting, and seizes on our sympathies more warmly than any other character in the book.

This, in the interests of art, it is necessary to protest against. The Foscos of ordinary life are not likely, we admit, to take encouragement from Mr Wilkie Collins; but if this gentleman has many followers in fiction, it is a matter of certainty that the disciples will exaggerate the faults of their leader, and choose his least pleasant peculiarities for special study. Already it is a not uncommon result of fictitious writings, to make the worse appear the better cause. We have just laid down a clever novel, called *East Lynne*,[1] which some inscrutable breath of popular liking has blown into momentary celebrity. It is occupied with the story of a woman who permitted herself, in passion and folly, to be seduced from her husband. From first to last it is she alone in whom the reader feels any interest. Her virtuous rival we should like to bundle to the door and be rid of, anyhow. The Magdalen herself, who is only moderately interesting while she is good, becomes, as soon as she is a Magdalen, doubly a heroine. It is evident that nohow, except by her wickedness and sufferings, could she have gained so strong a hold upon our sympathies. This is dangerous and foolish work, as well as false, both to Art and Nature. Nothing can be more wrong and fatal than to represent the flames of vice as a purifying fiery ordeal, through which the penitent is to come elevated and sublimed. The error of Mr Wilkie Collins is of a different kind, but it is perhaps even more dangerous. Fosco in suffering would be Fosco in collapse, totally unmanned and uninteresting. It is the perfect ease, comfort, and light-heartedness of the man—what virtuous people would call his 'simple tastes,' his thorough enjoyment of life, and all the pleasant things within reach—

[1] Mrs Henry Wood's *East Lynne* was published in 1861.

his charming vanity and amiableness, as well as his force, strength, and promptitude, that recommend him to our regard. Whatever the reason may be, few good men are permitted in books to enjoy their existence as this fat villain is permitted to enjoy his. He spreads himself out in the sun with a perfect pleasure and satisfaction, which it is exhilarating to behold. His crimes never give him an apparent twinge; his own complacent consciousness of the perfect cleverness with which they are carried out, confounds all compunctions. He is so smilingly aware of the successful evil he has done, and unaware of the guilt of it, that it seems heartless to take so innocent and genial a soul to task for his peccadilloes. Such is the great and radical drawback of the most notable of sensation novels. Fosco is, unquestionably, destined to be repeated to infinitude, as no successful work can apparently exist in this imitative age without creating a shoal of copyists; and with every fresh imitation the picture will take more and more objectionable shades. The violent stimulant of serial publication—of *weekly* publication, with its necessity for frequent and rapid recurrence of piquant situation and startling incident—is the thing of all others most likely to develop the germ, and bring it to fuller and darker bearing. What Mr Wilkie Collins has done with delicate care and laborious reticence, his followers will attempt without any such discretion. We have already had specimens, as many as are desirable, of what the detective policeman can do for the enlivenment of literature: and it is into the hands of the literary Detective that this school of story-telling must inevitably fall at last. He is not a collaborateur whom we welcome with any pleasure into the republic of letters. His appearance is neither favourable to taste nor morals. It is only in rare cases, even in real life, that bystanders side with those conspirators of justice; and in fiction it is almost a necessity that the criminal who is tracked through coil after coil of evidence should become interesting, as we see him thrust into a corner by his remorseless pursuers. The rise of a Sensation School of art in any department is a thing to be watched with jealous eyes; but nowhere is it so dangerous as in fiction, where the artist cannot resort to a daring physical plunge, as on the stage, or to a blaze of palpable colour, as in the picture-gallery, but must take the passions and emotions of life to make his effects withal. We will not deny that the principle may be used with high and pure results, or that we should have little fault to find with it were it always employed with as much skill and self-control as in the *Woman in White*; but that is an unreasonable hope; and it seems but too likely that Mr Wilkie Collins, in his remarkable novel, has given a new impulse to a kind of literature which must, more or less, find its inspiration in crime, and, more or less, make the criminal its hero.

The ordinary belief of the public, backed by recent experience, seems to be that there are few trades more easy than the writing of novels. Any man who entertains this opinion, would do well to take a backward glance over the early works of Mr Wilkie Collins. These productions, all of which have come into existence with elaborate prefaces, and expositions of a 'purpose,' will prove to the reader that the *Woman in White* is not a chance success or caprice of genius, but that the author has been long engaged in preparatory studies, and that the work in question is really the elaborate result of years of labour. Academical sketches and studies from the life are not always interesting to the general spectator; nor are painters apt to exhibit them, by way of showing how much pains were necessary before the picture could be composed, and the figures duly set and draped; yet when the great work is complete, there is an unquestionable interest in the fragments of suggestion from which, one by one, the perfect composition grew. We will not inquire whether the *Woman in White* is a sufficiently great work to merit such an exposition; but every reader who thinks so has it in his power to study the portfolio of sketches by which the author measured his strength. We confess that it has, up to a recent time, been a marvel to us what possible interest any human creature could be supposed to take in the motives which induced a rational man and tolerable writer to weave such a dreary web as the *Dead Secret*, or to commit to print and publicity such a revolting story as *Basil*. It appears, however, that the author knew what he was about; his last successful work has thrown a gleam of intelligibility even upon his prefaces, and it is with the respect due to persevering labour and difficulties overcome that we approach the book which shows how much he has profited by his probation. Let us not neglect such an opportunity for a moral. To judge this author by the portfolio of imperfect sketches which he liberally confided to the world before uncovering the picture for which they were made, nobody would have concluded him likely to open a new path for himself, or to produce a remarkable and thrilling effect by the most modest and subtle means. The sketches are often diffuse and washy—sometimes coarsely horrible—scarcely at all betraying that fine faculty of perception which can divine and seize upon the critical instant, neither too early nor too late, in which lies the whole pictorial force and interest of a lengthened scene. Mr Wilkie Collins has profited in the very highest degree by his preparatory labours. He has improved upon all his early works to an extent which proves in only too edifying and complete a way the benefits of perseverance and painstaking. The very excellence of the result tempts us to an ungracious regret. Would that those memoranda by which future generations may trace 'the steps by which he did ascend,' had but been less confidingly intrusted to the public! Such a disclosure of all the beginnings and early essays of a successful career is possible only to literature. Other crafts keep their experiments out of sight. Authors alone have that ingenuous confidence in the world, and belief in its candour and kindness, which emboldens them to submit the first utterances of the muse to its great ear, and confide to it all the particulars of their progress. Fortunately, the confidence is rarely misplaced. When the hour arrives, and the man becomes famous, the indulgent world applauds his success without pausing to remind him of his failures. Let us follow the charitable example. Mr Wilkie Collins has made many a stumble on the laborious ascent; his progress upward has been jolting and unharmonious by time; but now that he has reached a height upon which he can pause and receive the congratulations of his friends, let not ours be the hand to throw his earlier imperfections in his face. If he makes as much progress in time to come as he has done in the past, there is no predicting what future altitude may await the author of the *Woman in White*.

The novel itself is too well known to call for anything like a critical review at our hands. We need not discuss over again so familiar a tale, or dwell upon the characters which are, all but Fosco, undeniably subordinate to the story, and to the delicate succession of sensations by which that story is set forth. Mr Wilkie Collins insists upon the fact that readers have written to him expressing their interest in 'Laura,' and 'Miss Halcombe,' and 'Anne Catherick;' a fact, indeed, which it is very easy to account for, seeing that there could be no story but by means of these figures. But in reality the truth is, that one cares very little for these characters on their own account, and that Mr Hartright and Sir Percival Glyde and the rest are persons whom we regard with but the mildest interest so far as themselves are concerned. The distinguishing characteristic of the book (always excepting Fosco) is the power and delicacy of its sensation incidents; the simple manner in which they are brought out; generally the perfect naturalness of the fact, and always the extremely effective manner in which the critical moment and event strike into the tale, giving it a precision and distinctness which no other expedient could supply so well. Nothing can better illustrate the skill and self-control with which these effects are produced than the following scene, which is the first introduction of the 'Woman in White' to the pages which bear her name. . . .

[The reviewer then quotes an extract from ch. 4 of Walter Hartright's narrative, from 'The heat had been painfully oppressive . . .' to '. . . that suspiciously lonely place'.]

Few readers will be able to resist the mysterious thrill of this sudden touch. The sensation is distinct and indisputable. The silent woman lays her hand upon our shoulder as well as upon that of Mr Walter Hartright—yet nothing can be more simple and clear than the narrative, or more free fom exaggeration. There is nothing frightful or unnatural about her; one perceives how her shadow must fall on the white summer highway in the white moonlight, in the noiseless night. She is not a wandering ghost, but a wistful, helpless human creature; but the shock is as sudden, as startling, as unexpected and incomprehensible to us as it is to the hero of the tale. It is the first 'point' in the story; it is accomplished by the simplest means, and is in itself a perfectly harmless occurrence; yet the momentary thrill of that touch has an effect as powerful as the most startling event. It is, in fact, in its perfect simplicity, a sensation-scene of the most delicate and skilful kind.

Not much further on occurs the second effect in this singular picture. The whole plot of the story hinges upon the resemblance between the forlorn creature described above, and a beautiful girl, rich, fair, and happy, in whose prospects, at the moment the discovery is made, trouble or mishap seem to have no place. She is outside the drawing-room window of her home, walking upon a moonlit terrace, while Walter Hartright inside listens to sundry extracts from her mother's letters, read to him by her half-sister, Miss Halcombe, by way of throwing some light upon the strange woman in white. The young man, listening beside Miss Halcombe and her candle, has turned his eyes to the window, where he sees 'Miss Fairlie's figure, bright and soft in its snowy muslin dress—her face prettily framed by the white folds of the handkerchief which she had tied under her chin,' passing in the moonlight. . . .

[Quotes from ch. 8 of Hartright's narrative, from 'Miss Halcombe paused . . .' to ' "Pray call her in!" '.]

Nothing can be more delicately powerful than this second shock of surprise and alarm. It is a simple physical effect, if one may use such an expression. It is totally independent of character, and involves no particular issue, so far as can be foreseen at this point of the story. The scene itself is as tranquil as can be conceived—two young people indoors in a lighted room, with a pretty girl outside passing and repassing the uncovered window—yet the sensation is again indisputable. The reader's nerves are affected like the hero's. He feels the thrill of the untoward resemblance, an ominous painful mystery. He, too, is chilled by a confused and unexplainable alarm. Though the author anxiously explains that the elucidation of character has not been in his hands incompatible with the excitement of narrative, these two startling points of this story do not take their power from character, or from passion, or any intellectual or emotional influence. The effect is pure sensation, neither more nor less; and so much reticence, reserve, and delicacy is in the means employed, there is such an entire absence of exaggeration or any meretricious auxiliaries, that the reader feels his own sensibilities flattered by the impression made upon him.

It is unnecessary to enter into further description of a story so well known; nor will we quote the after sensation-scenes of a very closely-wrought plot, which naturally increases in excitement as it goes on, and perhaps affords no other touches, so emphatic and so entirely dependent upon the skill of the artist, as the above. When the very existence of the principal persons in the story is in question—when the strange country-house where Sir Percival carries his bride is mysteriously evacuated by one person after another, and the bright and resolute Marian becomes suddenly visible as the prisoner of a hidden sick-room—when Laura confronts Hartright by the grave where she is supposed to be buried—when Hartright and Fosco meet in the last struggle, which may end in death to both,—the excitement of the situation has a certain reality which makes the author's task easier. The scenes we have quoted owe their startling force entirely to the elaborate skill and cunning of the workman, and are, in this point of view, more notable than anything that comes after—demonstrations of successful art, which the critical eye cannot look upon without the highest approval. At the same time, the conduct of the drama is far from being unexceptionable. Sir Percival Glyde, who conducted himself before his marriage as astutely as Fosco himself could have done, becomes a very poor, passionate, unsuccessful rascal after that event—a miserable attempt at a villain, capable of deceiving nobody, such as novelists are fond of palming off upon us as impersonations of successful scoundrelism. This was no doubt necessary in order to the full development of Fosco; but had the author been as careful of character as he has been of story, he could not possibly have permitted this unlucky individual to conduct himself so cleverly in the beginning of his career, and so absurdly in the end. Consistency, which in actual life is by no means necessary to existence, is a law and necessity in art. It is indispensable that we should be able to recognize every important figure in the picture, whensoever and howsoever he or she may reappear. There is another still more radical defect in the conception of Laura. How a pure-minded and ingenuous young woman, put under no particular pressure—neither driven to it by domestic persecution, nor by the want of a home, nor even beguiled by the attractions of improved position—should, when nothing but an effort of will seemed necessary to deliver her from the engagement, voluntarily marry one man while conscious of preferring another, is a mystery which the clever mechanist who sets all in motion takes no trouble to solve. We are not even impressed with the idea that Laura's dead father had set any special charge upon her on the subject, or given the prospective marriage anything more solemn than his approval. Yet Mr Wilkie Collins drives his sensitive and delicate heroine, without any reason in the world for the sacrifice, into a marriage which she regards with horror; makes her drive away her lover, and half-kill herself in the effort to give him up, and rather holds her up as the victim of an elevated sense of duty, when, at the cost of all these agonies, she fulfils her engagement, and becomes the unhappy wife of Sir Percival Glyde. Bad morals under any explanation; but when no real reason exists, absolute folly as well, and an ineffaceable blot upon a character meant to be everything that is womanly and tender and pure. It was necessary to marry the two for the exigencies of the story; but the author of the story has shown himself too much a master of the arts of fiction to be tolerated in such a slovenly piece of work as this. A little more care in the arrangements of the marriage—a little less of voluntary action on the part of Laura—nay, even the hackneyed expedient of a solemn deathbed charge from her father, or obligation on his part to the undesirable bridegroom—would have given the heroine a much greater hold upon the sympathies of the reader, which, we are sorry to say, she loses entirely after the very first scenes. Neither is the secret which makes so much commotion in the beginning of the action, and proves at last so totally unimportant to the matter in hand, managed very skilfully. Some futile efforts were undeniably necessary to enhance the final success; but this thread, which, after we have followed it so long, is snapped so summarily, wants more careful interweaving with the web to make it effective. Mrs Catherick is a disagreeable apparition, and the bow extorted from her clergyman a false effect of the Dickens school. But these are lesser blemishes, which detract only momentarily from the value of a picture in which there is more genuine power of *sensation*, with less of the common arbitrary expedients for exciting it, than in any other contemporary production. . . .

35. W. M. Thackeray, from 'De Finibus', *Cornhill*

August 1862, vi, 285

The essay from which the following extract is taken appeared in the *Cornhill*, of which Thackeray was editor, as no. 23 of a series of 'Roundabout Papers'; it was later collected in *Early and Late Papers* (1867) and eventually incorporated in the complete *Round-about Papers* (1869). Another essay in the latter collection, 'The Notch on the Axe', contains a further reference to Collins's novel.

The passage below appears to be the only source for the legend, recounted by several biographers but not documented, that Thackeray sat up all night to finish *The Woman in White*. Amy Cruse tells the story more accurately but cites no source (*The Victorians and their Books* (1935), 322).

So is the author who excites and interests you worthy of your thanks and benedictions. I am troubled with fever and ague, that seizes me at odd intervals and prostrates me for a day. There is cold fit, for which, I am thankful to say, hot brandy-and-water is prescribed, and this induces hot fit, and so on. In one or two of these fits I have read novels with the most fearful contentment of mind. Once, on the Mississippi, it was my dearly beloved *Jacob Faithful*: once at Frankfort O.M., the delightful *Vingt Ans Après* of Monsieur Dumas: once at Tunbridge

Wells, the thrilling *Woman in White*: and these books gave me amusement from morning till sunset. I remember those ague fits with a great
deal of pleasure and gratitude. Think of a whole day in bed, and a good
novel for a companion No cares: no remorse about idleness: no visitors:
and the Woman in White or the Chevalier d'Artagnan to tell me
stories from dawn to night! 'Please, ma'am, my master's compliments,
and can he have the third volume?' (This message was sent to an
astonished friend and neighbour who lent me, volume by volume, the
W. in W.). . . .

36. Henry James, from an unsigned review, 'Miss Braddon', *Nation*

9 November 1865, i, 593–5

The essay by James (1843–1916) from which the following passage
is taken is a review of the New York edition (1865) of *Aurora Floyd*
by Mary Elizabeth Braddon (1837–1915), who had achieved fame
three years earlier with her sensation novel *Lady Audley's Secret*.
James's essay was reprinted in the posthumous volume *Notes and
Reviews* (Cambridge, Mass., 1921), 108–16.

[James observes that Miss Braddon 'created the sensation novel' with
Lady Audley's Secret.]

She had been preceded in the same path by Mr. Wilkie Collins, whose
Woman in White, with its diaries and letters and its general ponderosity,
was a kind of nineteenth century version of *Clarissa Harlowe*. Mind, we
say a nineteenth century version. To Mr. Collins belongs the credit of
having introduced into fiction those most mysterious of mysteries, the
mysteries which are at our own doors. This innovation gave a new
impetus to the literature of horrors. It was fatal to the authority of Mrs.

Radcliffe and her everlasting castle in the Apennines. What are the Apennines to us, or we to the Apennines? Instead of the terrors of *Udolpho*, we were treated to the terrors of the cheerful country-house and the busy London lodgings. And there is no doubt that these were infinitely the more terrible. Mrs. Radcliffe's mysteries were romances pure and simple; while those of Mr. Wilkie Collins were stern reality. The supernatural, which Mrs. Radcliffe constantly implies, though she generally saves her conscience, at the eleventh hour, by explaining it away, requires a powerful imagination in order to be as exciting as the natural, as Mr. Collins and Miss Braddon, without any imagination at all, know how to manage it. A good ghost-story, to be half as terrible as a good murder-story, must be connected at a hundred points with the common objects of life. The best ghost-story probably ever written —a tale published some years ago in *Blackwood's Magazine*—was constructed with an admirable understanding of this principle. Half of its force was derived from its prosaic, commonplace, daylight accessories. Less delicately terrible, perhaps, than the vagaries of departed spirits, but to the full as *interesting*, as the modern novel reader understands the word, are the numberless possible forms of human malignity. Crime, indeed, has always been a theme for dramatic poets; but with the old poets its dramatic interest lay in the fact that it compromised the criminal's moral repose. Whence else is the interest of *Orestes* and *Macbeth*? With Mr. Collins and Miss Braddon (our modern Euripides and Shakespeare) the interest of crime is in the fact that it compromises the criminal's personal safety. The play is a tragedy, not in virtue of an avenging deity, but in virtue of a preventive system of law; not through the presence of a company of fairies, but through that of an admirable organization of police detectives. Of course, the nearer the criminal and the detective are brought home to the reader, the more lively his 'sensation.' They are brought home to the reader by a happy choice of probable circumstances; and it is through their skill in the choice of these circumstances—their thorough-going realism—that Mr. Collins and Miss Braddon have become famous. . . .

We have said that although Mr. Collins anticipated Miss Braddon in the work of devising domestic mysteries adapted to the wants of a sternly prosaic age, she was yet the founder of the sensation novel. Mr. Collins's productions deserve a more respectable name. They are massive and elaborate constructions—monuments of mosaic work, for the proper mastery of which it would seem, at first, that an index and note-book were required. They are not so much works of art as works of science. To read *The Woman in White*, requires very much the same intellectual effort as to read Motley or Froude. We may say, therefore, that Mr. Collins being to Miss Braddon what Richardson is to Miss Austen, we date the novel of domestic mystery from the former lady, for the same reason that we date the novel of domestic tranquillity from the latter. . . .

37. Edward FitzGerald in his letters

1867-79

FitzGerald (1809-83), best known as the translator of Omar Khayyám, wrote a large number of attractive letters which form the record of a long life spent among books and authors. As the following extracts show, he has some claim to be regarded as the most distinguished constant reader of *The Woman in White*. The text of (a) and (d) is taken from *Letters of Edward FitzGerald* (1894), II, 90, 131; that of (b) and (c) from *FitzGerald: Selected Works*, ed. J. Richardson (1962), 642, 655-6; and that of (e) from *A FitzGerald Friendship*, ed. N. C. Hannay (New York, 1932), 126.

(a) Letter to Frederick Tennyson, 29 January 1867

But I am perhaps not a proper Judge of these high matters [he has been discussing his friend Spedding's edition of Bacon]. How should I? who have just, to my great sorrow, finished *The Woman in White* for the third time, once every last three Winters. I wish Sir Percival Glyde's death were a little less of the minor Theatre sort; then I would swallow all the rest as a wonderful Caricature, better than so many a sober Portrait. I really think of having a Herring-lugger I am building named 'Marian Halcombe', the brave Girl in the Story.

(b) Letter to W. F. Pollock, 11 November 1867

I have not yet revived my appetite for Novels: not even for my dear *Woman in White*: which I should like to have read to me; and which even now exerts a sort of magnetism in drawing me toward the corner of a dark Cupboard, or Closet, in which (like the proprietary Skeleton) she lies.

(c) Letter to W. F. Pollock, 7 December 1869

A lad comes to read at half-past seven till nine—stumbling at every other word, unless it be some Story that carries him along. So now we are upon the *Woman in White*: third [error for 'fourth'?] time of reading in my case: and I can't help getting frightened now.

(d) Letter to W. F. Pollock, 24 December 1871

[Jane Austen] is capital as far as she goes: but she never goes out of the Parlour; if but Magnus Troil, or Jack Bunce,[1] or even one of Fielding's Brutes, would but dash in upon the Gentility, and swear a round Oath or two! I must think the *Woman in White*, with her Count Fosco, far beyond all that.

[1] Characters in Sir Walter Scott's *The Pirate* (1822).

(e) Letter to Charles Donne, 6 January 1879

At a Desk all the Morning using my own Eyes in reading or writing: and at Night listening to another who reads me Sir Walter Scott, *The Woman in White, All the Year Round, Chamber's Miscellany,* & so on. . . .

NO NAME

Serialized in *All the Year Round* from 15 March 1862 to 17 January 1863; published in three volumes by Sampson Low before the end of 1862. A stage version in five acts was written in conjunction with W. B. Bernard in 1863 but never produced; a later version in four acts was produced in New York in 1871.

38. Charles Dickens, letters

24 January 1862–1 January 1863

The first two letters quoted from were written before serialization of the novel in *All the Year Round* began on 15 March. (d) indicates its success as a serial, and (e) provides evidence of Collins's request for Dickens's opinion and of the closeness of the latter's editorial scrutiny. The final extract suggests the immediate success of *No Name* in volume form.

Text from 'Nonesuch' edition, III, 282–4, 304, 308–9, 333.

(a) Letter to Collins, 24 January 1862

I have read the story as far as you have written it, with strong interest and great admiration. . . .

I find in the book every quality that made the success of the *Woman in White*, without the least sign of holding on to that success or being taken in tow by it. I have no doubt whatever of the public reception of what I have read. You may be quite certain of it. I could not be more so than I am.

You will excuse my saying, with a reference to what is to follow, something that may be already in your own mind. It seems to me that great care is needed not to tell the story too severely. In exact proportion as you play around it here and there, and mitigate the severity of your own sticking to it, you will enhance and intensify the power with which Magdalen holds on to her purpose. For this reason I should have given Mr. Pendril some touches of comicality, and should have generally lighted up the house with some such capital touches of whimsicality and humour as those with which you have irradiated the private theatricals.

This is the only suggestion in the critical way that comes into my mind. By-the-bye—except one. Look again to the scene where Magdalen, in Mr. Pendril's presence and that of Frank's father (who is excellent), checks off the items of the position one by one. She strikes me as doing this in too business-like and clerkly a way.

Wills clamours for the name, and that is most difficult to find.

[Twenty-seven suggestions for the novel's title follow, most of them of incredible triteness. Collins used none of them.]

(b) Letter to W. H. Wills, 28 January 1862

My suggestions to Wilkie as to altering what he has done, were very slight indeed; because he *cannot* alter it in any essential particular. They went mainly to the warning that it must inevitably come to pass that the more severely and persistently he tells the story, unrelieved by whimsical playing about it, the more he will detract from the steadiness and inflexibility of purpose in the girl. Contrast in that wise is most essential. She cannot possibly be brought out as he wants to bring her out, without it.

(c) Letter to Collins, 20 September 1862

I have gone through the Second Volume at a sitting, and I find it *wonderfully fine*. It goes on with an ever-rising power and force in it that fills me with admiration. It is as far before and beyond *The Woman in White* as *that* was beyond the wretched common level of fiction-writing. There are some touches in the Captain which no one but a born (and cultivated) writer could get near—could draw within hail of. And the originality of Mrs. Wragge, without compromise of her probability, involves a really great achievement. But they are all admirable; Mr. Noel Vanstone and the housekeeper, both in their way as meritorious as the rest; Magdalen wrought out with truth, energy, sentiment, and passion, of the very first water.

I cannot tell you with what a strange dash of pride as well as pleasure I read the great results of your hard work. Because, as you know, I was certain from the *Basil* days that you were the Writer who would come ahead of all the Field—being the only one who combined invention and power, both humourous and pathetic, with that invincible determination to work, and that profound conviction that nothing of worth is to be done without work, of which triflers and feigners have no conception. . . .

There is one slight slip, occurring more than once, which you have not corrected. Magdalen 'laid down,' and I think some one else 'laid down.' It is clear that she must either lay herself down, or lie down. To lay is a verb active, and to lie down is a verb neuter, consequently she lay down, or laid herself down.

(d) Letter to Collins, 12 October 1862

There is no doubt of *No Name*'s having attracted great attention lately, and made a strong impression. I have been in town and have heard of it on all sides.

(e) Letter to Collins, 14 October 1862

I have read those proofs carefully. They are very strong indeed.

I am not sure that I quite understand within what limitations you want my opinion of them. The only points that strike me as at all questionable are all details. But not to pass them over, here they are.

I find Mrs. Lecount's proceeding with the new will rather violently sudden, followed, as it is so immediately, by the death. Also, I do not quite like her referring to those drafts she has brought with her. It would be so very suspicious in the eyes of a suspicious man.

I forget whether you want that Laudanum bottle again. If not, I think Mrs. Lecount should break it before Noel Vanstone's eyes. Otherwise, while he is impressed with the danger he supposes himself to have escaped, he repeats it, on a smaller scale, by giving Mrs. Lecount an inducement to kill him, and leaving the means at hand.

I believe it would be *necessary* for a Testator signing his will to inform the witnesses of the fact of its being his will—though of its contents, of course, they would be ignorant. The legal form of attestation in use is: Signed, sealed, and delivered by so and so, the written-named Testator, *as and for his last will and testament,* in the presence of us, etc.

If the story were mine, I should decidedly not put into it the anticipation contained in the last line or two of Norah's postscript. But that is a moot point in art.

Throughout the whole of the thirty-sixth weekly part is there wanting some sense on the part of Noel Vanstone that he may not be legally married at all? This seems to me the most important question.

I do not quite follow the discussion between Noel and Lecount about the eight months' interval, and the puzzling of Magdalen by taking that number. Why? Mrs. Lecount says, 'People easily guess a year; people easily guess six months.' Suppose she did guess six months, she would only have to bestir herself so much the more. And it is clear that a plotter, bent upon losing no chance, would take the shortest likely time and not the longest. Then what is gained by eight?

Among the many excellent things in the proof, I noticed, as particularly admirable, the manner in which the amount of Mrs. Lecount's legacy is got at, and the bearing and discourse of the Scotch fly-driver.

(f) Letter to Collins, 1 January 1863

My dear Wilkie,—Many thanks for the book, the arrival of which has created an immense sensation in this palatial abode. I am delighted (but not surprised) to hear of its wonderful sale; all that I thought and said of it when you finished the second volume, I think and repeat of it now you have finished the third.

39. H. F. Chorley, unsigned review, *Athenaeum*

3 January 1863, 10–11

On Chorley, see headnote to No. 2.

No Name, which for some nine months past has fixed and retained curiosity in no common degree, is finished. Magdalen, the perverse heroine, whose heart-wrongs and strong desire to right a cruel injustice caused by her and her sister's illegitimacy led her into crime, falsehood, imposture, to the verge of theft even, is let off with a punishment gentle in proportion to the unscrupulous selfishness of her character: a period of agonized remorse and admitted failure—an illness which brings her to death's door; but she is then dismissed to restored fortune, and marriage with a man worth ten thousand of the fickle and feeble creature on whom her affections had at first fixed fast. This may be all right enough so far as the novelist's aims and ends are concerned, so far as the maintenance of suspense till the final hour of relief has been his purpose;—whether it be 'true to truth' is another matter, far less easy to decide in a phrase or two. The novel is, however, and in one sense deservedly, a great success, if not altogether a sound one; and this, not because of its total disregard of the artificial laws of poetical justice, but from certain faults and flaws which we shall attempt to indicate. Meanwhile, it is only fair to credit the author with increase of vigour and brightness. Passages of the story are admirably told, with a succinct clearness not to be over-estimated. The characters, if not always probable and too seldom agreeable, are painted in livelier colours than any in the former novels of Mr. Collins, 'Count Fosco', in *The Woman in White*, excepted. The work, in brief, is a work of Art; and doing, as we do, every credit to its author's skill, to his steady and unfaltering continuity in the contrivance and arrangement of incident, it is for the interest of artists that it should be looked into with a closeness of scrutiny which it would be absurd to apply to the heap of novels of its class which so rapidly accumulates at the time present. It would be superfluous minutely to trace out the story, point by point, while offering a few remarks which bear on the amount of its permanent value.

No Name must be pronounced incomplete as a work of Art if the character of Magdalen (which is, virtually, the book) fails to interest those who read the tale. Her deeds and expedients pique curiosity;—her good qualities, exhibited, not described, resolve themselves into beauty, great talent for personation, and indomitable will. She begins in the hour of prosperity by mimicry, in private theatricals, of the sister whom she loves most dearly. She chooses for her lover a weak pretty youth, that her fancy may deck and garland him, and her obstinacy take his part. She makes herself wretched on his account, because the event of her father's death, with its revelation of her illegitimacy and consequent pauperism, sends him away from beneath her protection. Friends are raised up for her; she will accept none of them. She will struggle out into action and revenge for herself; she will employ her beauty, her theatrical adroitness, her courage, to grasp back a fortune. In order to carry out her purposes she enlists into her service an unblushing scoundrel, whom she knows to be such. In reckless determination to carry through her purposes, she remains this man's associate and pupil for months, reckless of the agony she has caused to the affectionate sister and friend from whom she hides herself. She connives at every conceivable cheat and imposture to entrap into marriage a man whom she loathes as though he were a reptile. There must be surely coarseness, as well as meanness, in one capable of such actions and expedients as these. It is true that Mr. Collins indicates, and very powerfully, the inward repugnance which convulsed her during her solitary hours. The scene before her marriage, when she approaches the idea of self-destruction as an alternative, is most forcible. But her persistence in her evil purposes can only be explained by admitting that there existed in the heroine's character hard and (we repeat) coarse elements, which deprive her of our sympathy. . . . Mr. Collins delights in the intricacies of incident. More than two-thirds of the tale are devoted to Magdalen's stratagems, with all their hopes and fears. The 'favour and prettiness' with which it closes are too rapid, too unchequered, to be natural: even though a good novel, like every other good thing, must come to an end at last.

It may be suggested, then, that Mr. Collins has been so possessed with his story as to be unaware that its necessities give his heroine a colour and a character which he neither intended, nor may be able to perceive. More certain, however, is the fact, that too many of his leading characters are detestable. Capt. Wragge, though spiritedly hit off, is at the outset too transparent in the confessions of scoundrelism, made by him to Magdalen. His huge, half-witted wife, with her slatternly ways, her love of fine clothes, and her tender heart, is good. But too much time is spent with these people, and with the parties they are engaged to cozen and to blind,—Noel Vanstone, the weak miser, and Mrs. Lecount, his diabolically prudent housekeeper. Too small is the amount of healthy air let into the picture. The loveable characters—Norah, Miss Garth, and Kirke, Magdalen's redeemer,—are little more than sketches. Among the minor persons, Mazey, the tipsy old sailor, is the best.

Now, as to construction and incident. Few, if any other, novels could be named in which unforeseen death is so frequently appealed to as an incident necessary to carrying out the author's purpose. There are no fewer than five such catastrophes, each indispensable to the author's illustration of the conflict betwixt good and evil in Magdalen. It was necessary, perhaps, to avoid too long-drawn a strain on the woman who had contaminated herself by leaguing with a confessed scoundrel to carry out her plans of vengeance—and yet worse, by seducing into marriage and will-making the relative she loathed and had cause to loathe—that that man should be moved away, in order that a new argument for her wilfulness should be found in the failure of her purpose to possess a share of his fortune of which she had been despoiled. But are outlets like these broken so opportunely in real life? Mr. Collins being all for truth (as his Preface tells us), and being so largely true in many points, must bear the question, What is every man's experience? Do the husbands, to whom women sacrifice their truth and purity by fearful sale and barter for money, set their slaves free as soon as did Magdalen's husband? Did not Mr. Wilkie Collins make a summary end of Noel Vanstone because he felt that his wife could not have endured the consequences of her crime in wooing and wedding him, had he lived longer than to make the first will as she chose he should do, and the second one as her enemy the housekeeper, Mrs. Lecount, insisted on his doing? There are other 'sensation' effects than the stage ones of the 'Colleen Bawn' and the 'Peep o'Day'; and among these is the too profuse employment of the Destroyer. Mr. Collins pays sedulous attention to the weaving of his plot, and therefore, on reflection, or when weaving his next, may possibly feel that the amount of timely catastrophe is too large for the ease (which implies perfect credence) of the reader. We have a right to look to him for advance and progress, because, in his case, the earnest spirit of an artist is combined with no common creative and constructive powers.

40. Unsigned review, *Reader*

3 January 1863, i, 14–15

This review appeared in the opening number of the short-lived *Reader* (1863–7), the readership of which Ellegård (24) describes as 'upper to middle class'.

[The reviewer begins by describing No Name as a story pure and simple, written with virtually no moral purpose and with a total absence of 'reflections', directly or indirectly conveyed: 'it is a tale, and not a novel, in the modern sense of the word'.]

For our own part, we doubt very much whether the sensation school, of whom Mr. Collins is by far the ablest representative, will ever become genuinely popular in England. It is a plant of foreign growth. It comes to us from France, and it can only be imported in a mutilated condition. Without entering on the relative morality or immorality of French and English novelists, one may say generally that, with us, novels turn upon the vicissitudes of legitimate love and decorous affection; while in France they are based upon the working of those loves and passions which are not in accordance with our rules of respectability. Now, unlawful passions are inevitably replete with a variety of sensational situations, of which authorized love, however fervent, is devoid, and the consequence is that a sensation novel which cannot dwell upon seductions, intrigues, infidelities, and illegitimate connections, is like *Hamlet*, not only without the Prince, but without the Ghost and without Ophelia. If Magdalen Vanstone could have sacrificed her character without sacrificing the sympathy of an ordinary English reader, it is impossible to say to what heights of sensational grandeur *No Name* might not have risen. Unfortunately it was essential that Magdalen should not commit the one unpardonable sin of our English code, and the necessity of preserving her respectability to the end has sadly trammelled Mr. Collins's powers of invention. We doubt, too, whether the English language is as well adapted as the French to this peculiar class of literature. The pointed phraseology, the epigrammatic terseness, and the wonderful lucidity of the French language, give their writers an advantage in sensational writing not enjoyed by those who employ the richer and more subtle vocabulary of the English tongue.

At any rate we doubt if any English writer will carry this description of novel writing to a higher pitch of excellence than Mr. Collins. And yet, with all his many merits, we cannot help feeling that he does not belong to the same category as that to which in our own day Thackeray and Dickens and George Eliot have effected their entrance. However, we have no right to look a gift horse in the mouth. *No Name* does not profess to be anything more than an exciting story; and we have only made these remarks because we cannot help thinking that, with its author's unmistakable genius, he might rise to something higher than even a first-rate sensation novel. In the delineation of Captain Wragge and Old Mazey, Mr. Collins again gives evidence, that if he chose he might go deeper, in his power of describing character, than he has ever yet thought fit to do, except, perhaps, in *Basil*, the most powerful though the least popular of his works.

[The reviewer goes on to pay tribute to Collins's mastery of the serial form in *No Name*:]

Since it began, thousands of English households have studied its progress with unfailing interest . . . it is no small triumph to have constructed a story which, week after week, for nearly a year defied the divining powers of the most acute of novel readers, and surprised everybody at the end. . . .

41. Unsigned review, *Saturday Review*

17 January 1863, xv, 84–5

Mr. Wilkie Collins has again produced one of his ingenious puzzles. He has worked out once more a novel that is plot and nothing else but plot. *No Name* has all the faults, but it has all the merits, of this kind of fiction. It is a mere puzzle, in which the artist moves his puppets so as to make us wonder what is to be the end of them. We do not care, and are not meant to care, about the characters of the story. Indeed, nothing could be more unattractive than the main basis of the fiction. A girl, angry at finding that her illegitimacy deprives her of her father's money, determines to cheat the heir out of it by marrying him under an assumed name. The heir, a selfish foolish invalid, is protected by a sly, sleek housekeeper; and the whole point of the story, the one source of interest it possesses, is the contest between these two deceitful, wicked, obstinate women. Will the pretty bad girl get the fool to marry her, or will the adroit, audacious, catlike housekeeper keep the fool to herself? This is the riddle we are asked to follow to its solution. It is a game which we are invited to watch, because the turns of the game itself have an interest quite apart from the moral character of the players. All that criticism has to say against this reduction of fiction to a puzzle and a contest of low artifices is too obvious, and has been said too often, to make it necessary to repeat it here. It is more important to notice the merits of this sort of book. Criticism says that Mr. Wilkie Collins invents a puzzling plot, and does nothing more. This is true; but then it is so very difficult to invent a puzzling plot. Any one who has ever tried to sketch a story—and most clever young people have had moments when they fancied they could write one—will remember that there were many things that came at once when called for, and which the instinct or genius of the composer seemed quite ready to furnish. There were the descriptions of scenery; the moral reflections; the colour of the heroine's eyes and hair; the inner state of the head lover's mind; the views on the Church, and on the scheme of creation, and the true aim of life—all these welled up spontaneously in the breast of the fertile dreamer. But between him and an embodied dream there was the great barrier of an unimagined plot. Who was the heroine to be; and why was she to be unhappy; and who was to bring in the philosophy; and how on earth was it to come in naturally? These are the fatal questions which have caused so many possible novels of the single-volume kind to die unborn. A good plot—a plot that interests, excites, and properly balances bewilderment and explanation—is a very considerable effort of the mind, and one which demands great practice, patience, and inventiveness. To have devised and worked out the plot of *No Name* is a sign of mental qualities that are by no means common, and we do not wonder that Mr. Wilkie Collins is so well pleased with his productions as his preface shows him to be. In order to do him justice, we ought to compare him not only with writers of real genius, but with the authors of the other sort of current popular novel—the novel where there is no plot that could cost ten minutes' thought, but where there is any amount of digression, sentiment, and description. We shall then under-stand what Mr. Wilkie Collins means when he tells us that he regards himself as an artist in the construction of fiction. . . .

[The long central portion of this review, here omitted, discusses 'a tale called *Thalatta* . . . reprinted from *Fraser's Magazine*' as an example of 'the other sort of current popular novel'—formless and digressive. The comparison is very much to Collins's advantage.]

It is easy to see that a book of this sort presents as complete a contrast as possible to the works of Mr. Collins. He does not treat the novel as a literary vehicle. He has no views, no philosophy, no thoughts about reprobation or the Whigs. He does not sketch heroines, like the first girl in *Thalatta*, 'with fawn-like look and auburn eyes.' He does not trouble himself about dying statesmen. But he offers about as nearly even betting as he can contrive for and against a furious plausible young lady outwitting a wily housekeeper. When, by many a cunning stroke of art and an infinity of subtle contrivances, he at last lets it dawn upon us that it is really about five to four on Miss Magdalene, he has worked his work and fulfilled the mission of his heart. Which of the two kinds of novel is really the best, we will not attempt now to decide. But if art means something which requires labour and forethought, and a subordination of parts to a whole, then we can understand how it is that Mr. Collins—surveying the yearly crop of books of gushing meditations, published as fictions because a fawn-eyed maiden and a Viking make a little love in their pages, and knowing how little trouble they must have cost, in proportion to the pleasure they have afforded to the mind that produced them—boldly claims to be an artist.

42. H. L. Mansel, from an unsigned review, *Quarterly Review*

April 1863, cxiii, 495–6

Henry Longueville Mansel (1820–71), Oxford don and clergyman, became Waynflete Professor of Moral and Metaphysical Philosophy and Dean of St Paul's. His attack on the logical and moral bases of Collins's protest in *No Name* occurs in a review of twenty-four examples of sensation fiction: of the other novels discussed, only M. E. Braddon's *Lady Audley's Secret* (1862) is still remembered.

No Name is principally a protest against the law which determines the social position of illegitimate children. But the prosecution of this main purpose involves, as a subordinate purpose, a plea in behalf of the connexion to which such children owe their existence. Hence the . . . stage-trick of exhibiting the virtuous concubine in contrast to the vicious wife is brought forward to give effect to the piece. Andrew Vanstone, when a mere boy, is privately married in Canada to a wife whom he afterwards discovers to have been a woman of profligate character; but, inasmuch as her irregularities are all antenuptial, there is no pretext for dissolving the marriage, and the only resource of the husband is to pension her off, on condition that she shall never trouble him by asserting her conjugal rights. Mr. Vanstone then returns to England, and finds an accommodating young lady, who is content to discharge the duties and assume the name of his wife, without being too particular in demanding a legal right to them. On the death of his real wife, Mr. Vanstone marries the mother of his children, but is prevented by an untimely death from making a new will, his former one being invalidated by the second marriage. The consequence is that his property goes to the heir-at-law, and his children are left penniless, because a cruel jurisprudence does not permit them to be made legitimate by the subsequent marriage of their parents. Against this state of the law, Mr. Collins, through the mouth of the family solicitor, declaims in the following strain:—

I am far from defending the law of England, as it affects illegitimate offspring. On the contrary, I think it a disgrace to the nation. It visits the sins of the parents on the children; it encourages vice by depriving fathers and mothers of the strongest of all motives for making the atonement of marriage; and it claims to produce these two abominable results in the names of morality and religion. But it has no extraordinary oppression to answer for, in the case of these unhappy girls. The more merciful and Christian law of other countries, which allows the marriage of the parents to make the children legitimate, has no mercy on *these* children. The accident of their father having been married, when he first met with their mother, has made them the outcasts of the whole social community: it has placed them out of the pale of the Civil Law of Europe.

We have often heard an illegal connexion and its result euphemistically designated as a 'misfortune;' but this is the first time as far as we are aware, in which a lawful marriage has been denominated an 'accident.' Unfortunately for the author, it is of that kind which is known among logicians as an 'inseparable accident.' This, however, is not the only *fallacia accidentis* of the author's argument. Let us, as we are at liberty to do, suppose all the other accidents of the case reversed. Let us suppose that a heartless husband has deserted an innocent and amiable wife to live with an abandoned mistress, and that, late in life, having quarrelled with his virtuous relatives, he is enabled, by a marriage with his paramour, to provide himself with a ready-made family of lawful children, and to ruin the prospects of some exemplary and ill-used brother or nephew, upon whom the property is settled in the absence of direct heirs; thus securing, through the mercy of the law, the pleasures of adultery during his youth, and the advantages of matrimony in his riper years. Would not such materials, in the hands of a skilful story-teller, make quite as good a case against the new law which Mr. Collins would enact, as he has made against the old law which he desires to repeal? Does not he see that all the virtues which he heaps on the erring couple, and all the vices which he attributes to the lawful wife, are simply so much dust thrown in the eyes of the reader, to blind him to the real merits of the argument? Does he not see that the existing law would have been exactly as just, or exactly as unjust, had the forsaken wife been the most admirable of women, and her illegal successor the most shameless of harlots? Or can any law be contrived by human wisdom which may not be made to appear oppressive by this sort of special pleading? Does not the punishment of a felon inflict a stigma on his children? And should there be, therefore, no punishment for felony? . . .

[The rest of the review attacks the 'sententious platitudes' to be found in the reflective portions of the novel.]

43. Alexander Smith, unsigned review, *North British Review*

February 1863, xxxviii, 183–5

Smith (1830–67) was a Scottish poet and essayist. Under the title 'Novels and Novelists of the Day' he reviews a group of novels, his comments on *No Name* following a discussion of George Eliot's *Silas Marner*.

Mr Wilkie Collins is a writer of quite a different stamp from George Eliot, and in his own way he has achieved eminent successes. The interest of his books is absorbing, the ingenuity of his plots marvellous; and to go to bed after the perusal of the *Woman in White* or *No Name*, is like going to bed after supping on a pork-chop. Mr Collins can hide a secret better than any man, he is a master of mystery; but when once the secret is discovered, when once the mystery is unravelled, his books collapse at once, their interest perishes, they are flat as conundrums to which you have the answers. For to this writer plot and incident are all in all, character nothing. He has little spontaneity of humour, no reflection, no aphoristic wisdom, no poetry, but little painting of scenery, and, what there is, not of the highest kind. He relates his stories boldly and nakedly; he pursues his plot with the directness and pertinacity of a detective or a bloodhound. From the beginning of the first chapter of his work, he keeps his eye steadily fixed on the last. So long as you have his book open, you are spell-bound; whenever you close it, you feel you have been existing in a world of impossible incidents, and holding converse with monstrosities. The touches that make the whole world kin, the humour which is a perpetual delight, the pathos which makes sacred, are not in these books. Everything is tense, strained, and unnatural. The characters are preternaturally acute; they watch one another as keenly as duellists do when the seconds fall back and the rapiers cross. Then every trifling incident is charged with an oppressive importance: if a tea-cup is broken, it has a meaning, it is a link in a chain; you are certain to hear of it afterwards. In a short time, however, you discover the writer's trick. If a young lady goes into the garden for a moment before dinner, you know that some one is waiting for her behind the laurels. If two people talk together in a room in a hot summer day, and one raises the window a little, you know that a third is crouching on the gravel below, listening to every word, and who will be prepared to act upon it at the proper time. Everything in these books is feverish and excited; the reader is continually as if treading on bomb-shells, which may explode at any moment. The incidents follow each other rapidly, and they are generally of the most improbable description. Every chapter is a shock of astonishment; but in a little while the feeling of astonishment perishes, the sense of wonder is dulled by the repeated calls made upon it, the marvellous becomes commonplace; and if Mr Collins described a dead man walking out of his grave, the reader would peruse the startling sentences without a thrill—just as if such a proceeding was the most ordinary thing in the world.

The Woman in White is amazingly clever and ingenious. It contains, of course, a mystery, and the solution is skilfully hidden away under folds on folds of incident. The passion of curiosity is appealed to at the commencement, and so strongly is it roused that it carries one through to the close. The reader may dislike the book, despise the form of art of which it is an example, but, once started, he is certain to go on with it. The chief attraction gathers round Count Fosco; but this attraction is dissipated long before the story closes. The wily Count deteriorates as you make his acquaintance; he is found to be the most impudent of knaves. *No Name* possesses a simpler and more intense interest than *The Woman in White*, but it is a horrible and unnatural interest; the book enchains you, but you detest it while it enchains. The incidents at Aldborough, where Miss Magdalen, under the instructions of Captain Wragge, is striving to entrap Mr Noel Vanstone into marriage, and where Mrs Lecount is working to foil the conspirators, are cleverly told, but the repulsiveness of the matter disturbs the pleasure of the reader. Here, again, the actors are preternaturally acute; there is plot and counterplot, and the game of wits is played out as mercilessly as a duel. The reader is interested of course; but immediately on closing the book, he feels the unreality of the whole thing; he flings it off as he does the remembrance of a nightmare. There never was a young lady like Magdalen, there never was a scoundrel like Wragge, a fool like Vanstone, a housekeeper like Mrs Lecount. Such people have no representatives in the living world. Their proper place is the glare of blue lights on a stage sacred to the sensation drama. And yet there are excellent things in *No Name*. . . .

44. Mrs Oliphant, unsigned review, *Blackwood's Magazine*

August 1863, xciv, 170

This brief attack on Collins's novel occurs in an account of 'the faults of popular fiction—its tendency to detectivism, to criminalism—its imperfect and confused morality', as exemplified by the sensation novel. On Mrs Oliphant, see headnote to No. 34.

Mr. Wilkie Collins, after the skilful and startling complications of the *Woman in White*—his grand effort—has chosen, by way of making his heroine piquant and interesting in his next attempt, to throw her into a career of vulgar and aimless trickery and wickedness, with which it is impossible to have a shadow of sympathy, but from all the pollutions of which he intends us to believe that she emerges, at the cheap cost of a fever, as pure, as high-minded, and as spotless as the most dazzling white of heroines. The Magdalen of *No Name* does not go astray after the usual fashion of erring maidens in romance. Her pollution is decorous, and justified by law; and after all her endless deceptions and horrible marriage, it seems quite right to the author that she should be restored to society, and have a good husband and a happy home.

45. Unsigned review, *London Quarterly Review*

October 1866, xxvii, 107–8

The *London Quarterly* was a Methodist organ 'read by the educated middle class members and ministers of the denomination' (Ellegård, 31). Under the title 'Recent Novels: their Moral and Religious Teaching', the writer finds occasion to deplore the moral influence of much sensation fiction. This brief comment on *No Name* prefaces a fuller discussion of *Armadale* (see No. 50 below).

Mr. Collins is a clever, and for a time is sure to be a popular, writer; and the moral tone of his books is, therefore, the more to be lamented. In *No Name* he has employed all his genius so to gild one of the greatest offences a man can commit against the laws of morality and the well-being of society, as to hide its real character and excite sympathy for that which should be visited with stern reprobation. The tale is very powerful; the poison is distilled so subtly that the evil is wrought almost before suspicion is awakened; the art with which the whole is managed is so complete, that the mind unconsciously drifts on into an acquiescence in a state of things, which, were it free from the glamour which the author throws over the mental vision, it would at once condemn. There is no other of Mr. Collins's later books which is open to such serious exception; but we hesitate not to say that the tendency of all of them is to relax rather than to brace the moral tone of the reader.

Serialized in the *Cornhill* from November 1864 to June 1866, with illustrations by G. H. Thomas. Published in two volumes by Smith, Elder in May 1866, with a dedication to John Forster. In the same year Collins wrote, in collaboration with his friend the actor François Régnier, a dramatic version in three acts, never produced or published in England. A second version nine years later by Collins alone (*Miss Gwilt: a drama in five acts*) was produced at the Globe Theatre.

T. S. Eliot has described *Armadale* as being, after *The Woman in White* and *The Moonstone*, 'the best of Collins' romances' (Introduction to 'World's Classics' edition of *The Moonstone* (1928), ix).

46. Bishop Thirlwall, letters

1865–6

Connop Thirlwall (1797–1875), Bishop of St David's, historian and theologian, was an energetic correspondent on a wide variety of literary topics. He evidently read *Armadale* as it appeared in the *Cornhill*. Text from *Letters to a Friend by Bishop Thirlwall*, ed. A. P. Stanley (1881), 48, 61.

I *have* read that *Armadale*, drawn on by curiosity to see how such a very complicated skein is to be unravelled, but with very little enjoyment. Miss Gwilt is a tragic Becky Sharp, but immensely below her prototype. On the whole, I consider this class of novels as an unhappy invention, creating an insatiable demand which must be met by less and less wholesome food, and absorbing a great deal of ability which might be much better employed.

(19 December 1865)

We seem to be nearing land in *Armadale*. Is it not marvellous that anybody could have conceived it possible for Miss Gwilt to write such a journal? It is a comfort to think that she cannot go on much longer, and that almost the only doubt remaining is whether she is to poison or drown herself.

(3 March 1866)

47. H. F. Chorley, unsigned review, *Athenaeum*

2 June 1866, 732–3

On Chorley, see headnote to No. 2 above. The first part of this review is quoted in Hewlett's *Henry Fothergill Chorley: Autobiography, Memoir and Letters* (II, 119–21); Hewlett also notes an 'increase of severity in his censure' in the veteran reviewer's later criticisms (II, 105).

It is not pleasant to speak as we must speak of this powerful story; but in the interest of everything that is to be cherished in life, in poetry, in art, it is impossible to be over-explicit in the expression of judgment. Mr. Wilkie Collins stands in a position too distinguished among novelists not to be amenable to the plainest censure when he commits himself to a false course of literary creation.

Armadale is a 'sensation novel' with a vengeance,—one, however, which could hardly fail to follow *No Name*. Those who make plot their first consideration and humanity the second,—those, again, who represent the decencies of life as too often so many hypocrisies,—have placed themselves in a groove which goes, and must go, in a downward direction, whether as regards fiction or morals.

We are in a period of diseased invention, and the coming phase of it may be palsy. Mr. Collins belongs to the class of professing satirists who are eager to lay bare the 'blotches and blains' which fester beneath the skin and taint the blood of humanity. He is ready with those hackneyed and specious protests against the cant of conventionalism. These may amount to a cant more unwholesome than that against which it is aimed. This time the interest of his tale centres upon one of the most hardened female villains whose devices and desires have ever blackened fiction—a forger, a convicted adulteress, murderess, and thief, aged thirty-five,—a woman who deliberately, by the aid of a couple of wretches whose practices belong to the police-cells, but not to pages over which honest people should employ and enjoy their leisure, sits down to make her way to fortune and apparent respectability by imposture, deliberate murder and, lastly, by cold-blooded unfaithfulness to the man who had really loved her and rescued her from her bad life, and for whom she is said to have entertained her solitary feeling of real attachment. The Count Fosco of *The Woman in White* was a mild culprit as compared with Lydia Gwilt, assisted by her supporters, Mrs. Oldershaw (styled by her 'Mother Jezebel') and Doctor Downward. Doubtless such writhen creatures may live and breathe in 'the sinks and sewers' of society—engendered by the secret vices and infirmities of those who were answerable for their existence and who encourage their misdoings; but when we see them displayed in Fiction with all the loving care of a consummate artist, (and without any such genuine motive as led formerly Hogarth and latterly Mr. Dickens not to show a horror without a suggestion towards its cure,) we are oddly reminded of a line in Granger's West Indian poem, 'The Sugar Cane,'—

Now, Muse! let's sing of Rats!

What artist would choose vermin as his subjects? The serpents that wreathe a coil about the head of Da Vinci's Medusa, in the Florence Gallery, are mere accessories to the grand, fatal face. Here we have nothing so graceful, nothing that gets beyond the

Eye of newt and toe of frog

of the obsolete witch. The sorceress of *Armadale* (to display whom the novel was evidently constructed) writes, diarizes, confides, as familiarly as did Harriet Byron (a lady objected to as tedious by 'sensation' novelists), and to the last miscreants in the world to whom such a woman would have spoken out. She is described as a beautiful, accomplished, plausible lady, approaching middle age, who, after having passed her life in kennels and gambling-houses and casinos and jails, shows no trace in her demeanour of such associations, and by her graces entraps two young men and one old fool. The criminal dock, the prison, the companionship with a procuress, must tell even on an educated woman who had sunk to such infamy. Lydia Gwilt began her life in the midst of crime; and yet we find her writing to 'Mother Jezebel' and talking to herself about 'Beethoven's Sonatas'! With all his art in piling up events, Mr. Collins cannot but be said to have failed in a story of which the centre and in which the only being who excites curiosity is such a creature as this.

[Various incidents of the novel are criticized on grounds of morality and probability.]

These abominations are displayed with the concise neatness and excellent precision of language which distinguish Mr. Wilkie Collins; but these very great and cordially-acknowledged literary attributes only bring the monstrosity of invention into brighter relief. The end crowns the work. A new murder is now-a-days almost as hard a thing to find as a blue dahlia. After Lady Audley's well in the Lime Walk, after the revolving window of *Uncle Silas*, it was not easy to devise a horror which should frighten the world with some show of freshness.

While discussing this story as a work of art, it must be pointed out that every character is arranged so as to be subordinate to this horrible creature. . . .

The young lawyer, Pedgift, a sort of human sparrow, is so sharply and shrewdly touched as to satisfy every one that Mr. Wilkie Collins has power to fill a canvas with living, breathing creatures of a higher order than the obscene birds of night.

One word more. The novelist has never been more terse, more clear, more pictorial, than in the soliloquy, the dialogue and the descriptions of this his latest and most perverse novel. Unnatural (so we hold) as is Lydia Gwilt's diary, it is still capitally kept, if considered *per se*, as a piece of journalism. And the painter, to whom we are obliged for many life-like landscapes, has not yet painted anything better than his scene of the picnic on the Norfolk 'Broads,' where the arch-fiend of foolish Allan's dream presents herself on the edge of the pool!

48. Unsigned review, *Spectator*

9 June 1866, xxxix, 638–40

If Mr. Wilkie Collins is contented with the praise of not having hastily meditated or idly wrought out his new story, he may be sure that his claims to such praise will not be disputed. But the concluding sentences of his preface do away with the modest effect of the opening sentence, and plead for a less qualified verdict. 'Estimated by the Clap-trap morality of the present day, this may be a very daring book. Judged by the Christian morality which is of all time, it is only a book that is daring enough to speak the truth.' Mr. Wilkie Collins is fond of challenging his critics, and we see no cause to shrink from accepting his challenge. We have no love for Clap-trap morality, even when it is dignified with a large C, and we have never shown any wish to restrict the development of modern fiction within such narrow limits as exclude Crime, Fraud, and those kindred elements which Mr. Wilkie Collins honours with the same emphasis. But when we find a book daring enough to speak the truth, and appealing to Christian morality, we have a right to demand the whole truth, and some more reference to that morality than is contained in the modern tag which is called a preface. Is it, then, the whole truth about the world in which we live that it is peopled by a set of scoundrels qualified by a set of fools, and watched by retributive providence in the shape of attornies and spies? Is it the object of half the world to cheat the other half, and the object of the other half to put itself in the way of being cheated? Is it true that all women are idiots till they are twenty, intriguers and murderesses till they are forty, and customers of hags who restore decayed beauty till they are eighty? Do the hags and intriguers exchange cynical letters sparkling with the epigram of a practised writer, and do the murderesses keep journals of equal literary merit and equal power of mental anatomy? If the world is such Mr. Wilkie Collins is certainly daring and Christian. But if he has only taken disjointed facts, which at best are fragments of truth, and patched them together,—if he has expended his wonderful ingenuity in producing a discordant mosaic instead of a harmonious picture, his plea falls to the ground, and the fact that there are characters such as he has drawn, and actions such as he has described, does not warrant his overstepping the limits of decency, and revolting every human sentiment. This is what *Armadale* does. It gives us for its heroine a woman fouler than the refuse of the streets, who has lived to the ripe age of thirty-five, and through the horrors of forgery, murder, theft, bigamy, gaol, and attempted suicide, without any trace being left on her beauty. The plot turns on this woman's attempt to murder a boy whom she had first attempted to marry, and to pass herself off as his widow by means of her marriage to another boy who is secretly his namesake. And these attempts are told frankly in a diary, which, but for its unreality, would be simply loathsome, and which needs all the veneer of Mr. Wilkie Collins's easy style and allusive sparkle to disguise its actual meaning. If we needed any proof of our assertion we should point to Mr. Thomas's pictures. It is well that a novelist should see the effect produced by the images of his fancy on the man who has to give them form and shape. So long as Miss Gwilt is talking about Beethoven's sonatas, eclipsing Byron's sarcasm about girls in their teens, and Dickens's joke about church bells, we are tempted to forget the character of the speaker. But if we turn to the illustration no doubt is left in our mind:—

> Vice is a monster of so frightful mien,
> As to be hated needs but to be *seen*.

The other characters are so mild compared to the heroine that it is hardly worth while dwelling upon them. But the same test answers for them all. They are not characters, they are shadowy beings put in to answer the requirements of Mr. Wilkie Collins's plot. They do just as he tells them, and are led by the nose as he wants them. That he places them well and leads them cleverly is only to be expected of a writer who has raised 'plot interest' to the rank of a science. But he can do no more than this, he cannot leave them to act without him, he cannot even leave them free to follow the bent of those peculiarities he has imposed upon them. . . .

Mr. Wilkie Collins has himself acknowledged that it is not possible to tell a story successfully without presenting characters, and one reason why his novels never excite a higher feeling than curiosity is because the characters are sacrificed to the story. . . .

[The rest of this long review demonstrates with a wealth of detail that Collins 'has overreached himself by [his] ingenuity', and that 'the only proof of ingenuity in the book is the maintenance of a complication which of itself was improbable'.]

49. Unsigned review, *Saturday Review*

16 June 1866, xxi, 726–7

Mr. Wilkie Collins has given us, in his latest novel, one more instance of his strange capacity for weaving extraordinary plots. *Armadale*, from beginning to end, is a lurid labyrinth of improbabilities. It produces upon the reader the effect of a literary nightmare. Miss Gwilt, Mrs. Oldershaw, and Doctor Le Doux of the Sanatorium are enough to make any story in which they figure disagreeably sensational; and Mr. Collins seizes every possible opportunity of working up the horror they inspire to the highest point. If it were the object of art to make one's audience uncomfortable without letting them know why, Mr. Wilkie Collins would be beyond all doubt a consummate artist. To the accomplishment of this object he devotes great ingenuity, a curious genius for arranging and contriving mysteries, and a good deal of what may be called galvanic power. There is a sort of unearthly and deadly look about the heroes and heroines of his narrative, and though it is necessary for the purpose of the plot that they should keep moving, we feel that every one of their motions is due, not to a natural process, but to the sheer force and energy of the author's will. They dodge each other up and down the stage after the manner of puppets at a puppet-show, and after watching their twistings and turnings from first to last we come away full of admiration of the strings and the unseen fingers that are directing everything from behind the curtain. An ordinary novelist would let the villains murder their intended victim at once, and have done with it. Not so Mr. Wilkie Collins. A hundred agencies are brought into play to suspend our interest through two long volumes. Spies, detective officers, lawyers, and two or three virtuous and watchful amateurs counterplot day and night against the villains. Each dogs the other till he is tired, and when he is tired the other dogs him. They overhear each other's secrets from behind trees, or lurk unsuspected under windows, keeping diaries sometimes of their proceedings. To heighten the absorbing interest of this contest of intelligences, railways, telegraphy, post-offices, presentiments, and dreams are freely used; and the wonders of science do duty side by side with the marvels of the supernatural world. As a whole the effect is clever, powerful, and striking, though grotesque, monotonous, and, to use a French word, *bizarre*. There can be no mistake about the talent displayed. What strikes one as wanting is that humour which is the salt of all great genius, and that sense of proportion and beauty which is the soul of all real art.

The praise which *Armadale* merits for its ingenuity it cannot be said to deserve as a study of character. Its various heroes and heroines may or may not have each a parallel in real life; but, apart from the startling incidents with which they are brought into contact, they have little intrinsic interest in themselves. Miss Gwilt, and the two Armadales, the Milroys, and the Pedgifts are none of them capable of awakening our sympathy, and when they fill the whole foreground, unrelieved by any figures on which the eye can rest with pleasure, the effect of the whole is glaring and deadly, if not dull. Considering how much Miss Gwilt tells us of herself, and the length to which she prolongs her diary and her correspondence, it is singular how indistinct is the image she leaves upon the mind at the end, except that she is wicked and audacious, and that she has got very red hair. Her correspondent, Mrs. Oldershaw, occasionally tells her that her vivacity is charming, and a reputation for vivacity is accordingly one of the things she has to sustain. But her vivacity is precisely the same sort of vivacity as the vivacity of the younger Pedgift and the younger Bashwood, and consists apparently in a power of making by no means brilliant observations in rather flippant English. Place her side by side with Becky Sharp, in Mr. Thackeray's *Vanity Fair*, and it becomes apparent in a moment what one means by saying that *Armadale* is deficient in humour, and deficient as a real sketch of character and life. Becky Sharp is quite as great a sinner, but with all her vices is a bit of genuine human nature. Contrasted with her, Miss Gwilt is a waxwork figure displayed from time to time in every conceivable sort of garish light. Ozias Midwinter, upon the other hand, must be taken to be perhaps the most carefully executed portrait in the book. It would be impossible for a writer of the position of Mr. Wilkie Collins to avoid occasional touches in such an elaborate delineation which are really good, but, considering the amount of ability expended upon Midwinter, the result is decidedly disappointing. He is such a poor creature at the best that it is impossible to derive much pleasure or profit from the spectacle of his feeble mental and moral evolutions, and a virtuous and self-conscious goose who is at the mercy of his dreams and his visions is not enough to support the whole dead weight of Miss Gwilt, and the other characters, upon his shoulders. It is nearly as difficult to become excited over his fate as it is to be excited over Armadale's; and if Miss Gwilt had murdered both of them, and murdered herself afterwards, everyone would have been ready to allow that it would not have signified very much. In common with all writers who have felt the influence of Mr. Dickens, Mr. Wilkie Collins sometimes endeavours to quicken the narrative into liveliness by descending into caricature. As a caricaturist he is not successful, and we are disposed to think that he does not at all lighten the general effect by so doing. The scene, for example, in which Armadale and Miss Milroy examine *Blackstone*, for the purpose of making up their minds as to the legal validity of a secret marriage, falls short of being thoroughly witty or amusing. It is not human nature on the one side, and it is not genuine humour on the other, and a caricature which stands midway between the two is usually not worth constructing. . . .

[Quotes from Book 3, ch. 9: from ' "Page two hundred and eighty . . ." ' to ' ". . . on the next page" '.]

Clever though it may be, this species of writing is not interesting, and one passes from it, as indeed one passes from the whole of *Armadale*, with some admiration of the powers of the author, but without a sense of genuine pleasure enjoyed during the perusal.

Without the incidents of the plot, the characters in *Armadale* would be very wearisome; but it must be admitted that the plot makes a material difference. It is subtle and well-sustained, and the unity of purpose and aim which pervades it is very perceptible. Novelists in general would do well, not indeed to take the plots of Mr. Wilkie Collins as a model, but take a lesson from his patience, and from the resolution with which he makes every circumstance subordinate to his leading idea. The weak part in his plots, perhaps, is that he relies too much upon startling and improbable coincidences. *Le vrai n'est pas toujours le vraisemblable.*[1] The most remarkable coincidences may be found in real life; but when coincidences happen in shoals, one's faith in the novelist's conceptions becomes somewhat weakened. There is such a thing as economy in the free use of improbabilities, and though odd things do occur in the world, they do not keep on occurring to the same people every other day. But the story of *Armadale* hinges almost entirely on miraculous combinations, the arithmetical chances against which are simply infinite. Ozias Midwinter, who strikes up a warm intimacy by accident with Allan Armadale, happens to be his cousin, the other Allan.

---

[1] The truth is not always convincing.

The lady who throws herself overboard the steamer, and is casually saved by Arthur Blanchard, happens to be Miss Gwilt. Arthur Blanchard happens to catch cold and die after his wetting, thus devolving the inheritance on Allan Armadale. Armadale and Midwinter, sailing for pleasure out to sea, happen to fall in with, and pass the night on, the very same French brig, *La Grace de Dieu*, on board which, more than twenty years before, the father of the one had murdered the father of the other. Walking in Kensington Gardens, Mr. Brock, the clergyman, happens to overhear two women talking about Armadale, one of whom happens to be the fatal Miss Gwilt; just as Ozias Midwinter, passing one day through Glasgow, happens to overhear his father-in-law and a stranger conversing about himself. Mr. Wilkie Collins would perhaps reply that all this is fatality. If so, fatality certainly may work wonders in a novel, and the only pity is that we know so little about what fatality can or cannot do in real life. And, over and above all this, we have to grapple with the wonderful coincidence of the Dream, which forms the backbone of the whole work. About this Mr. Wilkie Collins vouchsafes a word to assist us in his appendix:—

My readers will perceive that I have purposely left them with reference to the Dream in this story in the position which they would naturally occupy in the case of a dream in real life—they are free to interpret it by the natural or the supernatural theory, as the bent of their own minds may incline them.

This is really a very funny confusion of thought. When a dream of the kind is proved upon decent authority to have actually been dreamed in 'real life,' and to have been followed up by such strange events as are recorded in *Armadale*, it will be time enough to examine into its rationale. As for the dream in the story, Mr. Wilkie Collins's readers, unless they are singularly simple-minded, will not be long in puzzling themselves between natural and supernatural. Being an invention of the author's fancy, it is much more simply accounted for on the theory that it has pleased Mr. Wilkie Collins to invent it. The only philosophical inquiry still possible after this solution is whether or not Mr. Wilkie Collins believes that such a train of incidents, *if* it happened in the world, would be referable to a natural or a supernatural origin—an inquiry towards which the mere fact of his imagining the fiction contributes nothing. It reminds us of Lord Dundreary's[1] metaphysical problem—'If you had a brother, do you think he would like cheese?'

It is impossible to avoid the conclusion that *Armadale* has not alto-

[1] In the play *Our American Cousin* (1858) by Tom Taylor.

gether satisfied its own author. In a short preface which seems written for purposes both of offence and of defence, Mr. Wilkie Collins half anticipates criticism, and half defies it. 'Viewed by the clap-trap morality of the day, this may be a very daring book. Judged by the Christian morality which is of all time, it is simply a book daring enough to speak the truth.' The habit of using a preface to deliver a clinical lecture on oneself, is not one that should be encouraged, and it is a little alarming to find Mr. Wilkie Collins employed in heaving stones at imaginary reviewers before any of them have come in sight. Nor do we understand wherein the 'truth' in particular of *Armadale* consists, unless it is in the fact that red-haired women do exist who are as wicked as Miss Gwilt, a fact which it is not our wish to deny. But we do not see why Mr. Wilkie Collins supposes that he is going to be made a victim to 'the clap-trap morality of the day.' Moralists of all kinds, clap-trap or otherwise, would prefer perhaps, in real life, to see Miss Gwilt occupying her proper position in the world, which, without offence to Mr. Wilkie Collins, we take to be the dock of the Old Bailey; but the real objection to *Armadale* is not that Miss Gwilt is too sinful to be drawn. The question is whether it is worth while drawing her, and what the picture comes to when it is painted. The chief flaw in it is not that it is pernicious, but that it is ugly. There is a criticism by Coleridge upon the painter Martin, which we should like Mr. Collins to read and digest. It sums up forcibly part of the criticism which most people will feel disposed to pass on *Armadale*. 'It seems to me that Martin never looks at nature except through bits of stained glass. He is never satisfied with any appearance that is not prodigious. He should endeavour to school his imagination into the apprehension of the true idea of the Beautiful.'[1]

[1] *Table Talk* (1835), under the date 31 May 1830.

50. Unsigned review, *London Quarterly Review*

October 1866, xxvii, 107–9

See headnote to No. 45 above.

Mr. Wilkie Collins has done more, perhaps, than almost any writer of the day to foster the taste for sensational stories. He is a pure story-teller, spending comparatively little care on anything but his plot; but in his own department he is unrivalled. There is no one who, with more consummate skill, can weave an exciting tale out of the most slight and unpromising materials, leading his reader on from point to point with ever-growing interest, concealing the mystery on which the whole depends till the proper time for disclosure comes, and, meanwhile, ever dangling it before the eye with an art that tantalizes even while it stimulates the curiosity. . . .

In *Armadale* we have a Miss Gwilt, a portrait drawn with masterly art, but one from which every rightly constituted mind turns with loathing. Is she, we ask, a type of any class to be found in society, or is she simply a horrible monstrosity? Are we to believe that there are women, holding respectable positions, received into honest and even Christian circles, who are carrying on a system of intrigue and wickedness which we have been accustomed to associate with the name of Italy, but which we fondly believed had no existence in this country? Apparently our novelists would have us receive this notion, so determined is the pertinacity with which they go on producing heroes and heroines of this style. Now it is a Count Fosco, now a Lady Audley, now a Miss Gwilt; and, however it may be said, that in these tales the Nemesis rarely fails to overtake the guilty, and that the retribution exacted is sometimes very terrible, it must still be felt that even this is insufficient to remove the impression produced by the continued reproduction of such characters. We go even further, and assert that the tendency of the multiplication of these tales is to create a class of such criminals, if they do not already exist. We can well believe that the writers themselves little calculate the extent of the evil they are helping to produce. They are pleased with present popularity and success; they find they have the power of amusing, and are satisfied to employ it, never pausing to look at the ulterior consequences they may produce in many minds. Not the less certainly, however, do they scatter impressions calculated to shake that mutual confidence by which societies and, above all, families are held together, to abate our love of simple unpretending virtue, in fact, almost to destroy our faith in its reality.

It is only due to the author of *Armadale* to say that he does not leave his readers shut up to contact with wickedness alone. *Armadale* does develop a great moral truth which cannot be too earnestly or too frequently enforced. It is so rare to find in these books any ethical lesson on which we can dwell with satisfaction, that it is the more incumbent on us to give this the mention it deserves. We think, indeed, it might have been developed in a wiser and healthier manner, that a Miss Gwilt was not necessary, even as a foil to Midwinter and Armadale, and perhaps that the familiarity with her evil is more likely to leave a lasting impression on those young and susceptible minds, which ought most carefully to be guarded from such influences, than the spectacle of the good by which it was ultimately overcome. Still, we must acknowledge the presence of this element, and the implied recognition of the power that, notwithstanding the many adverse forces with which it has to contend, secures the ultimate victory for the good. . . .

[The reviewer goes on to anticipate the objection that he is attaching undue significance to light literature: unacknowledged influences are often the most powerful, and 'books of relaxation' are 'just those which need to be most carefully watched'.]

51. Unsigned review, *Westminster Review*

October 1866, lxxxvi (n.s. xxx), 269–71

This review of *Armadale* follows a discussion of Charles Kingsley's *Hereward the Wake*.

There is no accounting for tastes, blubber for the Esquimaux, half-hatched eggs for the Chinese, and Sensational novels for the English. Everything must now be sensational. Professor Kingsley sensationalizes History, and Mr. Wilkie Collins daily life. One set of writers wear the sensational buskin, another the sensational sock. Just as in the Middle Ages people were afflicted with the Dancing Mania and Lycanthropy, sometimes barking like dogs, and sometimes mewing like cats, so now we have a Sensational Mania. Just, too, as those diseases always occurred in seasons of dearth and poverty, and attacked only the poor, so does the Sensational Mania in Literature burst out only in times of mental poverty, and afflict only the most poverty-stricken minds. From an epidemic, however, it has lately changed into an endemic. Its virus is spreading in all directions, from the penny journal to the shilling magazine, and from the shilling magazine to the thirty shillings volume. Bigamy is just now its typical form. Miss Braddon first brought the type into fashion. No novel can now possibly succeed without it. In real life money is sometimes obtained by marriage, but in literature only by bigamy. When Richardson, the showman, went about with his menagerie he had a big black baboon, whose habits were so filthy, and whose behaviour was so disgusting, that respectable people constantly remonstrated with him for exhibiting such an animal. Richardson's answer invariably was, 'Bless you, if it wasn't for that big black baboon I should be ruined; it attracts all the young girls in the country.' Now bigamy has been Miss Braddon's big black baboon, with which she has attracted all the young girls in the country. And now Mr. Wilkie Collins has set up a big black baboon on his own account. His big black baboon is Miss Gwilt, a bigamist, thief, gaol-bird, forgeress, murderess, and suicide.

This beats all Miss Braddon's big black baboons put together. And the interesting creature is brought forward under the plea of religion. She is heralded in with a fine preface about 'Christian morality.' But we must assure Mr. Wilkie Collins that this and his other moral reflections no more make his book religious than a Hindu drama is made religious because it begins with a prayer, or an Oxford prize poem because it ends with a 'Salem.' Mr. Wilkie Collins once nearly succeeded in making a mad woman popular, but he has now perfectly succeeded in making religion ridiculous. But besides the big black baboon there are a number of small baboons and monkeys, for by no stretch of language can they be called human creatures. The most prominent are a hag, who paints and enamels women's faces, and a doctor, whose services, when we are at first introduced to him, are apparently principally required by painted women. Lying, cheating, intriguing, and dreaming strange dreams are the characteristics of these animals. Some of them keep diaries, and some of them yachts.

The way in which the story is put together is certainly ingenious, but to admire the plot and to forget the characters is like admiring the frame instead of enjoying the picture. The story has all the interest, and also the literary power of a police report. It appeals to our curiosity, not to our imagination, or our feeling, or reason. And let us not do Mr. Wilkie Collins injustice. He tells us, and doubtless truly, that he has taken great pains, especially with certain descriptions of scenery and locality. This, however, only makes him rather like a cat, an animal which cares more for places than for persons. Character alone should be the central object of interest for a novelist. And Mr. Wilkie Collins cannot draw character. To slightly alter Pope's words,—

> Nothing so true, as what you once let fall,
> His novels have no characters at all;
> Matter too soft a lasting mark to bear,
> And best distinguished by black, brown, or fair.

So accordingly we have already had from him *The Woman in White*, and in the present novel we have Armadale the Fair and Armadale the Dark. Pedgift junior, who feels 'in his native element in Hyde Park,' who reads 'Pagan writers assisted by a crib,' and who is fond of fathering metaphorical rosebuds, is the nearest approach to a character. But Pedgift junior is after all a mere sketch, modelled after one of Mr. Dickens' comic young men. Again, too, Mr. Wilkie Collins informs us that he has very properly spared no pains in ensuring accuracy on all questions of Law, Medicine, and Chemistry. But we must add it is not artistic to tell this to the reader. The process of watching our dinner being cooked takes away our appetite.

Of the general tone of the tale we have already spoken. Further reprobation is useless. For to attempt to put down Sensationalism by words, is like trying to remove the hump off a camel's back with a poultice. Once there was a play called *The Spanish Tragedy*, very dull, imbecile to the verge of insanity. All the Elizabethan dramatists denounced it. Jonson satirized, and Shakespeare laughed at its folly. In vain. The play was more popular than any of Shakespeare's. The mob rushed to see its performance, for each act was full of horrors. Hanging, stabbing, shooting followed each other in every scene. Nine people were murdered in nearly as many ways. What Shakespeare could not do, we certainly cannot. Sensationalism must be left to be dealt with by time, and the improvement of the public taste. But it is worth while stopping to note, amidst all the boasted improvement of the nineteenth century, that whilst Miss Braddon's and Mr. Wilkie Collins' productions sell by thousands of copies, *Romola* with difficulty reaches a second edition.

52. Bret Harte, 'No Title. By W-lk-e C-ll-ns', *Condensed Novels*

1867

Bret Harte (1836–1902), American poet and writer of short stories, published in his *Condensed Novels* (1867) some clever parodies of Dickens, Charlotte Brontë, Marryat, and others. Although its title echoes that of *No Name*, this Collins parody pokes fun at both specific novels ('Count Moscow' is obviously Fosco of *The Woman in White*) and features common to many novels, such as his partiality for multiple narratives and for medical witnesses.

PROLOGUE.

The following advertisement appeared in the *Times* of the 17th of June, 1845:

WANTED.—A few young men for a light genteel employment. Address   J. W., P. O.

In the same paper, of the same date, in another column:

To LET.—That commodious and elegant family mansion, No. 27 Limehouse Road, Pultneyville, will be rented low to a respectable tenant if applied for immediately, the family being about to remove to the continent.

Under the local intelligence, in another column:

MISSING.—An unknown elderly gentleman a week ago left his lodgings in the Kent Road, since which nothing has been heard of him. He left no trace of his identity except a portmanteau containing a couple of shirts marked '209, WARD.'

To find the connection between the mysterious disappearance of the elderly gentleman and the anonymous communication, the relevancy of both these incidents to the letting of a commodious family mansion, and the dead secret involved in the three occurrences, is the task of the writer of this history.

A slim young man with spectacles, a large hat, drab gaiters, and a note-book, sat late that night with a copy of the *Times* before him, and a pencil which he rattled nervously between his teeth in the coffee-room of the 'Blue Dragon.'

CHAPTER I.

MARY JONES'S NARRATIVE.

I AM upper housemaid to the family that live at No. 27 Limehouse Road, Pultneyville. I have been requested by Mr. Wilkey Collings, which I takes the liberty of here stating is a gentleman born and bred, and has some consideration for the feelings of servants, and is not above reward-ing them for their trouble, which is more than you can say for some who ask questions and gets short answers enough, gracious knows, to tell what I know about them. I have been requested to tell my story in my own langwidge, though, being no schollard, mind cannot conceive. I think my master is a brute. Do not know that he has ever attempted to poison my missus—which is too good for him, and how she ever came to marry him, heart only can tell—but believe him to be capable of any such hatrosity. Have heard him swear dreadful because of not having his shaving water at 9 o'clock precisely. Do not know whether he ever forged a will or tried to get my missus' property although, not having confidence in the man, should not be surprised if he had done so. Believe that there was always something mysterious in his conduct. Remember distinctly how the family left home to go abroad. Was putting up my back hair, last Saturday morning, when I heard a ring. Says cook, 'That's missus' bell, and mind you hurry or the master 'ill know why.' Says I, 'Humbly thanking you mem, but taking advice of them as is competent to give it, I'll take my time.' Found missus dressing herself and master growling as usual. Says missus, quite calm and easy like, 'Mary, we begin to pack to-day.' 'What for, mem,' says I, taken aback. 'What's that hussy asking?' says master from the bedclothes quite savage like. 'For the Continent—Italy,' says missus—'Can you go Mary?' Her voice was quite gentle and saintlike, but I knew the struggle it cost, and says I, 'With *you* mem, to India's torrid clime, if required, but with African Gorillas,' says I, looking toward the bed, 'never.' 'Leave the room,' says master, starting up and catching of his bootjack. 'Why Charles!' says missus, 'how you talk!' affecting surprise. 'Do go

Mary,' says she, slipping a half-crown into my hand. I left the room scorning to take notice of the odious wretch's conduct.

Cannot say whether my master and missus were ever legally married. What with the dreadful state of morals now-a-days and them stories in the circulating libraries, innocent girls don't know into what society they might be obliged to take situations. Never saw missus' marriage certificate, though I have quite accidental-like looked in her desk when open, and would have seen it. Do not know of any lovers missus might have had. Believe she had a liking for John Thomas, footman, for she was always spiteful-like—poor lady—when we were together—though there was nothing between us, as Cook well knows, and dare not deny, and missus needn't have been jealous. Have never seen arsenic or Prussian acid in any of the private drawers—but have seen paregoric and camphor. One of my master's friends was a Count Moscow, a Russian papist—which I detested.

CHAPTER II.

THE SLIM YOUNG MAN'S STORY.

I AM by profession a reporter, and writer for the press. I live at Pultneyville. I have always had a passion for the marvelous, and have been distinguished for my facility in tracing out mysteries, and solving enigmatical occurrences. On the night of the 17th June, 1845, I left my offce and walked homeward. The night was bright and starlight. I was revolving in my mind the words of a singular item I had just read in the *Times*. I had reached the darkest portion of the road, and found myself mechanically repeating: 'An elderly gentleman a week ago left his lodgings on the Kent Road,' when suddenly I heard a step behind me.

I turned quickly, with an expression of horror in my face, and by the light of the newly risen moon beheld an elderly gentleman, with green cotton umbrella, approaching me. His hair, which was snow-white, was parted over a broad, open forehead. The expression of his face, slightly flushed, was that of amiability verging almost upon imbecility. There was a strange, inquiring look about the widely-opened mild blue eye—a look that might have been intensified to insanity, or modified to idiocy. As he passed me, he paused and partly turned his face, with a gesture of inquiry. I see him still, his white locks blowing in the evening breeze, his hat a little on the back of his head, and his figure painted in relief against the dark blue sky.

Suddenly he turned his mild eye full upon me. A weak smile played about his thin lips. In a voice which had something of the tremulousness of age and the self-satisfied chuckle of imbecility in it, he asked, pointing to the rising moon, 'Why?—Hush!'

He had dodged behind me, and appeared to be looking anxiously down the road. I could feel his aged frame shaking with terror as he laid his thin hands upon my shoulders and faced me in the direction of the supposed danger.

'Hush! did you not hear them coming?'

I listened; there was no sound but the soughing of the roadside trees in the evening wind. I endeavored to reassure him, with such success that in a few moments the old weak smile appeared on his benevolent face.

'Why?—' But the look of interrogation was succeeded by a hopeless blankness.

'Why!' I repeated with assuring accents:

'Why,' he said, a gleam of intelligence flickering over his face, 'is yonder moon, as she sails in the blue empyrean, casting a flood of light o'er hill and dale, like— Why,' he repeated, with a feeble smile, 'is yonder moon, as she sails in the blue empyrean—' He hesitated— stammered— and gazed at me hopelessly, with the tears dripping from his moist and widely-opened eyes.

I took his hand kindly in my own. 'Casting a shadow o'er hill and dale,' I repeated quietly, leading him up the subject, 'like— Come, now.'

'Ah!' he said, pressing my hand tremulously, 'you know it?'

'I do. Why is it like—the—eh—the commodious mansion on the Limehouse Road?'

A blank stare only followed. He shook his head sadly. 'Like the young men wanted for a light, genteel employment?'

He wagged his feeble old head cunningly.

'Or, Mr. Ward,' I said with bold confidence, 'like the mysterious disappearance from the Kent Road.'

The moment was full of suspense. He did not seem to hear me. Suddenly he turned.

'Ha!'

I darted forward. But he had vanished in the darkness.

CHAPTER III.

NO. 27 LIMEHOUSE ROAD.

It was a hot midsummer evening. Limehouse Road was deserted save by dust and a few rattling butchers' carts, and the bell of the muffin and crumpet man. A commodious mansion which stood on the right of the road as you enter Pultneyville surrounded by stately poplars and a high fence surmounted by a *chevaux de frise* of broken glass, looked to the passing and footsore pedestrian like the genius of seclusion and solitude. A bill announcing in the usual terms that the house was to let, hung from the bell at the servants' entrance.

As the shades of evening closed, and the long shadows of the poplars stretched across the road, a man carrying a small kettle stopped and gazed, first at the bill and then at the house. When he had reached the corner of the fence, he again stopped and looked cautiously up and down the road. Apparently satisfied with the result of his scrutiny, he deliberately sat himself down in the dark shadow of the fence, and at once busied himself in some employment, so well concealed as to be invisible to the gaze of passers-by. At the end of an hour he retired cautiously.

But not altogether unseen. A slim young man, with spectacles and note-book, stepped from behind a tree as the retreating figure of the intruder was lost in the twilight, and transferred from the fence to his note-book the freshly stenciled inscription—'S—T—1860—X.'

CHAPTER IV.

COUNT MOSCOW'S NARRATIVE.

I am a foreigner. Observe! To be a foreigner in England is to be mysterious, suspicious, intriguing. M. Collins has requested the history of my complicity with certain occurrences. It is nothing—bah—absolutely nothing.

I write with ease and fluency. Why should I not write? Tra la la! I am what you English call corpulent. Ha, ha! I am a pupil of Macchiavelli. I find it much better to disbelieve everything, and to approach my subject and wishes circuitously, than in a direct manner. You have observed that playful animal, the cat. Call it, and it does not come to you directly, but rubs itself against all the furniture in the room, and reaches you finally—and scratches. Ah, ha, scratches! I am of the feline species. People call me a villain—bah!

I know the family, living No. 27 Limehouse Road, I respect the gentleman—a fine, burly specimen of your Englishman—and Madame, charming, ravishing, delightful. When it became known to me that they designed to let their delightful residence, and visit foreign shores, I at once called upon them. I kissed the hand of madame. I embraced the great Englishman. Madame blushed slightly. The great Englishman shook my hand like a mastiff.

I began in that dexterous, insinuating manner, of which I am truly proud. I thought madame was ill. Ah—no. A change, then, was all that was required. I sat down at the piano and sang. In a few minutes madame retired. I was alone with my friend.

Seizing his hand, I began with every demonstration of courteous sympathy. I do not repeat my words, for my intention was conveyed more in accent, emphasis, and manner, than speech. I hinted to him that he had another wife living. I suggested that this was balanced—ha!—by his wife's lover. That, possibly, he wished to fly—hence the letting of his delightful mansion. That he regularly and systematically beat his wife in the English manner, and that she repeatedly deceived me. I talked of hope, of consolation, of remedy. I carelessly produced a bottle of strychnine and a small vial of stramonium from my pocket, and enlarged on the efficiency of drugs. His face, which had gradually become convulsed, suddenly became fixed with a frightful expression. He started to his feet, and roared: 'You d—d Frenchman!'

I instantly changed my tactics, and endeavored to embrace him. He kicked me twice, violently. I begged permission to kiss madame's hand. He replied by throwing me down stairs.

I am in bed with my head bound up, and beefsteaks upon my eyes, but still confident and buoyant. I have not lost faith in Macchiavelli. Tra la la! as they sing in the opera. I kiss everybody's hands.

CHAPTER V.

DR. DIGGS'S STATEMENT.

MY name is David Diggs. I am a surgeon living at No. 9 Tottenham Court. On the 15th of June, 1854, I was called to see an elderly gentleman lodging on the Kent Road. Found him highly excited, with strong febrile symptoms, pulse 120, increasing. Repeated incoherently what I judged to be the popular form of a conundrum. On closer examination found acute hydrocephalus and both lobes of the brain rapidly filling with water. In consultation with an eminent phrenologist, it was further discovered that all the organs were more or less obliterated except that of Comparison. Hence the patient was enabled to only distinguish the most common points of resemblance between objects, without drawing upon other faculties, such as Ideality or Language, for assistance. Later in the day found him sinking—being evidently unable to carry the most ordinary conundrum to a successful issue. Exhibited Tinct. Val., Ext. Opii, and Camphor, and prescribed quiet and emollients. On the 17th the patient was missing.

———

CHAPTER LAST.

STATEMENT OF THE PUBLISHER.

ON the 18th of June, Mr. Wilkie Collins left a roll of manuscript with us for publication, without title or direction, since which time he has not been heard from. In spite of the care of the proof-readers, and valuable literary assistance, it is feared that the continuity of the story has been destroyed by some accidental misplacing of chapters during its progress. How and what chapters are so misplaced, the publisher leaves to an indulgent public to discover.

THE MOONSTONE

Serialized in *All the Year Round* from 4 January to 8 August 1868; published in three volumes by William Tinsley in July 1868. A dramatic version was produced at the Olympic Theatre in 1877.

This has been the most widely-discussed of all Collins's novels. Notable appreciations include prefaces by T. S. Eliot (to the 'World's Classics' edition, 1928) and Dorothy Sayers ('Everyman' edition, 1945). For V. S. Pritchett (and many others) it inaugurates the modern detective story in England—'the long career of murder for murder's sake' (*The Living Novel* (1946), 74). A Freudian view may be found in L. A. Lawson's 'Wilkie Collins and *The Moonstone*', *American Imago*, 20 (1963), 61–79. Many critics have suggested that the Indian element in *Edwin Drood* may owe something to Collins's novel; for a possible influence on Trollope, see H. J. W. Milley, '*The Eustace Diamonds* and *The Moonstone*', *Studies in Philology*, 36 (1939), 651–63.

53. Charles Dickens, letters to W. H. Wills

30 June 1867 and 26 July 1868

Wills was Dickens's sub-editor on *All the Year Round*. Text from 'Nonesuch' edition, III, 534 and 660. K. Robinson suggests that the hostile comments in the second extract may be evidence of 'some kind of personal estrangement' between the two writers. It is worth noting, however, that Dickens's distaste for the 'construction' anticipates a similar observation by another practising novelist, Anthony Trollope (See No. 78, 2nd extract).

I have read the first 3 Nos. of Wilkie's story this morning, and have gone minutely through the plot of the rest to the last line. Of course it is a series of 'Narratives', and of course such and so many modes of action are open to such and such people; but it is a very curious story—wild, and yet domestic—with excellent character in it, great mystery, and nothing belonging to disguised women or the like. It is prepared with extraordinary care, and has every chance of being a hit. It is in many respects much better than anything he has done.

I quite agree with you about the *Moonstone*. The construction is wearisome beyond endurance, and there is a vein of obstinate conceit in it that makes enemies of readers.

54. Geraldine Jewsbury, unsigned review, *Athenaeum*

25 July 1868, 106

On the author of this review, see headnote to No. 11.

When persons are in a state of ravenous hunger they are eager only for food, and utterly ignore all delicate distinctions of cookery; it is only when this savage state has been somewhat allayed that they are capable of discerning and appreciating the genius of the *chef*. Those readers who have followed the fortunes of the mysterious Moonstone for many weeks, as it has appeared in tantalizing portions, will of course throw themselves headlong upon the latter portion of the third volume, now that the end is really come, and devour it without rest or pause; to take any deliberate breathing-time is quite out of the question, and we promise them a surprise that will find the most experienced novel-reader unprepared. The unravelment of the puzzle is a satisfactory reward for all the interest out of which they have been beguiled. When, however, they have read to the end, we recommend them to read the book over again from the beginning, and they will see, what on a first perusal they were too engrossed to observe, the carefully elaborate workmanship, and the wonderful construction of the story; the admirable manner in which every circumstance and incident is fitted together, and the skill with which the secret is kept to the last; so that even when all seems to have been discovered there is a final light thrown upon people and things which give them a significance they had not before. The 'epilogue' of *The Moonstone* is beautiful. It redeems the somewhat sordid detective element, by a strain of solemn and pathetic human interest. Few will read of the final destiny of *The Moonstone* without feeling the tears rise in their eyes as they catch the last glimpse of the three men, who have sacrificed their cast in the service of their God, when the vast crowd of worshippers opens for them, as they embrace each other and separate to begin their lonely and never-ending pilgrimage of expiation. The deepest emotion is certainly reserved to the last.

As to the various characters of the romance, they are secondary to the circumstances. The hero and heroine do not come out very distinctly, though we are quite willing to take them upon testimony. Ezra Jennings, the doctor's assistant, is the one personage who makes himself felt by the reader. The slight sketch of his history, left purposely without details, the beautiful and noble nature developed in spite of calumny, loneliness, and the pain of a deadly malady, is drawn with a firm and masterly hand; it has an aspect of reality which none of the other personages possess, though we fancy we should recognize old Betteredge if we were to meet him, even without a copy of *Robinson Crusoe* in his hand! We wish some means could have been found to save Rosanna Spearman. The cloud that hangs over her horrible death might have been lifted by a true artist, and she might have been allowed to live and recover her right mind, under the tender influence of her friend, 'Limping Lucy.' Mr. Godfrey Ablewhite, the distinguished philan-thropist and his lady worshippers, as seen by the light thrown on him by his ardent admirer, Miss Clack, is very cleverly managed; the reader suspects him, like Sergeant Cuff and Mr. Bruff; but the reader is destined to be quite as much taken by surprise as they were.

55. Unsigned review, *Spectator*

25 July 1868, xli, 881–2

The Moonstone is not worthy of Mr. Wilkie Collins's reputation as a novelist. We are no especial admirers of the department of art to which he has devoted himself, any more than we are of double acrostics, or anagrams, or any of the many kinds of puzzle on which it pleases some minds to exercise their ingenuity. Still if readers like a book containing little besides a plot, and that plot constructed solely to set them guessing, there is no particular reason why they should not be gratified. The making and guessing of conundrums are both harmless exercises of ingenuity, but when men of intellect engage in them they ought at least to succeed. If the work is to be done at all, the better it is done the nearer does it rise to a work of genuine intellectual interest. Hitherto Mr. Wilkie Collins has done his work well, has been among the makers of conundrum-novels something more than chief, the only one whose writing was endurable by cultivated taste. Few men who could read the *Woman in White* at all read it without pleasure, or forgot its one character, the subtle, cowardly, intellectual sybarite Count Fosco. The plot of *No Name* also was worked out with rare skill, such skill as to suggest a regret that it had not been all expanded on the heroine, Magdalen Vanstone, the born actress, and the single person in the story with a character at all. Captain Wragge only appears to have one, and is obliged to tell you every five minutes what kind of villain he is. The excessive and morbid improbability of *Armadale* could not destroy all its interest, or the curiosity of its readers in the proceedings of that vulgarized Becky Sharp, Miss Gwilt. In the *Moonstone*, however, we have no person who can in any way be described as a character, no one who interests us, no one who is human enough to excite even a faint emotion of dull curiosity as to his or her fate. The heroine is an impulsive girl, generally slanging somebody, whose single specialty seems to be that, believing her lover had stolen her diamond, she hates him and loves him both at once, but neither taxes him with the offence nor pardons him for committing it, a heroine who seems to have been borrowed from one of those old novels where everybody is miserable because nobody will talk common sense for five minutes. The hero has no qualities at all. In the beginning of the book Mr. Wilkie Collins had apparently an idea of describing a rather remarkable figure, a man who, educated in many countries, has so far imbibed their intellectual specialities that he by turns displays the French, German, Italian, and English side of his nature. The idea is not a bad one, for though no such human being ever existed, even a lay figure may be made interesting by carefully selected costume, but it is clumsily worked out even at first, through nonsensical talk about objective and subjective, and very soon found burdensome and abandoned; after which Franklin Blake becomes a person to whom all manner of fascinating qualities are attributed, but who does nothing remarkable except, indeed, cry when the girl he loves declares that he has stolen her jewellery. Of the minor characters Miss Clack is an absurd exaggeration of the bitter evangelical type, a woman who reveals her greed and spitefulness and love of power in broad splashes, not touches, in her own letters; Godfrey Ablewhite is the most ordinary of hypocrites; Gabriel Betteredge a butler like no butler the world ever saw, now a garrulous old goose, now shrewd enough to detect the effect of several educations on his interlocutor; and Mr. Bruff is a very inferior copy of Pedgift Senior in *Armadale*. . . . Such an array of dummies was never got together in any book of Mr. Wilkie Collins's before, or, we venture to say, in any book written by a man with the same literary reputation.

The plot is a little better than the characters, and very little. . . . [In his discussion of the story, the central idea of which he finds 'improbable', the reviewer grudgingly admits that Collins shows 'some of his accustomed power'. He concludes, however, that] the *Moonstone* gives the impression that he is weary of his own occupation, and puts together the pieces of his puzzle with little trouble and no interest. It is a pity, for even toys of that kind may as well be well made, and Mr. Wilkie Collins has it in him to be the very best puzzle-maker in the world.

56. Unsigned review, *Nation*

17 September 1868, vii, 235

Mr. Wilkie Collins's new book is very suggestive of a game called 'button,' which children used to play, and probably play now. A number of little folks being seated in a circle, each with hands placed palm to palm in front of him, one of the party, who holds a button, comes in turn to each of the others, and ostensibly drops it into his closed hands. Of course, but one of the party can receive it, but in each case the same motions are gone through with; and having made his rounds, the principal performer enquires, 'Who's got the button?' Each one, including him who has it, but who intentionally misleads the rest, guesses at the puzzle, and he who guesses right carries the button at the next trial. The *Moonstone* riddle is so like in its essential features to this child's-play, that it might very well have been suggested by it. Mr. Collins's art consists, in this particular case, in converting the button into a yellow diamond, worth thirty thousand pounds; in calling the players Hindoos, detective policemen, reformed thieves, noble ladies, and so on, and in thus more effectually distracting his reader's attention from the puzzle itself, which turns out at last, like most of Mr. Collins's mysteries, to have no vital connection with his characters, considered as human beings, but to be merely an extraneous matter thrown violently into the current of his story. It would perhaps be more correct to say that there is no story at all, and that the characters are mere puppets, grouped with more or less art around the thing the conjurer wishes to conceal until the time comes for displaying it. These books of his are, in their way, curiosities of literature. The word 'novel,' as applied to them, is an absurd misnomer, however that word is understood. There is nothing new in Mr. Collins's stories, if the reader has ever read a book of puzzles, and they serve none of the recognized purposes of the novel. They reflect neither nature nor human life; the actors whom they introduce are nothing but more or less ingenious pieces of mechanism, and they are all alike—like each other and like nothing else. They teach no moral lessons; they are unsuggestive of thought, and they appeal to no sentiment profounder than the idlest curiosity. They are simply conundrums. It is for this reason that Mr. Collins, wise in his generation, deprecates any attempts on the part of his critics to tell the plot of his stories. One commits, however, no breach of trust in speaking of the theatrical properties which supply, in our author's case, the place of dramatic ability. He cannot create a character, unless the solitary instance of Count Fosco be an exception; he can only dress a lay-figure with more or less of skill. Take his 'Moonstone,' for instance—which, as far as the real business of the plot is concerned, might as well have been a black bean or a horn button—call it a yellow diamond, stolen, centuries ago, from the forehead of an Indian idol, and make its recovery a part of the religion of three mysterious, lithe, swarthy East Indians in flowing white robes, and there is a chance of awakening, in the most hardened of novel-readers, a curiosity which would assuredly have slept over the possible whereabouts of a button.

But it is hardly worth while to go on. One might say of the book, that it is like a pantomime—the characters appear to speak, but really say nothing, and are merely conventional figures, and not characters at all. Mr. Collins ventriloquizes behind each of his puppets, in order to give a sufficient number of misleading sounds. But his art is bad, and he has not art enough—his voice always betrays him, and the reader is never deceived into thinking that it is anybody but Mr. Collins that is talking. We do not know of any books of which it is truer than of Mr.

Collins's to make the damaging remark, that nobody reads them twice, and that when the end of the first perusal is reached, everybody thinks his time has been wasted.

57. Unsigned review, *The Times*

3 October 1868, 4

This long review, here considerably shortened, fills almost four columns in the original version.

It would be unjust to the memory of Edgar Poe, or perhaps—to look further back still—to Mrs Radcliffe, to style Mr. Wilkie Collins the founder of the sensational school in novels, but he long ago placed himself at its head. He proved, indeed, at so early a period, his skill in the construction of a plot, that he has since been his own most formidable rival. His *Basil* displayed a more intense concentration than, perhaps, any of his later tales of tragic interest, of however painful a kind, but about one or two characters only; in *The Woman in White* he evinced that he could preserve the unity and concentration of interest while multiplying his actors and circumstances; and in the present story he has shown himself a master in the art of amalgamating the most unmalleable and inconsistent of facts—fatalism and Hindoo mysticism and devotion, English squirearchy, detectives, and housemaids—and seems to have taken by choice difficulties for his resources.

[A plot-summary follows, stopping short at the solution of the mystery: 'Who took the Moonstone, where it has been, where it is, together with the virtues and failings of medical theories and opium, we have not the cruelty to explain further to our readers.']

Mr. Wilkie Collins explains that the distinction between the present and former tales of his is that the attempt made in this is to 'trace the influence of character on circumstances,' and to show that the conduct of the several actors directs the course of those portions of the story in which they are concerned. . . .

[The principal characters are discussed in turn; the passage on Sergeant Cuff is given as a sample.]

Cuff is the inevitable detective, a character apparently so regularly retained on the establishment of sensational novelists that it would be convenient for a due appreciation of their new works to find appended to advertisements of them, along with extracts from critical journals, such remarks as 'Very true to life' and the like, dated from Scotland Yard. We cannot affect to love the police-court flavour these characters infuse into modern tales. But 'the great' Sergeant Cuff would almost reconcile one to the type. . . .

Into and among these characters rolls and revolves the Moonstone, with its mythical burden of misfortune. All the ill attends it of which its legend told. . . . Yet itself is a harmless diamond enough. It works its mischief by purely natural means; every one is the voluntary agent in his or her own undoing; and, after all, the mystery is found to be due to the professional pique of one country doctor, and is solved by another. The character of each of the real actors in the story is the centre of attraction within the orbit of its own circumstances, the actions of each in conformity with such person's character becoming in their turn circumstances on which the characters of the others have to operate. . . .

So much for Mr. Wilkie Collins's theory. His readers, probably far too soon for their retention of the scientific placidity necessary for the due weighing of the principles laid down in his preface, if they ever read it, will be caught in the vortex of his plot. The essence and secret of sensational novel-writing is to keep flashing a metaphorical bullseye up the particular dark archways where the thief is not lurking; to make the circumstances agree with one given explanation, which is not the true one; and to disguise as long as possible the fact that they agree also with a perfectly different conclusion. It is to present a real clue and a pseudo clue, and tempt the reader on to follow the pseudo clue till past the middle of the third volume. The whole school has this habit of laying eggs and hiding them. But Mr. Wilkie Collins has a complex variety of this propensity for secretiveness. He is not satisfied with one false clue, but is perpetually dropping clues, and, like a bird, by his demonstrative employment of various arts to lead his readers elsewhere, away from the spot where he originally induced them to fancy the nest was, only makes them more eagerly bent on keeping the old path. Every character in the book has his or her theory as to the mystery, and each of the theories is partly true. But then it is also partly, and that manifestly, false. So when, as often, a hint of the truth is let fall by one of them, the reader has by this time grown so suspicious that he refuses to accept it. . . .

Mr. Wilkie Collins never once quits his hold of his reader's interest. When one part of the mystery is solved, the interest in what remains becomes still more eager. The true test of writings like this, and one which *The Moonstone* will stand, is whether at each stage and break of the story a negative answer must be returned to the question whether the final dénouement be yet seen. . . . When the author shows his whole hand, and while he is revealing the procedure by which it was taken . . ., the interest even yet does not flag, and the reader traces each step to the goal which he sees before him in eager suspense and uncertainty, up to the last page, whether the real catastrophe be not still behind. Mr. Wilkie Collins has built his plot like an iron ship with the several compartments combining perfectly, but isolated and all watertight. . . .

The book has its shortcomings. There are some petty ambiguities and flaws in the plot. [Several examples follow.] There is, again, a certain pervading high-pressure tone about the characters which is exhausting. The medical men are so very medical; the lawyers are so very legal, and peruse abstracts of title with 'breathless excitement;' the politicians are so very political. . . . Every character is sure to have his pet theory as to life, and to be exceedingly epigrammatic. There is a superabundance of law; and lastly, and above all, every narrator makes too much a point of giving to his simplest statements the air of depositions taken before a police magistrate.

But some of these faults are very closely allied to the merits of the book. We could not spare one item of Miss Clack's 'patience' and 'abstinence from judging' others, though all pious ladies are not malignant; Betteredge's frequent stumblings into epigram are none too many; and the legal tediousness and preciseness of the ordinary course of the narrative arises from the same intellectual quality whence come the minute touches (each doing its own work without projecting the smallest shadow in front), which work up the reader's interest at any important crisis to boiling point. To object again, as some ungrateful readers probably may, that there is no desire to turn back to the first volume when the last is read and con over each separate detail fondly, is to complain that the tale belongs to a class in which in proportion to the intensity of interest in the catastrophe is the suddenness of the descent into acquiescence when that is reached; it is to murmur at Mr. Wilkie Collins because his primary aims are not those of Miss Austen or even Mr. Anthony Trollope. There is one positive and intrinsic defect in Mr. Wilkie Collins as a novelist. It is a want of what Mr. Matthew Arnold has called 'sweetness' and 'charm'. But those who admire the spectacle of ingenuity in the construction of a plot, and of the power of bringing home to the imagination the dreariness and terror of dreary and terrible scenes, should seek, and will find, it in *The Moonstone*.

58. Unsigned review, *Harper's New Monthly Magazine*

October 1868, xxxvii, 712–13

If there were such a word as 'story-wright,' corresponding to the term 'playwright,' Wilkie Collins would be styled the one great 'story-wright.' He indeed writes always good sound English, such as De Foe or Swift might have written; but he has none of the delicacies or manner-isms of style which characterize the works of Dickens and Thackeray. It would be hard to find in all his characteristic works a page which from mere form of expression any one could declare to be his rather than that of any other person who understands grammar and has at command a good store of good words. But Mr. Collins has the faculty of constructing a story in such a way that while no one when it is in progress shall even guess at its winding-up, yet when all is done the reader will wonder why he had not anticipated the end of the plot. Mr. Dickens somewhere complains that unscrupulous playwrights, taking one of his novels when half completed, 'adapted it to the stage,' antici-pating the event which was to have formed the climax. Thackeray seems never to have had a plot in his mind. In the preface to *Pendennis* he tells humorously how, until the last chapter was to be written, he did not know how the work was to end. No one who reads Dickens's

Mutual Friend will doubt that the final explanation of Mr. B
strange conduct never entered into the mind of the author until
after the story was begun. More odd still is the fate of Paul Emanu
Charlotte Bronte's *Villette*. Of ten critical readers of the story, five
be sure that he was drowned, and the other five will be just as sure that
he came home, married Lucy Snowe, and 'lived happily ever after.' No
such difficulties will confront the readers of any novel by Wilkie Collins.
They may not be able to even guess, while the story is in progress, how
it is to turn out. If they did guess, most likely their guesses would turn
out wrong. Mr. Collins possesses the faculty, almost amounting to
genius, of writing a novel. In the *Moonstone* he has come nearer to
success than in any of his former stories. If he has fallen short of producing a great novel, he has succeeded in making a most readable story.

59. Unsigned review, *Lippincott's Magazine*

December 1868, ii, 679–80

Lippincott's was a Philadelphia journal which later merged with
Scribner's.

I'm sick to death of novels with an earnest purpose. I'm sick to death of out-
bursts of eloquence, and large-minded philanthropy, and graphic descriptions,
and unsparing anatomy of the human heart, and all that sort of thing. Good
gracious me! Isn't it the original intention or purpose, or whatever you call it,
of a work of fiction, to set out distinctly by telling a story? And how many of
these books, I should like to know, do that? Why, so far as telling a story is
concerned, the greater part of them might as well be sermons as novels. Oh,
dear me! what I want is something that seizes hold of my interest, and makes
me forget when it is time to dress for dinner—something that keeps me reading,
reading, reading, in a breathless state, to find out the end.

Wilkie Collins' confession of faith as a novelist is comprised in the
above speech of his sprightly heroine, Miss Jessie Yelverton, in *The*

Queen of Hearts. He is emphatically a story-writer. He is unrivalled in the construction of an elaborate and intricate plot, and he certainly succeeds in making his readers 'go on reading, reading, reading, in a breathless state, to find out the end.'

Wilkie Collins' career has been a progressive one. There are some ardent novel-readers who will doubtless remember the publication, years ago, of *Antonina*, and a few years later of *Basil*—two books of singular power, but which, we believe, were failures; and no wonder. *Antonina*, a tale of the days of ancient Rome, was filled with ghastly pictures of famine, murder and other 'onpleasantnesses,' while *Basil* was a veritable literary nightmare. The very force and vigor of the author only served to add to the discomfort of the reader by making its painful pictures strangely vivid and impressive. The scarred face of the fiend, Mannion, and the fever-deathbed of Margaret Sherwin, have haunted many an imagination in persistent and uncomfortable fashion. Soon after Mr. Dickens commenced the publication of *Household Words*, there appeared in that periodical a number of short stories which were remarkable for the perfection of their style, the elaboration and originality of their plots and their general artistic finish. 'A Terribly Strange Bed,' 'Sister Rose,' 'The Yellow Mask,' etc., were praised, reprinted and universally read, and were afterward issued in book-form in various collections, under the titles of *After Dark*, *The Queen of Hearts*, etc. Then came a novel, *The Dead Secret*, also published in *Household Words*, in which the wonderful skill of the author in constructing and unfolding a plot was for the first time fully displayed. *The Woman in White* followed, and the claims of Wilkie Collins to be considered a great novelist were at once firmly established. *No Name* and *Armadale* succeeded—both, however, inferior to *The Woman in White*.

Wilkie Collins is, however, no mere weaver of intricate plots—no teller of elaborately constructed stories only. Few characters in modern fiction are as well drawn and sustained as that of Count Fosco, the cool, sensible, intellectual villain in *The Woman in White*, or the swindling but soft-hearted Captain Wragge in *No Name*. Collins also possesses, in common with Anthony Trollope, the power of delineating a heroine who shall be neither a dressed-up doll nor an impossible angel. Rosamond in *The Dead Secret*, Magdalen Vanstone in *No Name*, Marion Halcombe in *The Woman in White*, and Rachel Verinder in the book before us, bear witness to the truth of this assertion. Nor does his powerful mind and pencil fail when called upon to depict scenes of purer and gentler emotion. Rosamond, revealing the 'dead secret' to her blind husband, and the vigil of Rachel Verinder beside her sleeping lover, are pictures drawn with a touch truthful, delicate and tender as that of a woman.

The novel that now lies before us is the best that Mr. Collins has of late years given to the world, and we are inclined to consider it, with the one exception of *The Woman in White*, the best he has ever written. The story is singularly original; and when we remember the force and extent of Hindoo superstition, we can scarcely venture to pronounce it improbable. And how admirably is the story told! Clear, lucid and forcible in style, never straying into the alluring but pernicious paths of description or dissertation, the narrative moves onward in its unbroken and entrancing course. Let the impatient reader, hurrying to reach the dénouement, skip half a dozen pages. Instantly the thread of the story is broken, the tale becomes incomprehensible, the incidents lose their coherence. *The Moonstone* is a perfect work of art, and to remove any portion of the cunningly constructed fabric destroys the completeness and beauty of the whole. . . .

It would be well if some of the New England writers, who look upon a novel as a mere vehicle for the introduction of morbid and unwholesome metaphysical and psychological studies, or long dissertations on Art—well enough in their way perhaps, but strangely out of place in a story—would study the elements of their art from Wilkie Collins. . . .

MAN AND WIFE

Serialized in *Cassell's Magazine* (January–September 1870) and *Harper's Weekly* (December 1869–August 1870); published in three volumes by F. S. Ellis in June 1870. A dramatic version, published in 1870, was produced at the Prince of Wales's Theatre in 1873.

60. Unsigned review, *Saturday Review*

9 July 1870, xxx, 52–3

We must preface what we have to say upon Mr. Wilkie Collins's new novel by a statement which to some of our readers may possibly serve instead of any further criticism. We will confess to having taken the book, so to speak, at one draught. In spite of certain prejudices produced by causes to which we may presently refer, we found it too amusing to be laid down unfinished. And we may therefore say explicitly what we have illustrated by example, that *Man and Wife* is an exceedingly entertaining book, and that admirers of Mr. Wilkie Collins will probably admit it to be amongst his best performances.

Having attributed this cardinal virtue to the novel, there is perhaps little use in saying more; and yet we would willingly endeavour to solve a problem which has often occurred to us in reading it. Why, being so good, is it not a little better? There is so much undeniable cleverness, such an abundance of literary skill of a certain order, that we are almost puzzled by a certain sense of dissatisfaction which remains with us at the end of the third volume. It is not simply that the novel, like most of Mr. Collins's novels, depends upon a highly artificial plot, that strange coincidences happen with singular frequency, that the characters play hide and seek in a manner unknown in real life—not from want of sense, but obviously with the view of prolonging our suspense—and that it requires a clear head to remember the varying relations of the characters throughout the entanglements in which they are involved. We necessarily make up our minds to this kind of business when we sit down to a novel by Mr. Wilkie Collins; and in *Man and Wife* we do not get more than we expect, or than is inevitable in a work in his style. Ingenuity of construction is sufficiently rare in English writers to make us regard these peculiarities as at least a pleasant variation upon the ordinary run of novelists. But we have a suspicion that it is gained at a rather heavy price, and that in particular the reality of the characters is often sacrificed to the exigencies of the situation. We will take for examples one or two of the most prominent actors in *Man and Wife*. Perhaps the best character in the book is a shrewd, benevolent, and polished Scotch lawyer of the old school, called Sir Patrick Lundie. It is his special duty to be a useful family adviser to the extremely hot-headed and perverse young persons by whom he is surrounded. He is supposed to show the coolness and sagacity of an experienced man of the world, and always to find the right way out of every conceivable scrape. Now, so long as we deliver ourselves blindly to Mr. Collins's guidance, we are of course persuaded that this acute old gentleman is invariably right; at each stage of the proceedings his remarks are so sententious, and introduced with so much parade and such Burleigh-like shakings of the head, that we do not presume to differ from him. Yet when we venture to look back upon the story, to take off the blinkers with which Mr. Collins has provided us, and to form our own judgment of affairs, we begin to see that we have been taken in. Sir Patrick—in our judgment at least—not only blunders in the most mis-chievous manner, but we see the cause of his blundering. He is supposed to lay down the dictates of pure wisdom; he is really obliged to give that advice which will bring about interesting complications in the story. A good cool-headed lawyer under the circumstances suggested would probably have kept matters straight from the beginning—but then there would have been no novel; and consequently the only plan is to tell us at every moment that Sir Patrick is wonderfully wise, and to trust to our not thinking sufficiently to find out that Sir Patrick's advice is frequently silly in the extreme. When we have once reached this conclusion, we begin to suspect the whole story of a certain flimsiness. It is a highly ingenious puzzle, but won't bear picking to pieces. Follow your guide, and you will think that he has led you through an intricate labyrinth with wonderful skill. Trust to yourself, and you will see that he has been elaborately avoiding a straightforward and easy path. This, however, is a point which might be argued, and if we tried to give our reasons we should have to go into the plot more fully than is desirable. We will therefore turn to another character.

Miss Silvester is the heroine who is to suffer and to carry our sympathies along with her. Throughout the story she succeeds pretty well in so doing, but there is one little incident which has occurred before it opens, and which somehow is treated with wonderful leniency. Miss Silvester, who is a refined and intelligent lady, has been seduced under promise of marriage by a rough, brutal boor, whose only recommendations are that he is the son of a lord and has rowed stroke in a University boat-race. We will not say that this is improbable, or that it is immoral, or even that it is disagreeable. But we confess that we have a difficulty in putting together the two ends of Miss Silvester's life. The Miss Silvester of the novel is everything that is sensitive and modest and virtuous, and is rewarded by marrying a rich old gentleman of seventy, at the end of the book. The Miss Silvester of the previous epoch has been anything but virtuous, or even delicate, in her tastes. That such phenomena may occur as the supposed lapse from virtue of a pure and admirable girl is possible; that nobody should think much the worse of her after the discovery is, we will assume, also within the bounds of possibility; but a novelist who was painting character and sentiment rather than inventing clever situations would at least take the trouble to render so strangely mixed a character conceivable. Mr. Collins joins the beautiful woman to the fish without trying to conceal the transition. He puts the bits of his plots together with admirable skill, so far as the exterior is concerned, but does not seem to be conscious of the strange moral problems incidentally involved. That his machinery may work smoothly, a woman must be revoltingly abandoned at one moment, admirably virtuous directly afterwards, and none of her acquaintance must be shocked at her story. The result is that our imaginations entire refuse to accept her as a living woman at all; she is simply an actor playing two entirely different parts in distinct plays which have been somehow tacked together so cleverly that we cannot perceive the join. . . .

[The reviewer turns next to Collins's attack on athleticism.]

Geoffrey Delamayn is at least a vigorous portrait so far of an animal which we would hope to be imaginary. But we must remark that, in the first place, the more he is lowered, the more his victim, Miss Silvester, is degraded; no Roman lady could ever have been more degraded by connexion with a brutal gladiator; and our interest in the heroine is thus diminished. And, in the next place, Mr. Collins is so intent upon painting Mr. Delamayn's muscles and the absence of Mr. Delamayn's brains, that he forgets to make a man of him at all. We will not complain that Mr. Delamayn performs some impossible feats, and that it is very obvious that Mr. Collins's acquaintance with pedestrian performances is purely theoretical. Geoffery Delamayn, we should say, must have weighed at least thirteen stone, and was by no means the man for a four-mile race. But, letting this pass, it is curious to remark how singularly feeble a likeness he is of the undergraduate class which he is supposed to represent. There is not a touch of the genuine local colour about him. It would be absurd to compare Mr. Thomas Hughes as a literary artist with Mr. Collins, but Mr. Hughes's undergraduates and schoolboys are at any rate redolent of the place. They talk the slang, and have the ideas or the sentiments, which are caught at Oxford and Cambridge. Delamayn is a mere generic type of the strong, stupid, brutal man. He might be a prizefighter, or an officer in the Guards, or a backwoodsman; he might be of any age or any rank in life; he has not that indescribable air by which in real life we instantly recognise the young gentleman who is training for the University boat-race and being plucked for his degree. A realistic artist would enable us to tell from any of his conversations where was his standing, and almost at which University he had been trained. Mr. Collins, in his anxiety to produce bold contrasts, and to have a good vigorous figure well picked out in black and white, entirely neglects the more delicate colouring which makes a character really lifelike. He would have had a less tremendous ruffian, but a more really telling actor, if he had taken a less extreme case, and painted that queer variety of arrested development, the boy of man's stature, with good stupid impulses, clumsy shyness, and silly simplicity, whom we generally find distinguishing himself at athletic sports. We cannot, as we have said, assign Geoffrey Delamayn to any particular class or age, but we should say that the turf element was too strongly developed in him to make him a characteristic specimen of the ordinary undergraduate. He is not a boy of man's stature, but a youth of premature hardness and worldly cunning. Though such types are to be occasionally found, they are not the most characteristic nor, as it seems to us, the best adapted for Mr. Collins's design.

In this case Mr. Collins has been led into some extravagance by his moral purpose. How far he is right in that purpose, how far, as we rather think, he has overstated his case, we need not examine. If

Delamayn is something too much of a caricature, athleticism is greatly
in want of ridicule, and no harm will be done even by a little more
ferocious satire. With this assault upon a really serious evil is combined
an attack upon our incoherent system of marriage laws. Moral aims
generally spoil any novel in which they are prominent, and we think
that they have led in this case to some serious artistic faults. If one moral
is generally too much, two morals are surely unjustifiable. Mr. Collins
might be content with assaulting running and boat-racing without
breaking a lance at the same moment against all our marriage laws.
We must certainly decline to enter into the argument which he has
raised. But, after making all deductions, *Man and Wife* is an exciting and
spirited story, and though it is hardly of the kind which will bear two
readings, nobody is likely to repent of one.

61. Unsigned review, *Putnam's Magazine* (New York)

September 1870, xvi, 339–40

The discussion of *Man and Wife* is prefaced by a passage which
pays tribute to Dickens's genius as a creator of characters but
deplores his use of the novel 'to correct abuses', and the imitation
by his followers of this propagandist purpose.

We forgive this in Dickens, . . . and were it confined to him we should
say nothing about it. But unfortunately it is not confined to him, for,
being his weakest and worst trait, it is the very one which his imitators
have seized upon, and reproduced with most success. They have caught
the trick so completely that we cease to think of the great magician
whom these little jugglers have elbowed off the stage. What a brilliant
player, for instance, is Mr. Charles Reade, manipulating the balls of

prison-reform, mad-houses, and trades-unions; and how dextrous is
Mr. Wilkie Collins, with the abuses of Irish and Scottish marriages!
Mr. Collins is a man of genius, whose greatest defect is an excess of
cleverness in the construction of plots, and whose greatest excellence is
insight into character of a certain sort. His range is narrow, but within
that range he is a master. One character in his last novel ... is an
addition to Literature. We mean, of course, Geoffrey Delamayn, an
athlete, who exhibits in perfection the ultimate result of the extreme
physical training which is having its apotheosis in England. ... We
commend Geoffrey Delamayn to Mr. Collins' admirers, as being the
finest study of character that he has yet produced,—the natural result of
unnatural causes,—not such an arrested development as Mr. Kingsley's
Muscular Christian, but such a perfected development as Achilles, the
Achilles of the nineteenth century,—slow, good-tempered, restrained,
but brutal, cunning, murderous—the Muscular Pagan. We shall not
enter into the plot of *Man and Wife*, partly because it is difficult to
analyze the plots of Mr. Collins, and partly because the majority of
novel-readers must already be familiar with it. Our opinion is that it is
at once the simplest and the best that Mr. Collins has yet constructed;
and we trust it portends a turning on his part to the world of probable
occurrences. How clever he can be he has shown us over and over
again; let him show us now that he can be natural. And let him in
future drop social abuses, which Mr. Reade *will* make his own to the
end of the chapter. What we want is not reformers, but novelists—such
novelists as Dickens was in the early part of his career, as Thackeray was
all through his career, and as Mr. Collins can be when he chooses. He
has no equal in the art of telling a story, and but few equals in drawing
character when character 'pure and simple' is his object, as it evidently
was in several of the actors in *Man and Wife*, as Sir Patrick Lundie,
Bishopriggs, and Geoffrey Delamayn.

62. Mrs Oliphant, unsigned review, *Blackwood's Magazine*

November 1870, cviii, 628–31

On Mrs Oliphant, see headnote to No. 34. Reviewing *Man and Wife* as one of a group of recent books, she introduces it as 'one of the cleverest of recent works of fiction, a book which has done a great deal to revive the reputation of Mr Wilkie Collins in his own particular sphere of art'.

Man and Wife has probably by this time been read by most readers of fiction, and it has been largely commented upon by critics, so that it is unnecessary to enter into the details of a story which everybody knows. It is one of those tales founded on actual public grievances, which Mr. Dickens, we believe, was the first to bring into fashion, but which have been more boldly and successfully carried out by Mr. Charles Reade than by any other writer. Mr. Wilkie Collins has done it also; but his strength, which lies in plot and complication of incident, does not lend itself successfully to polemics. *Man and Wife*, however, is more distinctly didactic than any of his former works. Its *motif* is the abuse and irregularity of the laws of marriage—an abuse, however, of which he indirectly and unintentionally shows the limits, by proving beyond doubt that only a thoroughly heartless and unscrupulous villain could make them work real harm; and villains thoroughly unscrupulous are, thank heaven! not very common in the world. Mr. Wilkie Collins's strength is at the same time his weakness. To secure the necessary complications in his plot, he annuls the characters of his personages with the most extraordinary hardihood, and makes them act contrary to the commonest laws not only of conventional morality but of ordinary reason. For instance, in the apologue to this book he brings in a fine lady, a woman of rank, and, so far as he informs us, of unimpeached character, permitting her actually to see with her own eyes and hear with her own ears that the man who has been making a profession of love to her has

188

vilely deceived by a false marriage an honourable and good woman, who has for many years believed herself to be his wife. Yet as soon as the fraud is fully proved, and the heartbroken woman has been thrust into a corner to die, Lady Jane marries this monster, with no more than a pretty fie fie at his naughtiness! Has English society fallen so far, and English ladies become so indifferent to the distinction between virtue and vice, as to make this possible? or are we expected to believe it only because it was necessary to the plot?

Again, Anne the heroine is represented to us as one of the noblest of women. She is pure, proud, full of talent and mental power, with a faculty of attracting everybody, which is not so unusual in books as it is in real life. Yet she degrades herself to the lowest humiliation possible to a woman, becoming the victim of a brutal, brainless villain, whose sole quality is his personal strength, and the fame acquired by the fact that he rowed stroke in the Oxford crew, and has won a foot race or two. It is her desperate effort to get this brute to marry her in time to save her good name which causes all the complications of the tale; and of course we allow, as in the other case, that but for this the story could not have been. Mr. Collins gives his heroine's unaccountable fall as a proof of the dominion over the English imagination of muscularity, and the natural effects of its deification; without ever appearing to see that such a woman as he has drawn could not have made the sacrifice of her honour, her delicacy, and her pride, on any but the highest tragical impulse of self-devotion—an impulse which nothing in the hero's character or circumstances called for. . . .

One of the most powerful scenes in the book is that in which Anne, who has by this time conceived the most deadly terror of her seducer, makes up her mind to produce the document which proves her marriage to him, and the consequent nullity of the pretended marriage which he is trying to prove her to have entered into with another. It is to save that other and his young wife, Anne's dearest friend; but at the same time she is conscious that the step she is about to take will throw herself on the tender mercies of the infuriated brute thus forced to receive her as his wife. Her regard for her friend triumphs. She allows the paper to be produced, and her real position triumphantly proved. Nothing can be more tragical than the sacrifice which she supposes herself about to make; but though she has every reason to fear the last extremities of vengence—though she believes, and everybody else believes, her very life to be in danger—there is not one about her, though she is surrounded by lawyers, who has sufficient presence of mind to assure her that the law does not require her to give herself over to be killed, even to her husband. She allows him to lead her away pale as death and trembling with the certain conviction that she is to be butchered—a conviction which all her friends share. But no one says, Don't go—which in real life every one would have said. Again we allow the exigencies of the story; but Mr Wilkie Collins is not such a novice or weakling as to be unable, if he chooses to take the trouble, to build his story upon probable occurrences as easily as upon impossible ones. A wife who is ignorant and starving, who has no friends and no resources, has been known often enough, heaven knows, to follow her tyrant, in dumb helplessness and terror, to be kicked or beaten to death; but a lady with troops of friends, and at least one wily old lawyer entirely devoted to and trembling for her, could scarcely be compelled to follow such an example. Having said so much, we will not touch upon the deathly-faced weird woman Hester, who carries about with her her 'Confessions' of murder, and stops at every available moment to read that wonderful tale. Such a being belongs to the category of sprites and demons, and does not come within the bounds of criticism. It is impossible to judge by rules of nature and probability a creature utterly at variance with both.

But it is a curious fact that with all these outrages upon common sense, *Man and Wife* is full of power, and perhaps more exciting and interesting than if it had been more carefully constructed. It carries us back to the days of Mr. Wilkie Collins's old fame, though there is nothing in it equal to Count Fosco. Such a book may almost hope to be read even amid the distant sound of cannon, and by people three parts of whose mind are engaged in mourning the miseries or calculating the chances of the war.

Serialized in *Cassell's Magazine* (October 1871–March 1872); published in three volumes by Richard Bentley at the beginning of 1872.

63. D. E. Williams, unsigned review, *Athenaeum*

17 February 1872, 202–3

The author of this review is remembered as the biographer of Sir Thomas Lawrence, the painter.

It is impossible even to dip into *Poor Miss Finch* without at once recognizing the hand of its author. And yet the work is, in many respects, unlike any other of Mr. Wilkie Collins's many novels,—unlike *The Woman in White*, unlike *Armadale*, and, most of all, unlike *Basil*. It is dedicated to a lady, and it is worthy of its dedication. The rhapsodist weaves his plot *virginibus puerisque*.[1] The sanctifying influence of *Cassell's Magazine*—and, which is more, of *Cassell's Magazine* suffering from the intense re-action consequent upon *A Terrible Temptation*—is feebly apparent in every chapter. It is, in short, a sensation novel for Sunday reading, and, as such, can be confidently recommended to the notice of parents and guardians. There is a perjury in it, it is true; but as it is told by a distracted lover to enable him to get a marriage-licence, it is, after all, of the kind at which the gods laugh. And—the perjury excepted—there is no positive sin against the decalogue. There are no red-headed Messalinas, aged Jezebels, rascally doctors, or spurious baronets. Of the

[1] For young women and boys.

hidden horrors which made *Basil*, perhaps, the most powerfully characteristic of all Mr. Collins's achievements, there is not even a shadow. And
if it is a triumph to have demonstrated that the ordinary machinery of a
sensation novel can be turned to the purposes of edification by weekly
instalments, it is impossible to deny Mr. Collins credit for as large a
triumph as he may wish to claim. That the fifty-one chapters should be
full of plotting and counter-plotting, was inevitable. The good people
and the bad people scheme and counter-scheme, and overhear one
another, and write to one another, and intercept letters, and—the bad
people, that is to say—forge letters, and employ detectives, and work the
telegraph, and study law and science, and trip up and are tripped up in
turn with all the assiduity of clown and pantaloon in a pantomime. What
is delightful is, not that all this should be done,—for Mr. Wilkie Collins
has done as much before, and has done it far better,—but that it should
be done in so proper a spirit.

[A brief and ironic summary of the complexities of the plot follows.]

Each of Mr. Wilkie Collins's novels is a riddle, to the answer of
which each chapter brings us a degree nearer. The riddle propounded
in *Poor Miss Finch* is, 'whom will she marry?' And although we suspect
that fate will ultimately side with virtue, we yet must, in fairness, admit
that the story might quite well end either way, and that our interest—as
far as interest can be felt in a wax doll—is tolerably sustained.

Mr. Wilkie Collins is a very clever mechanist, and a very inferior
novelist,—even when judged by his two best works, *The Woman in
White* and *Armadale*. Each of these is clever, each is very interesting.
Each piques us as a Chinese puzzle might, or a charade, or an ingenious
mathematical problem, or a trick of sleight-of-hand with a pack of
cards. We read patiently on for chapter after chapter, working our way
inch by inch to the true answer. In what is essentially the last chapter the
answer suddenly bursts under our feet with a pop, and a bang, and a good
deal of harmless smoke, as at the springing of a theatrical mine. All is
over at once. We have all we wanted. Lucilla is married to Oscar. Who
cares to read further? We shut the book with a slam, much as experienced playgoers leave the theatre long before the curtain falls. Indeed,
that the reader should—apart from the mechanism of its plot—take the
faintest interest in one of Mr. Collins's novels, would argue him easily
interested; and that he should care to read through even *The Woman in
White* a second time—except upon the assumption that he has forgotten
the answer to it—would be almost incredible; for the truth is, that

clever as Mr. Collins is—and his cleverness is beyond all question—in the construction of his riddles, he has not yet called into existence a single character worthy to find its way to 'Kennaquhair.' Abstract from Count Fosco that he is fat, that he speaks a somewhat Italian and hyperbolical English, that he keeps white mice and canaries, and that he plays selections from *Israel in Egitto*, and we have left as ordinary a rogue as ever disgraced a novel. Abstract from Miss Gwilt her red hair, or from Geoffrey Delamayn his big muscles, or from Herr Grosse (the great character in *Poor Miss Finch*) his love of lunch, his Anglo-German oaths, and his general shabbiness and fatness,—in each case we have left us the very sorriest residue. Mr. Collins holds, we believe, that 'the main element in the attraction of all stories is the interest of curiosity and the excitement of surprise.' To this he does not add the analysis of human nature. He is no 'psychologist,' and seems to feel towards any such over-refinement as Mrs. Squeers felt when she boasted that she was 'no grammarian, thank Heaven.' The little subtle touches that make up such a character as Mrs. Poyser, or Colonel Newcome, or even Captain Cuttle, and the clever little nothings by which such a character is indicated, are apparently beneath or beyond Mr. Collins's power. He paints in distemper, with good strong colour, primary, bright, and plenty of it: he turns on the limelight: *voilà tout*. We have persons, not characters. And, for a tale in which the labyrinthine contortions of the plot are everything, persons do fully as good service as characters, while they entail far less labour on the author. The popular delusion that Fosco is a carefully-drawn character, is dispelled the moment we compare him with Herr Grosse. Fosco is a fat, gluttonous, accomplished Italian: Grosse is a fat, gluttonous, learned German. Grosse would make a capital villain, exactly as Fosco would have made a capital surgeon. All that Mr. Collins apparently attempts in his actors is to secure a certain definite individuality. This he effects by the most extrinsic devices, which are neither part of nor in any way consonant with the character itself. . . .

It is easy, then, to see why *Poor Miss Finch* is not to be compared to Mr. Collins's other works. The plotting has, for the ordinary reader, no sufficient *raison d'être*. Miss Finch would be—were she not 'poor' Miss Finch—such a limp lay-figure, that neither does the lover who nearly loses her win our sympathy, nor the villain who nearly deceives her arouse our indignation. We crave matter more stirring to justify mechanism so elaborate. We feel that even Miss Gwilt and her wicked red hair would be a pleasant foil to Miss Finch, and her Madonna-di-

San-Sisto face; and are hardly sure that even such horrors as those of *Basil* would not be, in a certain sense, a relief.

And yet, as far as the story will allow him, Mr. Wilkie Collins is himself. He has many good points, sufficient to justify his popularity. His English is always passable, often good, sometimes incisive. He has a certain sense of humour, although too obviously modelled during his apprenticeship to *Household Words*. . . . And, in addition to his sense of fun, it must be placed to Mr. Collins's credit that he is never tedious. Not a single ethical diatribe—in spite of temptations the most terrible— lurks from the first cover to the last of the three volumes. That the writer of a serial tale should be capable of such self-control is no small matter of commendation.

Mr. Wilkie Collins probably does not himself expect that any of his works will live. He certainly has no right to expect immortality for *Miss Finch*. But it is something to be *facile princeps*,[1] even in a transient school. And to novelists of his own kind Mr. Collins stands as stands the author of *Guy Livingstone* to his three or four copyists. He has made what may be called the 'detective' novel his own, and—for comparisons are unnecessary—need fear no rival. He takes so much and such evident trouble over what he writes, and his workmanship is so good and so conscientious, that the result is always, of its kind, as good as can be got. Many a man in his position would write five novels in every three years. But Mr. Collins respects his readers, and, *pro tanto*, his readers respect Mr. Collins. No one ever yet began one of his novels to throw it aside. It is possible that, having read one, we may not care to begin a second; but if we once begin it we shall most certainly finish it; for although Mr. Collins has grave defects, he has no positive faults. That Miss Gwilt is not Vivien, that Fosco—to go more widely a-field—is not, say, the Earl of Crabs, is what was to have been expected; but for ingenuity, for cleverness, for power of rousing curiosity and keeping interest alive, Mr. Collins stands altogether alone. The art is not a high art, perhaps; but he has mastered it, and mastered it—as his books show —by honest industry. To judge him fairly, we must not go out of our way to compare him with Thackeray or with George Eliot. He writes with no other object than to amuse; and—judged by his object—he achieves a substantial success. In not one of his best tales can we foresee the plot, or even guess at its result, save in so far as he chooses to help us. There is no sameness about him; nor does he ever inflict upon us a *mauvais quart d'heure*.[2] *Armadale*, *The Woman in White*, and *Man and*

---

[1] Easily the first.   [2] A painful (or perhaps dull) passage.

Wife, are as good as those who read six novels a year have any right to expect, and better by far than those can expect who read a novel a month. And if *Poor Miss Finch* is not as good as others, it is not that Mr. Collins's hand has in any way lost its cunning, but simply that the subject is one on which he could hardly be expected to work with zeal. He is at his best when his puppets are either in the dock or being fitted for it; exactly as his tales read best when we get them by instalments of three or four chapters at a time. In *Poor Miss Finch*, as it appears in its three-volumed form, neither of these conditions are fulfilled. And yet, although *Miss Finch* is, for Mr. Collins, weak, and although we hope he will return again with all speed to his favourite topics, (can nothing be made out of the disappearance of Mr. Bauer?) we none the less feel bound to express our opinion that, if not as good a novel as might have been written by Mr. Collins, *Poor Miss Finch* is yet, of its kind, far too good a novel to have been written by any one else.

64. Unsigned review, *Saturday Review*

2 March 1872, xxxiii, 282–3

Our prolific novelists are all mannerists, more or less, but no one of them is more of a mannerist than Mr. Wilkie Collins. Were his title-pages suppressed, the least critical of circulating library subscribers might be trusted to pronounce decisively on the authorship of his productions. For his is not mere mannerism of style—although that is marked enough—but a very decided mannerism of mind. He has considerable powers of imagination, but it is plain that his imagination works and schemes with patient deliberation. He plans his stories as a plodding chamber counsel might draw a settlement, elaborating details with the conscientiousness of a man who guards himself against flaws, and realizes his grave responsibilities. The plot must work plausibly, even where it is to be startlingly sensational, and accordingly the wilder its episodes the more realistic are the minutiæ of its every-day life. It is the art of Defoe adapted to a species of writing which in the days of Defoe was not yet in fashion. There can be no doubt that Mr. Collins has studied the tastes of his public, and in certain instances has pleased them—we will not say pandered to them—with great success. But novels constructed like the *Woman in White* will less than any others bear indefinite repetition. It is hard to cap a climax of sustained and of intricate interest, and one great success in that particular line makes an author his own most formidable rival. Each successive work becomes more of a strain and an effort, and he has to go further afield to grasp the leading conception which is to produce his latest effect. His conception in itself may do the greatest honour to his ingenuity, and yet because it is farfetched it is likely enough to fail of interesting his readers. We should say this is very much the case with *Poor Miss Finch*. In *Poor Miss Finch* we find all the author's characteristic faults and merits, and each intensified. As his faults are of a sort that irritate, we fear they may be found to outweigh the merits; and yet the merits are unmistakable. The plot is constructed with Mr. Collins's customary care, and excellent situations are continually rising out of it. The conception of the heroine entitles him to the credit of the originality he claims for it. There is evidence of observation and research in the information which Mr. Collins has collected, and he uses it in a way that surprises without positively shocking us. And yet we find the book wanting in the two primary essentials of a novel; the heroine fails to charm, and the story flags when it begins to interest us.

In the first place, *Poor Miss Finch* is a surgical and a medical novel. Now we are willing to admit that passions sufficiently intense, and situations sufficiently sublime, may be born of pain and physical afflictions. We know that Poor Miss Finch's special burden of blindness has lent itself before now to the noblest purposes of poetry and romance. But then those authors who have turned it to their professional purposes have idealized it gracefully, resting lightly even on the sightless eyeballs, dealing with the thoughts and following the mournful fancies of a mind driven to prey upon itself. Mr. Wilkie Collins recognizes this in his preface, and takes credit for handling the subject of his choice in an original and more natural manner. He undertakes to interpret faithfully what others have misrepresented for artistic purposes—to represent a blind person acting and speaking as she would really act and speak. The professed moral of his story is to show 'that the conditions of human happiness are independent of bodily affliction, and that it is even possible for bodily affliction itself to take its place among the ingredients of happiness.' How far he has succeeded in the latter part of his design it is difficult to say, for we do not see how a story based on circumstances purely fictitious can prove anything. But, with regard to the former, we have little doubt that Mr. Wilkie Collins has made his blind girl more faithful to nature in thought, act, and speech than Lord Lytton's Nydia. What then? Fidelity is, after all, not the foundation of all fiction. We set Murillo's fanciful Madonnas higher than his realistic monks, and so we prefer the work of art that suggests to us bright impressions and graceful fancies.

[The shortcomings of the hero and heroine are expounded at length.]

We have said that Mr. Collins runs the lines of his story on the familiar model. There is the invariable personage who acts annotator or chorus, and the book turns at last into the inevitable journal, although, singularly enough, not till the third volume. It is a Madame Pratolungo whom Mr. Collins has selected to tell us the story, and we recollect few personages in the range of his fantastical creations who can boast a more eccentric individuality, or one worse sustained. She is by birth and breeding a Frenchwoman, although, in spite of her protestations to the contrary, nature and Mr. Collins have made her essentially English. She is the widow of a Republican adventurer, and professes to have inherited her husband's principles. But the apostrophes to the Universal Republic, the affected invectives against the rich, which jar on us often at first as excessively out of place and character, gradually become rarer and almost vanish, until they reappear towards the close in an expiring flicker, a tardy tribute to consistency. Madame Pratolungo is in reality a frank, honest-hearted Englishwoman. Notwithstanding the French varnish which Mr. Collins rubs on, and the occasional twaddle he puts into her mouth, and in spite of her odd Republican antecedents, she is eminently practical in thought and action. The worst of it is that her twaddle takes the shape of humour, and Mr. Collins's strong side is certainly not the humorous. He sets about amusing us with the same conscientious conviction that he brings to the construction of his plot, and therefore his failure is not surprising. He seems to think that a joke is like a drama, and that its merit is to be judged by the number of repetitions, forgetting altogether that it is the same set of people who have to sit them out. We should be sorry to calculate how often he invites us to laugh at Madame Pratolungo's 'poor papa,' so brave and so impressionable—a scampish old *roué*, whose wonted fires lived in their ashes, and were always burning his daughter's fingers. Then there is the

Reverend Finch, the heroine's father, so called systematically through-out the volumes, which leads us to surmise that our critical acumen must be at fault when we detect no joke in the omission of the Christian name. Mr. Finch's prolific wife is distinctly comic, but the comedy is of the sort in which Mr. Charles Reade indulged so generously in a recent work—comedy that may be classed in the midwifery department of this medical novel. Little Jicks, one of Mr. Finch's children, promised very well, but she was probably too light to suit a form of humour which generally reminds us of a bear dancing in *sabots*, and always coming down heavily in the same place. To sum up, we should say *Poor Miss Finch* ought to be popular with readers who appreciate ingenuity, are indifferent to poetry, and unsusceptible of the ludicrous. It is un-questionably clever in its way, and these are not times when omnivorous novel-readers can afford to neglect anything with substantial pretensions to cleverness.

65. From an unsigned review, *Nation*

7 March 1872, xiv, 158–9

[After outlining the plot, the reviewer continues:]

That the story is interesting in a certain way cannot be denied. There is a judicious combination of tragedy of a certain sort and comedy of a certain sort. And then, too, the way that the villain has of entering the room just as the innocent hero has left; the way in which scraps of paper thrown aside as carelessly as we throw away old envelopes, turn up again a hundred pages later, and nearly break off a marriage and drive two lovers to despair; the mysterious influence that the most ordinary and everyday acts exercise upon the plot of the story, all combine in giving us the impression of a sort of civilized romanticism, of a fairy-land under the control of the police of the present day, that at certain moments makes such stories far from unreadable. But again, when we look at the story more coolly, we find around so petty a building such a lofty scaffolding, so many derricks, cranes, and pulleys, and, when the tale is finished, so little done in comparison with the immense preparations that have been made, that one is rather curious about the quality of mind that can produce such wonderfully intricate skeletons of stories without the power of more completely hiding the dry bones with the better-known and more attractive covering that we see in the life about us. For what is the aim of this story? That the blind should marry the dark-blue? There is then an excellent opening for some novelist, distracted for a plot, to write about the love of the color-blind for the jaundiced. Is it that twin-brothers should not pretend to be one another—that two minutes after we have left a room we should put our heads in the door to see if our deadliest foe is maligning us in our absence? But how petty, how exceedingly unreal seem just those stories that are so evidently most anxious to preserve the air of realism. Whatever may be said against the vanity of existence, it is not all a combination of missing trains, listening behind doors, and mysterious meetings. That is all that Mr. Collins sees in it, and therein lies his weakness. On the whole, the story may perhaps be recommended to persons about to take a long railway journey, or who, when at sea, are just well enough to sit up and read without growing dizzy.

66. Unsigned review, *Canadian Monthly & National Review*

May 1872, i, 477–9

Poor Miss Finch is contrasted in this review with another recent novel, George MacDonald's *Wilfred Cumbermede* (1872).

[Collins] does not trouble himself about psychology, subjective analysis, or the how and the why of individual character. To his view 'the main element in the attraction of all stories is the interest of curiosity and the excitement of surprise.' Life is a sort of chess-board, in which the pieces have indeed a different value; but this arises not from anything in the material of which they are made, but from the particular moves to which, by the laws of the game, they are restricted. The on-looker must, of course, be mystified as to the progress of the game, but he must make no mistake about the value of the pieces. By one or two strong daubs of colouring, Mr. Wilkie Collins marks his men beyond the possibility of mistake. In 'Poor Miss Finch,' the author begins by enumerating his human stock-in-trade—'a blind girl, two (twin) brothers, a skilful surgeon and a curious foreign woman.' To which needs only be added a little nitrate of silver, administered to one of the brothers to give him a blue face, for the purpose not of distinction, but of confusion—and you have all the materials of Mr. Wilkie Collins' legerdemain. Madame Pratolungo is a very companionable governess, and the story of the blind girl, though rather too finely drawn out, is touchingly told. Herr Grosse is a sort of reformed Count Fosco; he is skilful in his profession, fond of Mayonnaise, and addicted to an unearthly style of swearing, perfectly incomprehensible to us, unless a residence in New York may account for it. We shall not attempt any sketch of the plot, because that would be high treason in the author's eyes. *Poor Miss Finch* is perhaps, scarcely equal to some of Mr. Collins' former works, but it is sure to be read with interest from cover to cover, by any one who once takes it up.

Later Novels
1875–89

The ten novels from *The Law and the Lady* to *Blind Love* are here dealt with much more summarily; for a discussion of their reception, and further quotations from reviews, see Introduction, pp. 20–9.

THE LAW AND THE LADY

1875

---

67. Unsigned review, *Saturday Review*

13 March 1875, xxxix, 357–8

Mr. Wilkie Collins has the art of telling a secret at greater length than any one else, whether writer or merely speaker, that we have ever happened to come across. He wins his audience, as a clever child draws away her companions from their games, by the promise of telling them a secret; but when they are caught he does not quite so quickly let them go. The secret fills three whole volumes. We doubt, however, if it altogether repays the trouble of getting at it. Mr. Collins has done well in first publishing the story in weekly parts; for we should imagine any reader of common sense, when once he had the story in his hand, would save himself the labour of following the lengthy clue by going to the end by the shortest of all cuts. Mr. Collins perhaps has the same excuse as the sign-painter who, whatever was the name of the inn that he was hired to adorn, painted every sign a red lion, for the good reason that a red lion was all he had learnt to paint. So Mr. Collins tells secrets, for secrets are all that he has learnt to tell. Characters he cannot draw, and manners he cannot sketch. He can tie knots that are almost as ingenious as the knot of Gordius, and can form a puzzle that would be no discredit to a Chinaman. Untying knots and unravelling puzzles is at best but very dull work, though to people of a sluggish mind it would seem to be as pleasant as any other occupation. Mr. Collins begins to tie his knot in the first page of his story; he spends the reader's time by giving him clue after clue, each of which turns out to be a false one; and does not let him unravel the mystery till the last chapter has been reached. . . .

[The remainder of this long review is devoted to an ironic summary of the complexities and absurdities of Collins's plot.]

THE TWO DESTINIES

1876

---

68. Unsigned review, *Saturday Review*

20 January 1877, xliii, 89–90

This is an amazingly silly book. Indeed it is almost silly enough to be amusing through its very absurdity. It records, if we have counted rightly, three attempts at suicide, two plots to murder, one case of bigamy, two bankruptcies, one sanguinary attack by Indians, three visions, numberless dreams, and one shipwreck. The nearest approach to a tolerable character in the work is the hero's mother, and even she is of the most foolish type of womankind conceivable to the human imagination. Indeed the characters generally are so weak and so sketchily drawn as to be beneath criticism. . . .

[The reviewer continues at length, and in similar vein, with an analysis of the story.]

THE FALLEN LEAVES

1879

69. Unsigned review, *Saturday Review*

2 August 1879, xlviii, 148–9

'In my opinion,' says Tristram Shandy, 'to write a book is, for all the world, like humming a song—be but in tune with yourself, 'tis no matter how high or how low you take it.' Mr. Wilkie Collins is certainly in tune with himself from the first page to the last of *Fallen Leaves*. He takes it low enough we must admit, but then he keeps low throughout. All his characters are forced and unnatural, and no less so are the incidents of his story. Everything, in fact, is so extravagant, so absurd, and so grossly improbable that a kind of low harmony is preserved throughout. We are not so much shocked as perhaps we ought to be by any one chapter, as each separate chapter is in strict keeping with all the rest. The story is as unpleasant as a story can well be; but then it is unpleasant throughout. It is not wholesome reading, but then its unwholesomeness is, as it were, sustained. Mr. Collins would seem to be aware that his book is likely to meet with severe criticism, and he thus guards himself against it in a kind of preface:—

Experience of the reception of The Fallen Leaves by intelligent readers, who have followed the course of the periodical publication at home and abroad, has satisfied me that the design of the work speaks for itself, and that the scrupulous delicacy of treatment, in certain portions of the story, has been as justly appreciated as I could wish. Having nothing to explain, and (so far as my choice of subject is concerned) nothing to excuse, I leave my book, without any prefatory pleading for it, to make its appeal to the reading public on such merits as it may possess.

Certainly there is nothing of 'prefatory pleading' in what the author says here. He does not plead, but asserts, and asserts roundly. Like Clive he is astonished at his own moderation. He has had to deal with a set of degraded wretches. He has had to take his readers among the lowest outcasts, and he has not been for one moment indelicate. On the contrary, there is, as he tells us, 'scrupulous delicacy of treatment in certain portions of the story.' He himself knows this, and intelligent readers have justly appreciated it. ' "You are a moral man," said Mr. Snawley. "I rather believe I am, sir," replied Squeers. "I have the satisfaction to know you are, sir," said Mr. Snawley. "I asked one of your references, and he said you were pious." "Well, sir, I hope I am a little in that line," replied Squeers.' Mr. Collins has his references also, both at home and abroad. As we learn by the title-page, 'translations into the French, German, Italian, and Dutch languages are published by arrangement with the author.' No doubt this prefatory testimonial will be published with all the translations, and Frenchmen, Germans, Italians, and Dutchmen will all alike know that Mr. Collins is famous for his scrupulous delicacy of treatment of a very unsavoury subject. They will know this, moreover, not only on the testimony of his own countrymen, who might speak with a fond partiality, but on that of intelligent readers abroad. It will be noticed that Mr. Collins claims for himself this scrupulous delicacy only in certain portions of his story. Is he, we might ask him, scrupulously delicate when he describes the open mouth of the quartermaster of an American steamer, 'from which the unspat tobacco-juice trickled in little brown streams'? Where, in these days of word-painting, as it is called, are we to draw the line? Sailors too often have nasty habits; but that does not justify an author in disgusting his readers with nasty descriptions. Does Mr. Collins display this scrupulous delicacy for which he is so famed, in the account that he gives of an infamous hag, who is suffering under an attack of delirium tremens in the kitchen of a thieves' lodging house? . . .

[The reviewer's attack on Collins's story and characters, and his claims to 'delicacy of treatment', is pursued at length.]

JEZEBEL'S DAUGHTER

1880

---

70. Unsigned review, *Spectator*

15 May 1880, liii, 627–8

In the dedication of this book to his Italian friend and translator, Signor
Alberto Caccia, Mr. Collins takes occasion to remark that he respects
his art far too sincerely to permit limits to be wantonly assigned to it
which are imposed in no other civilised country on the face of the
earth; that he has never asserted a truer claim to the best and noblest
sympathies of Christian readers than in presenting to them the character
of the innocent victims of infamy; and that he knows that the wholesome audience of the nation at large has done liberal justice to his books.
He then goes on to allude to the 'interesting moral problem' which he
has worked out in the present volumes, and affirms that the events in
which the two chief personages play their parts have been combined
with all possible care, and have been derived to the best of his ability,
from natural and simple causes.

It would seem, therefore, that Mr. Collins is inclined to take himself
quite seriously. It is the more interesting to know this, inasmuch as the
ordinary reader of Mr. Collins's books might conceivably fail to discover it from the evidence of the books themselves. It has been popularly
supposed that Mr. Collins was a mighty weaver of plots, and that the
dissemination of his works was in direct proportion to the intricacy of
his webs. When the ordinary reader thinks of Wilkie Collins, he
connects him in his mind with memories of *The Woman in White*, *The
Moonstone*, and *After Dark*; whereas Mr. Collins himself has all the time
been pluming himself on *The New Magdalen*, *The Law and the Lady*, and
Fallen Leaves,—and this by no means because of the awful or entertaining ingenuity with which the dénouements were worked out, but
because they enlighten humanity in regard to certain moral problems

of deep and momentous import, and hold up to nature a mirror which educates the soul even more than it diverts the understanding. The plots are there, it is true, but are no more than the necessary vehicle for the inculcation of profound ideas; they are not to be regarded as owning any intrinsic value beyond this. And Mr. Collins objects to the squeamishness of English taste; he vindicates the superiority of art to bigoted and temporary fashions in morals, and wishes, apparently, to give his readers to eat of the Tree of the Knowledge of Good and Evil as freely as M. Zola does, or as M. Théophile Gautier did.

All this goes to show one of two things: either that a public may be lamentably mistaken in its author, or that the author may be curiously mistaken about himself. Is Mr. Collins, in fact as he declares himself to be in purpose, a moral reformer, or is he merely an ingenious storyteller? Are his ends greater than his means, or are his means so cunningly devised as to make his ends comparatively insignificant or invisible? Do his puppets exist solely for the sake of the dance, or is the dance contrived to elucidate the mechanism of the puppets? Or, to approach the matter from another side, is a noble warmth at the heart, or a creepy sensation down the spine, the commoner consequence of reading one of Mr. Collins's novels? and can it be that Mr. Collins, incapacitated by the nature of the case from feeling the creepy sensation himself, has incautiously leapt to the conclusion that it is incumbent upon him to feel the warmth at the heart? . . .

When a novelist has written so long or so much that he begins to lose the pleasure of creation, and to suspect his ideas of a lack of freshness, he will generally (if he goes on writing at all) endeavour to justify himself in doing so by claiming a motive and a value for his work loftier and more abstract than satisfied him before. His quips and cranks have grown stale, and no longer produce their former effect; but since he cannot afford to be neglected, he must needs strive to arrest attention by blustering about his 'motives.'

As regards Mr. Wilkie Collins, . . . we are the less disposed to press hard upon him because, in *Jezebel's Daughter*, he is nearly as entertaining as he ever was, and the only trace of moral or elevated motive that the book contains is to be found in the above-mentioned dedication. The story is told in the fantastically realistic way which Mr. Collins has uniformly affected, and which, as much as anything else, classes him with those who possess inventiveness, as distinguished from imagination. In other words, Mr. Collins has not the power to bring an object or an event so vividly before his mind as to feel safe in removing it from the strictest relation to time, space, and cause. His ideas must grow laboriously out of the earth; they can never come to him from the sky; and as he lacks imagination himself, he inevitably postulates the lack of it in his reader, and in the effort to make him believe that he is reading a genuine 'narrative,' he succeeds in never letting him forget that he himself is penning unmitigated fiction. The story is intended to be very horrible, but what is true of all Mr. Collins's stories is true also of this,— in his most horrible moments he is never otherwise than entertaining, except when he commits a breach of good-taste. And the reason is not far to seek; it lies in the unlifelikeness of the *dramatis personae*. You may place a character in the most appalling situation; you may subject him to the most inhuman tortures, mental or physical, and the most tender-hearted reader will not much mind, so long as he is persuaded that the character in question could never by any possibility have existed. If Mr. Collins possessed the faculty of making us believe in his fictitious people, the mind refuses to contemplate the appalling effects he would have achieved. Unfortunately, this is a sword that cuts both ways, or rather, it is as blunt of one edge as it is of the other. If Mr. Collins cannot terrify us, neither can he stir our tenderer emotions; if we do not lament when he mourns, neither do we dance when he pipes. But the reader sits with a pleased grin of suspense and curiosity widening his features, and he reads and reads, and does not want to leave off till he comes to the end. Say what you will, it is capital entertainment, smoothly and artfully prepared by a workman who knows the use of his tools. But why should Mr. Collins try to make us believe that Jezebel, the modern Lucrezia Borgia, who will poison you as soon as look at you, is at bottom what Artemus Ward or Mr. Barnum would call a 'moral figger,'—is redeemed, in other words, by the supremacy of her maternal affection? This redemption is so palpably lugged in by the head and ears, and is in itself so grotesquely preposterous, that we should have supposed even Mr. Collins might have hesitated to suggest it. But he has done so in accordance with a fashion which was perhaps introduced by Dickens, and which has been violently developed since his time, the fashion of discovering exquisite traits of generosity, tenderness, and nobility in natures the most lost and degraded. It is a cheap and tawdry form of sentimentality; it would ascribe to the author a more than ordinary power of seeing into the depths of a millstone; but, so far as our knowledge and belief go, it rests upon a foundation of fact so small as to be practically non-existent. A man or a woman is wicked exactly in proportion as he or she is selfish; and no wicked person can ever do a 'good' action from other than a selfish motive. Moral deformity is as much a matter of growth, organisation, and permanence as is physical deformity; and the latter can be thrown aside at a moment's warning, just as little as the former. But alas! some artists have so little regard for the integrity of nature, that they would be willing to let the sun rise in the west, if thereby they might create a more striking effect of light and shade for their lay-figure. If Mr. Collins would only consent to let his stories alone, and not insist upon our taking out of the bag more than was ever put into it, or other than it is capable of holding, he would save himself much trouble, and his readers a good deal of yawning.

THE BLACK ROBE

1881

71. E. A. Dillwyn, from an unsigned review, *Spectator*

7 May 1881, liv, 606–7

Although the review is generally unfavourable, the reviewer (herself a minor novelist) concludes rather surprisingly by recommending the novel for its readability.

The chief fault of the book is the unnaturalness which pervades it, and which is met with in plot, situations, and people alike. Many novels seem, as it were, to enlarge our circle of friends when an author shows us persons whom he has really known; and his work is often a vehicle of introducing us to himself, at all events, because he is very apt to take his knowledge of the human race from that member of it with whom he is most intimately acquainted, and to put somewhat of his own identity into the various individuals whom he depicts. But Mr. Wilkie Collins has not chosen to do this, and, consequently, his book lacks human nature. His characters come and go, and he is clever enough to keep the reader amused in following their progress; but, with one exception [the housekeeper Miss Notman], they do not give the idea of studies from life. . . .

HEART AND SCIENCE

1883

72. Unsigned review, *Academy*

28 April 1883, xxiii, 290

In several respects, which are too obvious to stand in need of being pointed out, the genius of Mr. Wilkie Collins resembles that of Edgar Poe; and, like Poe, Mr. Collins has invited the public into his workshop, exhibited his materials and tools, and affably expounded the methods by which the finished product comes to be what it is. Indeed, while the American story-teller wrote only one essay on 'The Philosophy of Composition,' the English novelist has written at least two or three Prefaces any one of which might put in a claim to the title. In the Preface to *Heart and Science*, Mr. Collins again takes his readers into his confidence, and gives them various pieces of information, of which the most important is his declaration that, while in all his works he had endeavoured to combine the character and humour which the British public love with the incident and dramatic situation for which he thinks the said public does not care, his latest work is one in which we are to 'find the scales inclining, on the whole, in favour of character and humour.' In spite of his Prefaces, however, it seems to me that we learn more of Mr. Wilkie Collins's methods from his books themselves than from what he has to tell us about them; and the reader who can distinguish any quality in *Heart and Science* which differentiates it from the majority of its numerous predecessors must be a reader whose critical perceptions have been refined to a pitch of rare subtlety. Certainly the plot, *qua* plot, is not nearly so complex as the plots of *The Woman in White* and *The Moonstone*, and it therefore absorbs a smaller proportion of the total interest of the story; but of the special interest of 'character and humour' there is neither more nor less than in any of the writer's previous works. Even the fact that *Heart and Science* is in part polemical (being not merely a novel, but an anti-vivisection manifesto) does not set it in a place apart, for in one or two previous books Mr. Wilkie Collins has said his say concerning current controversies in as effective a manner as the limitations of the vehicle would allow; and here he is not less successful than in *Man and Wife* in the difficult task of mixing art and argument. That he is wholly successful cannot be said, for *Heart and Science* will be found more entertaining than convincing, save by those who do not need to be convinced. The vivisecting Dr. Benjulia is certainly repulsive enough, and it is quite possible that he may have his original in real life. But neither he nor the scientific Mrs. Gallilee, with her talk of 'radiant energy' and 'sonorous vibrations,' can be accepted as a type; and, therefore, the conception, though interesting enough as an artistic product, has really no polemical value. The ordinary novel-reader will not, however, enjoy them less on this account; and, whatever else may be said of Benjulia, it must be declared that he is a singularly interesting and, in a way, fascinating creation. Mr. Wilkie Collins can deal strongly with a strong situation, but he has done nothing more powerful than his sketch of Benjulia's last hours, after his discovery that the one hope of his life had vanished, and that the loathsome labour of years had been in vain. For reasons which I have not space to give, Mrs. Gallilee is, I think, less successful. But Mr. Gallilee and the unscientific and illiterate Zoe are capital examples of genuine and unforced humour; and the book, as a whole, is thoroughly readable and enthralling from its first page to its last.

73. ?E. D. Cook, unsigned review, *Athenaeum*

28 April 1883, 538–9

The *Athenaeum* records indicate the reviewer of this and Collins's three preceding novels only with the surname Cook; the most likely candidate seems to be Edward Dutton Cook (1829–83), novelist and critic.

The awkward sound of *Heart and Science*, the title of Mr. Wilkie Collins's new book, will perhaps help to make people remember it; but though it is better than some of the author's later works it is not equal to his best. He has hampered himself by trying to write with a purpose. Novel-readers as a rule are supposed to omit prefaces. It will be well if they do so in this case, for they will learn from the two prefaces to *Heart and Science* that the author's purpose is to help the cause of the anti-vivisectionists; that there is a good deal of science in the book; and that the physiological part of it is quite correct, the manuscript having been submitted to an eminent London surgeon. All this sounds depressing enough; but fortunately Mr. Wilkie Collins is far too experienced and too skilful a novelist to be able to allow himself to be dull. The reader who has read the prefaces soon forgets them and the threatened anti-vivisection and science when he finds himself quickly launched into the midst of a story which opens in the author's best manner. In the first preface, which is addressed 'to readers in general,' it is stated that the novel is one of character and humour rather than of incident and dramatic situation. Mr. Wilkie Collins seems to have misjudged his own work. The merits of it really are those which are the merits of so many of the author's books: that the plot is well contrived at starting; that coincidences are cleverly managed; that the reader's interest is seized at the outset and constantly roused again; that there is an air of mystery about the principal characters, and an uncertainty about what will happen which makes one guess for a solution as one goes along, and change one's mind over and over again; that the details are accurate;

and that the dramatic effects are excellent. It may be readily admitted that Mr. Wilkie Collins is justified in saying that he has borne in mind the value of temperate advocacy, but the truth is that he is so much more an artist than an advocate that, on the whole, his novel is good enough to make one almost fail to notice that it was written against vivisection. Unfortunately the story has a weak ending. After imagining all sorts of strange possibilities the reader finds out at last that in truth there was very little plot at all. The second preface, 'to readers in particular,' points out the care that has been taken to have the science accurate. It is almost painful to think of the trouble that has been thrown away. Prof. Ferrier on the *Localization of Cerebral Disease*, *Chambers's Encyclopædia*, and a long list of books have been consulted, to say nothing of newspapers and magazines; but all that has been got from them is a phrase here and there to round off a sentence and raise a laugh at a learned lady. It seems almost a pity that a lawyer was not consulted too. One of the characters is a solicitor, and if accuracy in legal matters is as important as correctness in science, it would have been well to have avoided the mistake of sending a person to look for a will at Doctors' Commons instead of Somerset House. A lawyer could also have given some useful information on the subject of the guardianship of infants, a department of the law with which Mr. Wilkie Collins seems not to be familiar.

74. J. A. Noble, from an unsigned review, *Spectator*

26 May 1883, lvi, 679–81

James Ashcroft Noble was for many years in charge of the reviewing of fiction for the *Spectator*. It seems possible that his review, which bears the title 'An Anti-Vivisection Novel', may in some degree reflect the opinions of the journal's editor, R. H. Hutton, who had served on a Royal Commission which opposed experiments on animals (see R. A. Colby, ' "How it Strikes a Contemporary": the "Spectator" as Critic', *Nineteenth Century Fiction*, xi (1956), 194).

Mr. Wilkie Collins, as his custom is, gives in the forefront of his latest book a semi-descriptive, semi-critical preface, which is, unlike the majority of such compositions, certain to be read. 'In the abstract,' as Sydney Smith's Scotch young lady would put it, a preface to a work of art is a work of supererogation, possibly an impertinence; for such a work ought not to need explanation or supplement, while, as for criticism, readers can supply that for themselves, and resent it as cordially as they resent unsolicited advice. Mr. Wilkie Collins, however, can do for a preface what Swift, according to Stella, could do for a broomstick,—he can make it entertaining, which he does partly by the sheer force of a bright and perfectly lucid style, pleasantly salted with the special kind of humour which never fails him, but mainly by his delightfully confidential manner, which probably leads some simpleminded readers to think that, having been told how the books are written, they could write them for themselves, 'if they had a mind.'

In this particular preface, Mr. Wilkie Collins returns to an old theory of his, and insists that the qualities in fiction which find most favour with the British public are character and humour, and that incident and dramatic situation only find a second place in their favour. He tells us that he has 'always tried to combine the different merits of a good novel in one and the same book,' but that he has 'never succeeded in keeping an equal balance,' and that in the present story we shall 'find the scales inclining, on the whole, in favour of character and humour.' Perhaps Mr. Wilkie Collins hardly states the case quite correctly. The ordinary novel-reader of the day does indeed, value character and humour, but he values also incident and dramatic situation, as is amply proved by the continued popularity of the writer's own book, *The Woman in White*; and we are inclined to think that he values most of all the simple skill in the art of narration which is one of Mr. Wilkie Collins's strongest points. Whether there be much or little story in a novel, the reader demands that it shall be well told, and it is in this telling of a story that Mr. Wilkie Collins is supreme. There is less plot in *Heart and Science* than in many of the writer's previous works, but we do not find this out until we have closed the third volume; for what there is of story is so deftly managed, that we have in reading it the feeling of plot, just as in reading such an unrhymed poem as 'Tears, Idle Tears,' we have the feeling of rhyme.

When we began to speak about this preface we were, however, thinking not of such matters as these, but of the announcement that *Heart and Science* has been written partly as a contribution to the literature of the Anti-vivisection movement. We are not sure that this announcement is not a mistake, for if a novel have a distinct purpose apart from mere entertainment, it is, perhaps, better for several reasons that it should be left to reveal itself; but Mr. Collins has probably sufficient confidence both in himself and his cause to feel that he will lose little by thus showing his hand. We have never been able to see the force of an objection frequently brought against the polemical novel, that it attempts to substitute an appeal to the imagination and the feelings for the logical arguments which are asserted to be the only legitimate weapons in controversy. The heart, the conscience, and the imagination have their own arguments, not less than the reason; and when Mr. Collins traces in one of his characters 'the result of the habitual practice of cruelty (no matter under what pretence) in fatally deteriorating the nature of man,' he is making as genuine a contribution to the settlement of a vexed question as that made by the physiologist who proves, by hard fact, that vivisection has been misleading to science, as well as repulsive to morality. . . .

[The rest of this substantial review is mainly devoted to an account of the character of Dr. Benjulia—'a curiously interesting psychological study'. The reviewer concludes by praising Collins's humour and by recommending the story as 'thoroughly interesting . . . most fascinating . . . and . . . none the worse' for its propagandist purpose.]

'I SAY NO'

1884

75. From an unsigned review, *Saturday Review*

22 November 1884, lviii, 665–6

One of the penalties which the voracious novel-reader suffers lies in the too intimate knowledge he acquires of the novelist's method and mechanism. The Castle of Udolpho is no longer enchanting, and instead of being stored with the arcana of romance, is compacted of the dry devices of the modern stage, with its sliding doors and traps and wooden ingenuities. The novels of Mr. Wilkie Collins attract chiefly by their ingenious construction, and, if not always conceived in the spirit of an artist, are almost invariably excellent displays of invention and artifice. In all of them the mystery is the thing. It is veiled by a finely-spun tissue of diverse webs that are ever shifting under the magician's charm, and a very pretty dance it leads the easily-persuaded intelligence. It is sometimes almost divulged at the outset, and passes through more or less transparent eclipse until revealed, when, it must be owned, the revelation is not always imposing or surprising. In *I Say No* it is assuredly a very ridiculous mouse creeping timid and ashamed from one of the innumerable crannies of the labouring mountain. Early in the story it is seen that the mystery is no mystery, and should never have greatly exercised the minds of any of the characters. No one but the inexperienced reader, whom we frankly envy, could be deluded by the sundry false scents which the novelist trails across the true and obvious track. The reader who cannot forget the excitement of *The Moonstone* or *The Woman in White* is not likely to be drawn like a young hound from the pursuit of a mystery so early scented as in *I Say No*. This is his, and our, misfortune and the penalty of experience. The disappointment must not be altogether charged to Mr. Wilkie Collins. His story is told with the old force and dramatic skill. The plot is a genuine construction, a matter to be gratefully acknowledged in these days. The story is eminently readable, as is to be expected, and the attention is fixed in the first chapter and sustained to the last. . . .

[After a brief discussion of the story, the reviewer praises Collins's characterization, finding many of the characters] drawn with the simple graphic touches Mr. Wilkie Collins uses with masterly effect; they attract and interest with a strange vitality despite their manifest burlesque and the extreme improbabilities of the story. . . .

THE EVIL GENIUS

1886

76. John Dennis, from an unsigned review, *Spectator*

4 December 1886, lix, 1628

The opening paragraph of a review which offers a plot-summary and two long quotations from the novel, and concludes by finding it 'extremely clever'. Nothing seems to be known of Dennis except that he reviewed regularly for the *Spectator*.

Mr. Wilkie Collins has one at least of the prime requisites of a novelist. His object, from the first chapter to the last, is to tell his story. He does not trouble the reader with wearisome reflections or picturesque descriptions, neither does he exercise any of the arts by which a tale that could be easily told in two volumes is expanded into three. He knows how to make a plot and how to develop it, gifts which some recent novelists affect to despise, probably because they do not possess them. Mr. Collins, in the early days of his novel-writing, was in the habit of inventing a secret or puzzle which taxed the reader's curiosity to unravel. This rather childish exercise of ingenuity was dearer to him, or easier, than the delineation of character; neither did he give much heed to verisimilitude, and perhaps regarded improbabilities as an aid to the faith demanded of the novel-reader. In his latest work, there is no skein to be disentangled, and no accidents or coincidences more remarkable than we are accustomed to in fiction. The novel before us commands the reader's attention throughout. He is never tempted to lay it down, neither does he come to passages he can afford to skip. It is full of dramatic scenes, and might, we think, be readily transformed into a sensational drama. . . .

77. J. A. Noble, from an unsigned review, *Spectator*

26 January 1889, lxii, 120

On Noble, see headnote to No. 74. He begins by comparing the 'intellectual scheme' of the novel to that of *Armadale*—both works reading like 'implicit protests against the fatalism which is more or less bound up with any full acceptance of the modern doctrine of heredity'.

Perhaps, however, we are considering too curiously, and breaking an intellectual butterfly upon a critical wheel. Mr. Wilkie Collins may occasionally have a theory to illustrate, but he always has a story to tell, and the story is of more importance both to him and his readers than the theory. As a mere story it will, we think, be generally admitted, by both critical and non-critical readers, that it is not one of its author's conspicuous successes. The narrative style is as good, or nearly as good as ever, but the tale is somewhat burdened with needless complexities. For example, Mr. Gracedieu's extraordinary scheme of bringing up the two girls who are supposed to be sisters in ignorance of their respective ages was not merely impracticable in itself—as the elder would naturally remember the infancy of the younger—but was calculated to defeat the very end it was intended to serve by suggesting to some curious person that something was being concealed. Mr. Gracedieu's special aim was, of course, to prevent the fact that Eunice was the daughter of a murderess from being disclosed to the world by the malignant Miss Chance; but the danger seems far too shadowy to justify such an exceedingly cumbrous and inconvenient method of averting it, and the consequence is that the plot seems much less workmanlike and inevitable than Mr. Wilkie Collins's plots are wont to be. Then, too, there is an almost entire absence of the author's peculiar humour, which is always one of the most refreshing elements in his books; and when we add that among all the characters there is not one which appeals very strongly to the reader's interest, it will be seen that we regard *The Legacy of Cain* as a comparative failure. We say comparative, because to a writer with such a wonderful gift of narration as that possessed by Mr. Wilkie Collins, absolute failure is all but impossible.

78. The unpalatable taste of the construction

1883

From Anthony Trollope's *Autobiography*.

Trollope (1815–82) produced forty-seven novels between 1847 and his death; his career is thus roughly contemporary with that of Collins. The *Autobiography*, published posthumously, was completed by 1876. Text from the 'Oxford Trollope' edition (1950).

Among English novels of the present day, and among English novelists, a great division is made. There are sensational novels and anti-sensational, sensational novelists and anti-sensational; sensational readers and anti-sensational. The novelists who are considered to be anti-sensational are generally called realistic. I am realistic. My friend Wilkie Collins is generally supposed to be sensational. The readers who prefer the one are supposed to take delight in the elucidation of character. They who hold by the other are charmed by the construction and gradual development of a plot. All this is, I think, a mistake—which mistake arises from the inability of the imperfect artist to be at the same time realistic and sensational. A good novel should be both, and both in the highest degree. If a novel fail in either, there is a failure in Art. . . .

(pp. 226–7)

Of Wilkie Collins it is impossible for a true critic not to speak with admiration, because he has excelled all his contemporaries in a certain most difficult branch of his art; but as it is a branch which I have not myself at all cultivated, it is not unnatural that his work should be very much lost upon me individually. When I sit down to write a novel I do not at all know, and I do not very much care, how it is to end. Wilkie Collins seems so to construct his that he not only, before writing, plans everything on, down to the minutest detail, from the beginning to the end; but then plots it all back again, to see that there is no piece of necessary dovetailing which does not dove-tail with absolute accuracy. The construction is most minute and most wonderful. But I can never lose the taste of the construction. The author seems always to be warning me to remember that something happened at exactly half-past two o'clock on Tuesday morning; or that a woman disappeared from the road just fifteen yards beyond the fourth milestone. One is constrained by mysteries and hemmed in by difficulties, knowing, however, that the mysteries will be made clear, and the difficulties overcome at the end of the third volume. Such work gives me no pleasure. I am, however, quite prepared to acknowledge that the want of pleasure comes from fault of my intellect. . . .

(pp. 256–7)

79. A Canadian appreciation

November 1878

J. L. Stewart, 'Wilkie Collins as a Novelist', *Rose-Belford's Canadian Monthly & National Review*, November 1878, i, 586–601.

Collins's popularity in North America at this time is attested by this long, though not very critically penetrating, survey of his novels from *The Woman in White* to *The Law and the Lady*, here drastically abridged. Curiously enough, the writer makes no reference to *Armadale* or *The Moonstone*.

Rose-Belford's was a Toronto journal formed in 1878 by merging the *Canadian Monthly & National Review* with *Belford's Monthly Magazine*. It was later to serialize both *The Fallen Leaves* and *The Black Robe*.

Wilkie Collins has one of those well-balanced minds in which the constructive and didactic faculties exist in pretty equal proportions. He is an earnest moralist, with story-telling and plot-constructing capacities of a high order, and his productions appeal to the minds of the idle and the earnest alike.

With perfect appreciation of the necessity for concealing the lesson he wishes to teach, and full faith in his ability to make the incidents impart the instruction he seeks to give, he sets himself to the task, primarily, of simply telling a story. 'I have always,' he says, in his preface to *The Woman in White*, 'held the old-fashioned opinion that the primary object of a work of fiction should be to tell a story. It may be impossible, in novel writing, to present characters successfully without telling a story; but it is not possible to tell a story successfully without presenting characters.'

In this method of working he differs widely from many of his distinguished contemporaries, whose character drawing is evidently first in their thoughts, and must thank his dramatic genius rather than his theory for the permanent value attached to his works. . . .

The Woman in White, which is esteemed the ablest of his works, is one of the best examples we have in modern fiction of the union of a plot of absorbing interest with characters at once original, strong and pleasing. The presentation of the characters is merely incidental to the telling of the story, I admit, but their conception was a primary instead of a secondary part of the author's work. Laura Fairlie, that lovely and lovable piece of inanity, gets almost as strong a hold on us as she does on Walter Hartright. She is a fine example of the strength of feminine weakness. Hartright and Marian Halcombe, the 'magnificent Marian' of the 'grand grey eyes' (not the only one of Collins's women with this particular description of eyes), devote their lives to her service, and it seems right that they should do so. She clings to them and trusts them, and that is all the reward they ask or expect. If it were not for her great misfortunes she would hardly keep her place in the reader's affections, and even as it is we can hardly repress a sigh of regret when her marriage with Walter deprives Marian of the possibility of ever seeing her unspoken affection returned. It does not seem right, although it is supremely natural, that the helpless Laura should win all the strong man's devotion, while the glorious creature who united her efforts with his, in their almost hopeless struggle against the conspiracy of which Laura was the victim, should inspire nothing but a sisterly affection. Such women as she are able to stand alone in this world, and a merciful Providence provides that the men shall fall in love chiefly with the less gifted and self-reliant—with those who are not able to take care of themselves.

Anne Catherick excites a curiosity which is not gratified by results, but the interest awakened in her is not at all out of proportion to her importance in the plot. The manner in which the attention is kept fixed upon her, in the expectation that she will make an important revelation respecting Sir Percival Glyde, when it is a purely passive part which she is destined to play in the great crisis of the story, is very skilful.

Walter Hartright, that fine specimen of constancy, devotion, fearlessness and uprightness; Mr. Fairlie, a unique study of refined selfishness; Pesca, the excitable Italian; Mrs. Vesey, the amiable old lady who 'sat through life'; Sir Percival Glyde, that combination of strong passion and pliant yielding to his evil genius; Mr. Gilmore, the solicitor, who reassuringly informs his clients that they have entrusted their affairs to 'good hands;' Mrs. Michelson, with her charming faith in the angelic character of Count Fosco; and Madame Fosco, with her doglike devotion to her husband, and her inability to distinguish good from evil when he is an interested party, are all faithfully drawn characters.

The great personage of the book, however, is Fosco himself. He is a wonderfully clear-cut type of a somewhat mythical class. With great skill in music, chemistry, and diplomacy; with a magnetic power over men and women; with vast capacities for work; with the faculty of combination well developed; with great executive ability; and with a title and some fortune, he is nothing but a spy in his public capacity and a rascal in private life. Nothing but principle is wanting to make him a leader of men, a statesman, a great diplomatist, or an honoured member of a learned profession. His breezy brusqueness, oily affability, consummate impudence, infectious good spirits, and unwearying activity, make him the life of every scene in which he appears. His management of the brutal Sir Percival, his mastery over his wife, his sublime effrontery, his irrepressible vehemence when he quarrels with the physician's treatment of Marian, his intimate relations with his birds and white mice, his charming manifestations of personal vanity, his hearty and unhesitating yielding to circumstances which he sees to be too much for even his genius to contend with, and, most of all, the one weakness he manifests—his overpowering admiration of Marian Halcombe—keep his corpulent form fresh in the mind of the reader. His charming frankness, when he does not consider it worth while to wear the mask of virtue, is enough to make him friends. It is in perfect good faith, and not at all as a satirist seeking to be smart, that he argues that crime is a good friend as often as it is an enemy, and points for proof to the Howards passing virtuous misery in hovels to minister to misery in prisons. He is sincere, also, when he claims to be virtuous because he carefully avoided unnecessary crime in the perpetration of the great outrage that robbed an unoffending lady of reason, liberty and identity. The reader who can not forget his cold-blooded cruelty, and forgive his offences far enough to look pityingly on the mangled remains which his widow weeps over in the morgue, lacks the charity which all should feel for erring and fallen humanity.

The life at Blackwater, when the helpless Laura is struggling in the toils, and the crazy Anne is hovering around with her supposed secret, is painted with graphic realism; the several steps in the unwinding of the coil of conspiracy which bring Walter slowly but surely to the end, enchain the reader's unwearying attention; and the double retribution is brought about in a dramatic and by no means improbable manner.

Most of the writers who find fault with the institutions of their country

—with its legal, medical and theological doctrines and practices—have remedies to propose for all the ills they discover; but Wilkie Collins contents himself generally with pointing out the evils that exist, leaving to others the work of devising the cure. In this respect he presents a marked contrast to Charles Reade, who prescribes minutely for everything from tight lacing to the treatment to the insane, teaches the doctors how to deal with sprains, and defines the changes that should be made in the statutes.

In *The Woman in White* the author indicates, rather than presents and denounces, the evil effects which may result from the law of inheritance, and in *The Law and the Lady* the Scotch verdict of 'not proven' is the objective point at which the reformer aims. . . .

[A long discussion of the latter novel follows.]

In *Man and Wife* the author is so earnestly intent on satirizing and denouncing the mania for muscular sports, that he forgets the barriers which art erects between the story and the moral. His animus is so plain as to weaken the force of his satire, and he violates the proprieties of novel writing so far as to descend to downright invective in his own person. This weakens the work as an attack on muscular development, and mars it as a story. Those who are not ardent admirers of manly sports will wonder what excited this man's anger, and those who are will resent his severity instead of listening to his reasons. No man with good muscular development can read this book without feeling a desire to try the effect of a right-hander on the author, so unmeasured is its condemnation of muscle culture. . . .

[The discussion of *Man and Wife* continues at length.]

Poor Miss Finch, the next most notable production of Wilkie Collins's pen, is about the only one of his more important works without an undisguised attack on some popular institution, practice or doctrine. As a work of art, it approaches perfection. The materials are handled with consummate skill, but they lack the elements of wide popularity. Probabilities are weighed carefully, the springs of action are studied thoughtfully, and the characters are true to themselves in all their sayings and doings. There are no vicious dwarfs, with supernatural cunning; no madmen, with conflicting and unfathomable impulses, at large in society; no supernaturally gifted persons who favour us at the beginning with a prophetic view of the end. These people are men and women all the time, and submit to the limitations which a wise

Providence imposes on human powers. The story's greatest strength is its pathos. The blind lady who is the central figure of the tale, moves our tenderest compassion at the first, and retains her place in our affections and her claim on our pity to the last. . . .

[Continued at length.]

All readers of Wilkie Collins must have been impressed with the importance of the supernatural element in his writings. He appeals skilfully to the public taste for the marvellous, and gains readers by doing so. He shrewdly suspects that all men have an element of what is scornfully called superstition in their veins, and does not hesitate to cater for it. . . .

Wilkie Collins well knowing the world's tendency in this direction, and desiring also not to outrage the opposing sentiment, gives many striking examples of occult phenomena, and leaves his readers to place their own interpretation on them. *The Two Destinies* is nothing if not ghostly. The leading characters see visions, believe in them, obey their behests, and are never deceived by them. Their faith is whole, and the author's appears to be whole also. There is no pretence at a common-place explanation—no suggestion of natural agencies by which the strange results might have been produced. . . .

[The latter part of the article examines *The Two Destinies*, *The New Magdalen*, the play *The Frozen Deep* and some of the shorter tales, and offers some observations on Collins as a social satirist.]

No writer understands better than Wilkie Collins the peculiar charm of autobiographical literature, and he employs this style almost always. It is made still more interesting, in *The Woman in White*, by allowing each of the characters to tell the portion of the story in which he was the prominent actor. There is one element in these autobiographies, which I have already hinted at, that amuses us at first, then seems unnatural, and is finally accepted as real. I refer to the charming naïveté with which the writers proudly relate things which make them ridiculous, themselves wholly unconscious of the laughter they are exciting. It must be conceded by every one with an eye to the ludicrous that this is common enough in real life, and a slight exercise of the memory will recall sufficient incidents to justify the author. Count Fosco's cold-blooded confession of criminal motives, and his proud mention of his own 'impenetrable calm,' are perfectly in keeping with the rest of his character. Mr. Fairlie's chapter completes his character as no description or dialogue would have done, and his interruption of the serious narrative to complain that Fanny's shoes would creak is not out of keeping with his ideas on the relative importance of events. One could not stand a very long look at the world, from Fairlie's point of view, but a chapter or so is very entertaining. Madame Pratolungo [in *Poor Miss Finch*] is another very amusing illustration of this peculiarity. The relation of her experience as the wife of a patriot, her pledges to adhere to the political philosophy of her late husband, and the prophesies of the downfall of kings, seem so broadly ironical that it is hard to believe her perfectly sincere, and we take off our hats mockingly and cheer at her fervent farewell prediction:—'The world is getting converted to my way of thinking; the Pratolungo programme, my friends, is coming to the front with giant steps. Long live the Republic!'

80. The last survivor: an essay in rehabilitation

April 1888

Harry Quilter, 'A Living Story-teller', *Contemporary Review*, April 1888, lv, 572–93.

Quilter (1851–1907), artist, art critic and journalist, was a regular contributor to the *Contemporary Review*. He is remembered for his celebrated and prolonged quarrel with Whistler. See also Introduction, p. 29.

In times of change, such as the present, when fresh growths are continually struggling up into daylight, there is some danger that older and, hitherto, well-loved forms of art and literature may disappear almost unheeded, and that, while we stand gladly watching the bean-stalk-like rise of our new specimens, we may become just a little ungrateful to those authors who have gladdened us in former days. Yet something is due to the old age of the great who have filled us with the fruit of their genius, although their ancient quiet claim may be easily neglected amidst the press of new things and the din of louder and fresher voices which to-day echo round us.

Not always is it either just or wise to wait for the hour when an author's lips are silent before we bestow full recognition for what we have gained from his work, and it is more than ungrateful to allow the last years to pass unregarded of one who for a long life has, with un-flinching industry and unabated purpose, poured out his brains, not only for our amusement, but in accordance with many noble impulses, and in defence of many a worthy cause.

There is living amongst us at the present time the last of that group of great novelists whose works will make the fiction of the Victorian era for ever famous, and, despite the fact that in earlier days his merits were widely recognized, despite the fact that his books are even now translated as soon as written into nearly every European language, de-spite the fact that his readers in America alone are still numbered by hundreds of thousands, above all, despite the fact that he has done work which of its kind has not only never been surpassed, but has never even been approached—notwithstanding all these things, it is but rarely we hear the name of Wilkie Collins mentioned in England nowadays, that we read a word in his praise, or hear of the slightest claim being made on his behalf.

If, therefore, in the following pages, I may seem to dwell more on the merits than deficiencies of Mr. Wilkie Collins' writing, I would remind my readers that this article is professedly an eulogium, an attempt to thank the author for pleasure received, and to bring clearly before a somewhat unwilling public the nature and the quality of his literary achievements.

What then are the qualities of Mr. Wilkie Collins which separate him from the other novelists of his time, and which constitute his special claim upon our admiration? The chief of these can fortunately be stated very shortly and simply: this author has told stories better than they have ever been told in the world before, and probably better than they will ever be told again.

Now, in this art of story-telling, Charles Reade, Dickens, and Wilkie Collins were all past masters, but they were masters with a difference, and, since the art is almost a forgotten one, it is worth while to note in what the difference consisted. In some ways it is true that Dickens wrote stories uncommonly badly: he was always wandering away from his point; he seldom overcame the temptation to put in half a dozen new characters, whether they were needed or not; he exaggerated his types to such an extent that one continually feels personally angry with them and him; and in all sorts of irrelevant places he sticks in superfluous eccentric people and amusing incidents which it needs our utmost ingenuity and tolerance to weave into the substance of his plot. But in another way he tells his story equally well, giving to it an overpowering sense of vitality, touching it on one side and another till it gains something of the multiplicity, and the light and shadow of life itself; above all, clinging to it desperately just when it is on the verge of escaping him, catching the reader's interest as it were by the hair of the head, and compelling his attention by sheer force of genius.

Charles Reade's method is more methodical, and far less elaborate: its science consists in a perfectly clearly conceived, dramatic, and continuous narrative, the progress of which is never arrested from commencement to finish, which is subject to no interruption, and burdened with no unnecessary additions. The essential difference between his method and that of the other writers whom I have mentioned, is that it is entirely a personal one; he has always his characters by the throat, and, so to speak, pinches their windpipe hard, and shouts in their ear, 'You say so-and-so;' he then takes his unfortunate puppet by the throat, and shoves him lustily through whatever part he has to play in the drama. Bristling with facts and arguments, bubbling over with power and wit, indifferent to rebuffs, and impervious to ridicule, this author's personality and his story shoulder their way together through each of his books, till, after reading two or three of them, it becomes really doubtful of whom we know the most, the man who writes, or the men and women whom he writes about.

And now let us turn to the subject of our article, notice the peculiarities of his method, and see how entirely it differs from that of either Dickens or Reade.

With that of Dickens, in so far as the method of narrating the story is concerned, it has evidently little affinity. The narrative is not only plain and direct, but unencumbered to an extraordinary degree; it is scarcely an exaggeration to say that in several of his books there is hardly a phrase, much less a character, which could be spared without loss to the story. The plot is only elaborate in the sense of being intricately woven, not for its possession of any large amount of detail, or for its development necessitating many characters. On the other hand, the method diverges from that of Reade by its absolute impersonality; the author practically never speaks *in propria persona*, or, if he does so, he speaks as a voice only, leaving us quite in the dark as to all personal idiosyncrasy. But the difference to be noted lies deeper than that, for in Wilkie Collins' stories the result is brought about by a sustained and definite action and reaction of character and circumstance, which is only in a very minor degree present in either Dickens or Reade.

It would be fair to say of the latter authors that their characters might have acted in many other stories, but of Collins that his stories could not have been acted by any other characters. The connection with the special story is, in the first case, superficial; in the second, essential. I am not seeking now, be it remembered, to compare these men to the advantage or disadvantage of any one of them; I am trying only to point out differences. What is needed at the present day is that we should admire all three a great deal more than we do, not that we should admire one at the expense of the others.

Mr. Wilkie Collins' first essay in novel-writing was an historical romance entitled *Antonina; or, the Fall of Rome*, and is remarkable chiefly for the fact that though it possessed various merits, such as considerable power of descriptive writing, and clear perception of character, yet it affords us no hint of the author's special faculty—the power of concentrating the interest of the story, and bringing all the actions of his characters into close relation with it. It is, in my opinion, a very dull and quite unreadable book; and so the public apparently thought, for the work created no stir, and even after the author had achieved popularity, was seldom spoken of, much less read.

Well, we need only say that the book was a failure; whatever Mr. Wilkie Collins' gifts might be, it was evident he had not as yet found their right direction. Accordingly, in the next story there is an entirely new departure, and *Basil* takes us from ancient Rome to the very centre of modern London life: the story practically begins in an omnibus, and the chief characters are a managing clerk, and a linendraper's daughter.

When I think of the period in which this novel was written and published, I confess I find it difficult to understand the tolerance that must have been shown it by the Press, for it is as frank in its dealings with a certain phase of the affections as Daudet himself, and, indeed, I believe it was attacked in certain quarters on this score.*

* Ten years after the books was published, Collins wrote in the preface to a new edition, 'I allowed the prurient misinterpretation of certain perfectly innocent passages in this book to assert itself as offensively as it pleased, without troubling myself to protest against an expression of opinion which aroused in me no other feeling than a feeling of contempt'.

[A brief plot-summary follows.]

This, it will be observed, is a tolerably strong story, and can hardly be said to be a pleasant one; nor would it be worth while dwelling on the subject were it not that it shows the rise in our author of that peculiar faculty, the development of which was afterwards to render him unrivalled in his line. A single powerful motive, a single sustained purpose, runs throughout the book; towards it everything tends, and in connection with it every incident occurs. Characters come and go in entire subordination to the part they have to play in the story, and yet they do this naturally. The action of the book depends on the influence exercised by character over circumstance; the determining impulse of each event can be traced back to the mental idiosyncrasy of one or the other of the chief personages. It is this which makes the book organic, and from this method of treatment Mr. Wilkie Collins in each of his succeeding books has, with rare exceptions, never departed. Those who are interested in physiological contrasts, can trace with pleasure throughout *Basil* the manner in which the varying idiosyncrasies and motives, of the people concerned, combine to produce the catastrophe of the book—the pride of Basil's father; the over-credulity and timorousness of Basil himself: the terrified submission of Mrs. Sherwin, the mother of the heroine; the meanness and selfishness of her husband; the vanity and heartlessness of Margaret herself, are all as much factors in the catastrophe as the deliberate, cold-blooded scheming of the villain of the story. Gradually, as one reads the book, a sense of inevitable calamity mingles with our interest: the final catastrophe comes almost as a relief. Here is the secret of Collins' power as a story-teller; other authors may construct a plot with as great ingenuity, or tell us a story of as entrancing interest, but no other writer has so well succeeded in producing upon his readers the same sense of inevitableness and reality; these plots are not only *possible*, they are *imperative*; not only might things have happened thus; they could not have happened otherwise.

Let us consider the means by which the author attained this perfection of tale-telling. Before we speak of his method in detail, hear what, in Mr. Collins' personal opinion, a work of fiction should be.

Believing that the Novel and the Play are twin-sisters in the family of Fiction; that the one is a drama narrated, and the other is a drama acted; and that all the strong and deep emotions which the Play-writer is privileged to excite, the Novel-writer is privileged to excite also, I have not thought it either politic or necessary, while adhering to realities, to adhere to every-day realities only. In other words, I have not stooped so low as to assure myself of the reader's belief in the probability of my story, by never once calling on him for the exercise of his faith. Those extraordinary accidents and events which happen to few men, seemed to me to be as legitimate materials for fiction to work with—when there was a good object in using them—as the ordinary accidents and events which may, and do, happen to us all. By appealing to genuine sources of interest *within* the reader's own experience, I could certainly gain his attention to begin with; but it would be only by appealing to other sources (as genuine in their way) *beyond* his own experience, that I could hope to fix his interest and excite his suspense, to occupy his deeper feelings, or to stir his nobler thoughts.

No statement could be more precise, or, with regard to the art of fiction, more correct; it is not only true, but it covers, either expressly or by implication, the whole ground of legitimate story-telling. To have something worth the telling, and to say it in the clearest and most vivid manner, and to say it in such a way as to excite the reader's suspense, stir his emotion, and excite his nobler aspirations—this is to be a story-teller indeed; and who would not be proud if his work satisfied such conditions? At the risk of wearying my readers, I will repeat that on such or similar principles all our great novelists have hitherto worked. The chief foundation of the art of fiction is the drama, as every one who has heard a Neapolitan or an Eastern story-teller will readily admit; and the reason of this is that the most perfect presentment of a human being is not the analysis of his motives, but the embodiment of himself; the presenting him, so to speak, on the stage of your book, and letting him act there as he would do 'on the boards,' or as he would in that life of which his action 'on the boards' is an imitation. In other words, for the purpose of story-telling, the dramatic is a more powerful form than the literary, than the analytical. Moreover, this form becomes more imperative in proportion to the interest of the story which is being told; indeed, at crucial moments even the most analytical of fiction writers are forced into the simple dramatic methods; when they come to the point, their characters act their parts, not narrate them. One great difference between Wilkie Collins and other writers, who more or less appreciate the force of this truth, is that he constructs his stories throughout on the above-mentioned principle; his characters reveal alike themselves and the work on which they are engaged, by their actions and speech. The author tells us comparatively little about them, and in many minor instances he tells us absolutely nothing. Think, for example, of the old servant, Gabriel Betteredge, in *The Moonstone*, who exhibits himself so clearly by means of his diary in the first few pages of the book that we know him as intimately as our personal friends.

[Quotes from ch. 2 of the 'First Period' of the novel: from ' "Well, there I was in clover, . . ." ' to ' ". . . my experience of it" '.]

To return to our analysis of Mr. Wilkie Collins' method; we find, on examining the books closely, that the essential strength of the various stories consists in their possession of two attributes which at first sight seem somewhat conflicting. These are the attributes of mystery and simplicity. No books are ever at the same time so straight-forward and so intricate; the straightforwardness is in the execution, in the march of the narrative, the clear presentment of the characters, but the goal is nowhere in sight, nor to the end of the book does the reader know whither he is being led. There is throughout, however, a feeling of sustained purpose, a connection of action, and a development of character, which impresses the reader with the conviction of the author's sanity and trustworthiness. However intricate the plot may be, however numerous the people, we feel more and more certain, with every page we read, that every detail and every action, nay, even every speech, is helping on the development of some purpose, which we can-not guess, but dimly foreshadow. The conviction that this is so, holds the interest as in a vice, and excites an attention to the less obvious parts of the story, which is proportionately intensified in its more exciting portions. I know no writer, for instance, living or dead, who has been able to touch the facts of Nature with so keen a human interest, and weld them so firmly to the incidents and emotions of his story. Descrip-tions of Nature in Mr. Wilkie Collins' hands, no matter how simply realistic they may appear in every detail, become, when viewed as a whole, in entire harmony with, and of considerable importance to, the purpose of his book; and it is strange to notice how uniformly successful this author has been in imparting to each description the exact senti-ment which was dramatically appropriate to the part of the story in which it appears. Here is an instance from *Armadale*—a description of a picnic party to the Norfolk Broads, remarkable not only for its delicate truth to Nature, but for a suggestiveness and underlying sense of mystery which help to prepare the way for the fulfilment of the first vision in Armadale's dream [Book II, ch. 8]:—

An hour's steady driving from the Major's cottage had taken young Armadale and his guests beyond the limits of Midwinter's solitary walk, and was now bringing them nearer and nearer to one of the strangest and loveliest aspects of Nature, which the inland landscape, not of Norfolk only, but of all England, can show. Little by little, the face of the country began to change as the carriage approached the remote and lonely district of the Broads. The wheat-fields and turnip-fields became perceptibly fewer, and the fat green grazing-grounds on either side grew wider and wider in their smooth and sweeping range. Heaps of dry rushes and reeds, laid up for the basket-maker and the thatcher, began to appear at the roadside. The old gabled cottages of the early part of the drive dwindled and disappeared, and huts with mud walls rose in their place. With the ancient church towers, and the wind and water mills, which had hitherto been the only lofty objects seen over the low marshy flat, there now rose all round the horizon, gliding slow and distant behind fringes of pollard willows, the sails of invisible boats moving on invisible waters. All the strange and startling anomalies presented by an inland agricultural district, isolated from other districts by its intricate surrounding network of pools and streams—holding its communication and carrying its produce by water instead of land—began to present themselves in closer and closer succession. Nets appeared on cottage palings; little flat-bottomed boats lay strangely at rest among the flowers in cottage gardens; farmers' men passed to and fro, clad in composite costume of the coast and the field, in sailors' hats and fishermen's boots, and ploughmen's smocks,—and even yet the low-lying labyrinth of waters, embosomed in its mystery of solitude, was a hidden labyrinth still. A minute more, and the carriages took a sudden turn from the hard high-road into a little weedy lane; the wheels ran noiselessly on the damp and spongy ground. A lonely outlying cottage appeared, with its litter of nets and boats. A few yards farther on, and the last morsel of the firm earth suddenly ended in a tiny creek and quay. One turn more, to the end of the quay, and there, spreading its great sheet of water, far, and bright, and smooth, on the right hand and the left—there, as pure in its spotless blue, as still in its heavenly peacefulness, as the summer sky above it, was the first of the Norfolk Broads.

It is worth while looking at that passage carefully for a moment, if only to notice the excessive ingenuity with which the author passes, without the slightest jerk, from pure description of Nature to the continuation of his narrative. You are taken, as it were, into the carriage as it passes these various details of house, and field, and labourer; and still, as you go on, you are thinking of the Broad, and wondering why you cannot see it, till at the very last moment the reader arrives with the picnic party, and is ready to share their forthcoming experiences. This may seem a small point to dwell upon, but it is by the observance of small points such as these that Mr. Collins succeeds in impressing us with the reality of his stories. No reader can skip a description such as the one we have quoted; it is welded into the story, not laid upon it.

The fact is, our author feels what every great landscape painter has always felt, and shown in his pictures, that the interest of landscape for most people depends on its relation to ourselves, the associations with which it is connected, and the significance with which it impresses us; and, feeling this, he immensely heightens the power of his narrative, by connecting the occurrence of certain incidents with places which lend themselves, by their natural characteristics, to the emotions which he wishes to excite. In this special portion of *Armadale* he is seeking to prepare the reader's mind for the fulfilment of a dream vision, in a manner which is to leave the reader in doubt whether the fulfilment be accidental or no. Every line of this description of the Broads echoes back to the former description of the dream, and helps to arouse that sense of mystery, strangeness, and loneliness, which will prepare the reader's mind for 'strange matters.'

Let us recur to those characters which, as a rule, are the pivots on which the interest of a novel turns—the hero and heroine, and their love relations.

Throughout all Collins' finer novels the interest turns not on these characters alone, but is almost equally concerned with every personage mentioned in the book. The hero and heroine in *Basil*, for instance, are treated with neither more nor less respect by the author than the rest of the 'cast.' The so-called hero of *The Woman in White* disappears for some hundreds of pages in the most vital portion of the book, without our even noticing his absence. *Armadale* and *The Moonstone* have quite certainly no hero or heroine at all; and though *No Name* is concerned almost entirely with the fortunes of one erring girl, she is never regarded from the heroine point of view, and is indeed, considering her earlier life, perhaps the most faulty character in the book. The result, to the present writer at least, is a delicious sense of freedom—one's interest has not been concentrated entirely in the fortunes of two personages, both of whom may to special readers be personally uninteresting—and our trust in the author's impartiality becomes absolute, when we mark the even-handed justice he displays towards his creations.

Hide and Seek, the book which followed *Basil* in order of date, shows a great advance in the development of Mr. Wilkie Collins' literary power. It is at once a more pleasant story, and a better work of art; the interest, instead of being centred in a solitary figure, is distributed amongst the characters of the story, and there is far less strained action necessary on their part to bring about the final solution. The book, too, has a definite moral purpose, which, though never obtruded, is, in the end, satisfactorily achieved. It tries to show that it is perfectly possible, with a little kindness on one side, and a little resolution and patience on the other, that the life of a girl afflicted with even such a terrible calamity as that of being deaf and dumb, need not necessarily be either sorrowful to herself, or burdensome to her companions. In fact, in *Hide and Seek*, instead of representing the person afflicted in this manner as an object of pity, the author insists throughout, and in the end wins the reader's assent to his assertion, that Mary Blyth's is a happy life.

I have called this the main purpose of the book, but it is a purpose which, though always traceable, is for the most part kept in the background. The plot turns upon an incident (or rather upon the consequences of an incident) which has happened before the story begins, and, briefly put, shows how a brother who, with infinite difficulty, discovers the story of his only sister's desertion and death, foregoes his vengeance upon the man who was responsible for both, for the sake of his friend, the betrayer's son, who has been turned out of doors by his father as a scapegrace.

In the order of Mr. Wilkie Collins' novels this work holds a very important place, not only for the increase of power of which I have spoken, but because it is the first in which the author's peculiar gift of humour distinctly shows itself; neither *Basil* nor *Armadale* contains, to the best of my recollection, any indication of humorous faculty; they are, to use a painter's expression, 'a little tight' in their workmanship, the youth of the writer showing in a sort of self-conscious restraint, which does not allow him to look to the right hand or the left, to let himself go for a moment. But in *Hide and Seek* the author is not a bit afraid of his reader; he is not only going to tell him a story, he is going to tell it in his own way; and the result is a book which, despite its somewhat stern narrative and sorrowful episodes, yet literally brims over with humour, and shows the keenest appreciation of the humorous points of its various situations. I use this word 'humour' advisedly, for 'funny,' in the correct sense of the term, Mr. Wilkie Collins is not, either here or in his later novels. There is a mordant quality about his laughter which is alien to the spirit of fun; he laughs like a man who has known what it is to weep. In conclusion, I would say that the detailed charm of *Hide and Seek* lies in its minor sketches, especially in those of the artist and his bedridden wife, which are touched with the most gentle and yet incisive hand, and which show us two entirely lovable and generously imperfect people. In its slight way, I know nothing in fiction prettier or more genuinely pathetic than the study of the good-hearted, ambitious, but comparatively incompetent artist, who, after his wife's first attack of serious illness, gives up his dreams of becoming a great historical and mythological painter, and, finding that he can sell for a few pounds his studies of still-life, deliberately restricts his art to the purpose of producing these insignificant pictures, in order to give his ailing wife every luxury and resource which she might have had, had he been a man of fortune as well as a man of heart.

Those who call Mr. Collins a sensational writer, would do well to study many passages such as these, which occur throughout his works—passages which show that he can not only deal with the strongest motives or the greatest eccentricities of human nature, but that he can understand, and love to linger long over, these tender every-day affections, 'which have one by one, and little by little, raised man from being no higher than the brute, to be only a little lower than the angels.'

Here is the account of how the apparently fruitless, unselfish devotion to his art in happier days recompenses the artist when the time of his affliction comes, when, after the first shock of his grief is over, he is able to turn his big canvases to the wall, and set to work again on the humbler scale which is sanctified by a more human interest:—

[Quotes from the opening chapter: from 'On the first day . . .' to '. . . permitted to them to subdue'.]

It would be pleasant to say that the story which followed *Hide and Seek* showed a further development of our author's art in the qualities of which I have been speaking. But I find this book, on the contrary, less humorous, less genuine, and less tender than the one which preceded it; on the other hand, it is certainly more concentrated, and therefore, taken as a whole, more powerful. Its weakness, as a work of art, consists in the fact that for the protagonist of the story our sympathies are never aroused, and thus, despite the author's utmost efforts, he fails to interest us in Sarah Leeson and her mistress' secret. I think the reason for this is twofold. In the first place, Sarah Leeson is introduced to us from the very beginning with the burden of this secret overshadowing her; there is no special reason why we should care for this woman, who, from our first acquaintance with her, passes shrinking up and down the staircases, and sits trembling in the corridor. And, in the second place, the author in this instance has prepared his subject too elaborately; he makes his secret as if it were a pancake, and keeps tossing it about from one pan to the other, and hiding it, and seeking it, and missing it, and getting nearer to it, and farther from it again, till at last the poor thing is scrabbled over with incident and description, as if it had been raked with a small-tooth comb, and still we do not know what it is, and, when we do know, we feel inclined to say: 'Oh! is that all?' as at the end of a pointless story. And yet the book is full of ingenuity, and, as in a house built by some misguided architect, we are continually opening doors that only reveal dark cupboards, and running up and down passages and steps, only to find ourselves where we started. The book is especially poor in its minor characters; Uncle Joseph, the German upholsterer, for example, with the music-box that Mozart gave to his grandfather, becomes, despite his virtues, a perfect nuisance to the reader. He is that most annoying of all the creations of the novelist, a good man with a tiresome eccentricity which we are not allowed to forget for a single moment, introduced, of course, as a *Deus ex machinâ*, and to give relief to the more sombre portions of the story. Uncle Joseph never fairly gets into the plot at all; he, so to speak, dances about outside it, to the sound of his eternal music-box, and to the weariness of the reader. Perhaps one exception should in justice be made concerning the minor characters of *The Dead Secret*, and that is in favour of Mr. Phippen, the dyspeptic philosopher, who weighs his bread, and measures his tea, and yet, nevertheless, sees bilious spots dancing in front of him as he takes his morning constitutional. Mr. Phippen is delightful, but, most unfortunately, he only occurs in one scene of the story.

The Dead Secret would have been much improved had the author allowed his humorous faculty to have a little freer play. As it is, the book has sufficient interest to make you read it, but not sufficient to make you regret the revelation of the secret when it comes at last. With *The Dead Secret* ends what I should feel inclined to call the early period of Mr. Wilkie Collins' art; by the time the next book (*The Woman in White*) is published, the writer has entirely mastered his business, his 'soft-shell' stage is at an end, and, as he would say himself, for good or evil the man stands revealed before us.

I do not purpose to say much, or indeed anything, in detail, about the plot of *The Woman in White*; it is too well known to need description, nor are its merits such as can be easily explained in a brief outline; but of the character-drawing in this book, and its connection with the plot, it is necessary to speak somewhat minutely. This is the first book in which Mr. Wilkie Collins succeeds in entirely holding the reader's interest by the story itself, taken in connection with the characters by whom it is carried out. Gradually to this point has the author's power grown—to this point of welding together circumstance and character, and showing their interdependencies, and the results that arise from their mutual action and reaction. Two weak points, and only two weak points, I find in the construction. Anne Catherick is of necessity un-interesting, not only on account of the character itself, but because by the exigencies of the plot she is bound to be sacrificed fruitlessly, and so the author is forbidden by every rule of dramatic propriety to really arouse our interest in her; this, therefore, is felt as a deficiency necessi-tated by the plot itself, and as such may be excused, if not pardoned. The second point is to me a far more important one, as it is no less than an error in the actual art of the novel-writer—an error which would be almost unpardonable, were it not that our inartistic English public practically insist on such a mistake being committed in nine books out of ten. The point of which I am speaking is the anti-climax of Count Fosco's death and Walter Hartright's trip to Paris. The book should end —the book actually does end, as far as all interest is concerned—in the scene between Count Fosco and Walter Hartright, in which the former confesses his share in the conspiracy; this is not only the finest situation, but the finest scene, in the book—a scene which in its combination of dialogue and narrative, and its dramatic power, has probably never been surpassed in fiction; and then, lo and behold! we have some twenty more pages, containing a perfectly useless narrative of the erasure of Laura Fairlie's name from the tombstone, and the subsequent journey of Hartright to Paris, followed by his discovery of Count Fosco's body in the Morgue. Let us commit that worst of all impertinences—that of teaching a man his own business—and say boldly that the last episode of this novel should have been Hartright's departure from Count Fosco's lodgings, and his catching sight, as he left, of that Italian member of the 'Brotherhood' (to which the Count belonged) whom Hartright had noticed on two previous occasions watching him. So the villain would have departed into the darkness whence he came, with the shadow of Nemesis stealing after him, and we should have been spared that irri-tating feeling, so common to readers of English fiction, that all our stories must be saddled with a definite moral ending, wherein every personage is rewarded or punished according to his deserts; must also have all their incidents neatly finished up—as if the world ended at the end of the third volume. With these blemishes, and perhaps a slight feeling of disappointment with regard to the character of Hartright himself, the adverse criticism of *The Woman in White* must end. It is a book which made an era in novel-writing, and may be said to have opened up a new view of the art—a view on which a whole subsequent school has been founded; and yet, despite the thousands of so-called sensational novels which the last thirty years have seen, this book remains now easily first, and this results from simple conditions, and rests upon the fact that the author has been able to combine a very true and noble human feeling with his more passionate and tragical interests. The crimes of Count Fosco and Sir Percival Glyde would lose half their dramatic intensity, were they not contrasted with the unswerving sisterly devotion of Marian Halcombe, and the unselfish love of Walter Hartright; and these again would have little power to move us, were they not surrounded and, as it were, upheld by a multitude of other characters, for the most part indicated by slight touches, who are yet living, breathing realities. Walter's mother; Signor Pesca, the teacher of Italian; Miss Vesey, the old companion; Mr. Fairlie, the selfish *dilettante*; grim Mrs. Catherick herself—all of these are there, and not there only to play their part in the story, but to impress us with a sense of the every-day world, with its commonplace interests and actions, and so relieve and render natural the more salient portions of the story.

The most interesting character of the story is of course Count Fosco, who stands out from the villains of contemporary fiction as an almost solitary example of a scoundrel who makes no damnable faces over his villany, and whose part in the story is not only to bring about the catastrophe. For Fosco in *The Woman in White* has, as he had in life, two almost distinct individualities, one of which issues in his overflowing vanity, his resplendent waistcoats, his white mice, and his passion for Rossini's music; while the other sits silently by in the shadow, waiting its time to strike the long-planned blow of the conspiracy. Perhaps the strongest part of the interest, which *The Woman in White* inspires, is due to the conviction with which the author succeeds in impressing us of Count Fosco's capability for better things, of the strange recesses in his character. We keep saying to ourselves, 'What might not this man have done?' The overpowering influence of great strength of character, even when the direction of that strength is in the main an evil one, has never been shown in a work of fiction at once more subtly and more powerfully than here; it is not too much to say that the reader himself feels the fascination of the man, and feels it, too, without losing his horror at his cold-bloodedness and crime. By clear, bold, broad touches is this effect produced, without a moment's pause in the course of the story.

I can only extract a small portion of the description of the Count which appears in Marian Halcombe's diary, but even this will be sufficient to show the power and subtlety of the author's analysis, and the clearness of outline with which from the first this character is presented:—

[Three short extracts follow from ch. 2 of Marian Halcombe's narrative in the 'Second Epoch' of the novel, ending with the account of Fosco's white mice and canaries.]

In this description it is that the author's genius for depicting character shows its utmost height, for if Count Fosco had not been a human villain, the story of *The Woman in White* would have been unbearable: the cowardly, tyrannous selfishness of Sir Percival Glyde, the weak submission of his wife, the magnificent devotion to her sister of Marian Halcombe, would have had no foil and no relief. As it is, the woman and the man, Marian Halcombe and Count Fosco, the good and the evil spirits, stand opposite to one another, and fight for their respective interests amidst the weaker characters whose fortunes they decide, and, as I have said, so subtly is the villain conceived, that the balance of sympathy is never altogether on the side of his antagonist. Ought it to be?

That is the question to which the answer would not have been doubtful fifty years ago, and that is the question to which the affirmative answer, given by many people, has caused so much adverse criticism on Mr. Wilkie Collins' novels.

The answer which I should give to it here would be as follows:— That directly our sympathies are entirely withdrawn from any character whatsoever in a work of fiction, that character has for us practically no existence. It is a mere compound of words and phrases, and has no more the power to affect as a warning, than to encourage as an example. Out of the pages of *Frankenstein* there is no such thing as an unadulterated monster. Unless we can trace in any given character of fiction some possible likeness to ourselves, we cannot be either with or against it. Take away the little touches which make Count Fosco human—his fondness for his wife, his bravery, his tenderness to animals, his love of music, his overflowing, harmless vanity—and you take away the whole vital quality of the man, and leave merely a bundle of attributes, for which no human being can afford to care. Another, and perhaps a better, instance of our author's perception of this truth is in the sympathy which he arouses in us for Captain Wragge (who is an unscrupulous little swindler in *No Name*), in the description of one of his interviews with the heroine, Magdalen Vanstone. The girl has been tried past her power of endurance, and has, in an outbreak of temper, said hard things to the Captain. Her apology touches some kindly feeling in the little swindler's heart, and there seems to be an instant glad recognition of the fact that he was not wholly base, in the way in which this momentary impulse is described by the author. . . .

Some two years subsequently to *The Woman in White* (our author has rarely had less than two years to prepare each of his important novels), *No Name*, from which the above quotation is taken, appeared; —a book which, despite several minor blemishes, is, in my opinion, the most fascinating, as *Armadale* is the most important, of all Mr. Wilkie Collins' works. 'Here is one more book that depicts the struggle of a human creature under those opposing influences of Good and Evil which we have all felt, which we have all known.' These words, which I have extracted from the Preface, form the key-note of the book which tells the story of Magdalen Vanstone, her sins, her repentance, and her punishment. Space forbids me to say anything of the plot or the details of this work, but, in justice to the author, it must be pointed out that no better proof could be desired of his genuineness as an artist than its mere existence, considering the circumstances under which it was written. Think for a moment how keen was the temptation to an author, who had at last, after ten years of fiction-writing, made a gigantic and indubitable success in a very special and original manner, to repeat in his next work the same method, and try to catch the public in a similar way. On the contrary, he waits for two years, and then starts on an entirely different plan, content to let the author of *The Woman in White* be forgotten while he solicits our favour as the author of *No Name*. And why? Here is the explanation in his own words:—

To pass from the characters to the story, it will be seen that the narrative related in these pages has been constructed on a plan which differs from the plan followed in my last novel [*The Woman in White*] and in some other of my books published at an earlier date. The only secret contained in this book is revealed midway in the first volume. From that point all the main events of the story are purposely foreshadowed before they take place, my present design being to rouse the reader's interest in following the train of circumstances by which these foreseen events are brought about. In trying this new ground, I am not turning my back in doubt on the ground which I have passed over already; my one object in following a new course is to enlarge the range of my studies in the art of writing fiction, and to vary the form in which I make my appeal to the reader, as attractively as I can.

Nowadays, I confess that I know no novel-writer who could honestly put the above in a Preface. . . .

The book which succeeded *No Name* was *Armadale*, which, on the whole, must be considered the greatest of Mr. Wilkie Collins' novels.

It has all the interest and sustained purpose of *The Woman in White*, while it is drawn on a much larger scale, and shows a much wider knowledge of character. If it were only for the intricacy of the plot, and for the manner in which that plot is worked out over the lapse of years, and by means of a large number of diverse characters, the work would remain of typical excellence; but it is more than this. It is an attempt, and a successful attempt, to deal from the imaginative point of view with the doctrines of heredity, both physical and moral. The causes of the story are all in the first generation, and all its incidents are in the second generation and the results of the earlier action. It is a story of the effects produced by a woman's weakness and a man's crime—a weakness which is reflected, though on the good side instead of the bad, in the succeeding generation; and a crime, of which the strength alone survives in the child of its author, inspiring him with a passionate determination to shield the life of the son of the man whom his father murdered, at all hazards to his own life, and at all costs to his own happiness. This is the better nature of the chief actor of the book, but along with it there exists a more morbid strain of feeling, which prompts him to doubt whether, despite all his efforts, he will not bring fatal mischance to his friend, and the vital portion of the book is the story of his mental struggle, of the incidents which affected it, and of the final catastrophe through which the solution is found.

What I have ventured to call the mental and moral doctrine of heredity, is, amongst other causes, worked out by the author making the instrument of danger to the son, the same woman, who, as a child, was the instrument of his mother's deception. This character, who stands to the female villains of fiction in the same relation that Count Fosco does to the male, lingers in the memory, despite her crimes and her heartlessness, with an almost terrible insistency; and in her final punishment, brought about, as it is, with a daring truth to reality, by her fulfilment of the one good instinct of her nature, we feel almost as much for her as though all her acts had been equally blameless with her death for the man she loved. I am here, no doubt, treading on delicate ground; we should have, the moralists tell us, no sympathy with a criminal who only suffers for her sins without abjuring them; but, human nature being what it is, I confess to a sympathy with Mr. Wilkie Collins' disposition to find something which is admirable, or at least lovable, in even the black sheep of the community. They are so much in the hands of fate, that we may well afford to be a little extra kind to them. Such is a hint of the story of *Armadale*, and of the motives that inspire it; but

I can give no idea of the richness of incident with which these main motives are surrounded, or with which they are worked out, or of the wealth of character-perception which the book displays, or of its unforced and many-sided humour, or of the power of its culminating tragedy.

In an earlier portion of this paper I have given a quotation from *Armadale* in order to show Mr. Collins' power of interweaving natural scenery and human emotion. Here is another little extract to substantiate what I have said as to the humour of the book:—

[Quotes from ch. 2 of Book the Second: from 'The gardener, who still stood . . .' to '. . . hobbled slowly out of view'.]

I have said that with *Armadale* the power of Wilkie Collins, in my opinion, culminated, but the book which succeeded it was certainly more immediately popular, and, by those who like their fiction of a light character, is generally regarded as this author's most amusing work. It is certainly one, if it be the least important, of his four finest novels; and, if we consider it purely from the point of view of handicraft, I do not know that it does not deserve to be placed first of all, if only because of the unhesitating clearness and rapidity of the narrative, and the manner in which the reader's attention is never allowed to falter for a single instant. It contains also two studies of character which are, in their way, unique—that of Gabriel Betteredge, the old family servant, devoted to his pipe and his *Robinson Crusoe*, and that of Sergeant Cuff, the one detective in fiction whom it is a pleasure to remember. The story of the book is well known. It deals with the theft of a celebrated diamond, entitled the *Moonstone*, and its final restitution to the Hindoo idol which represents Brahma in his character of the 'Moongod.' I have given instances before in this article of our author's tenderness, his perception and delineation of character, his natural sympathy, his humour, and his concentration of dramatic effect; let me here give a single instance of his imaginative faculty—the account of how the stone is set once more in the forehead of the great idol by the three Brahmins who have compassed its recovery:—

[Quotes from the closing chapter of the novel: from 'Looking back down the hill . . .' to ' ". . . Who can tell?" '.]

With this instance, these notes, in which I have endeavoured to show something of the nature, and give some idea of the extent, of Mr. Wilkie Collins' genius, may fitly come to a close. It has been my

endeavour less to criticise the writer's style than to reveal the breadth
and power of his genius by the most indisputable of all methods, the
method of quotation. I have endeavoured to advance nothing which I
was not prepared to prove, and which, so far as my space has allowed
me, I have not afforded the reader the opportunity to verify; and I have
carefully foreborne to contrast Mr. Collins' work with that of special
living writers, who may be at the present moment in greater popular
favour. No one will feel more keenly than myself the inadequacy of
this paper from a literary point of view; but I shall be content if it help
ever so little in the appreciation of this author, who has probably given
more keen and harmless pleasure to the last generation than any living
writer, and yet for whom I seldom hear a generous word spoken, or
read a criticism which recognizes the service he has done, the genius he
has shown, and the noble purpose which has always directed his work.

Think for a moment; it is not yet too late to take off our hats to the
great story-teller, and say, as a nation, what thousands of readers must
have frequently felt, and said privately: 'We thank you heartily.'

81. The English Gaboriau

September 1889

Unsigned obituary notice, *Athenaeum*, 28 September 1889, 418.
The first part briefly summarizes Collins's early career.

Antonina was followed in 1852 by *Basil*, a much more skilful novel,
though crude in some parts and coarse in others. Soon after that he
made Dickens's acquaintance, which ripened into close and lasting
friendship, and thus came under a stronger and worthier literary influence than Bulwer's. Much of his most skilful work was done for *Household Words* and *All the Year Round*, beginning with *After Dark* in 1856,
and culminating in *The Woman in White* in 1859, though some may

consider that he reached higher levels in *Armadale*, which appeared in the *Cornhill* in 1866, and in *The Moonstone*, produced two years later. His other novels make a long catalogue, including particularly *Man and Wife* and *The New Magdalen*, the latter even more effective when it was converted into a play than as a novel, and, as a play, the most successful of his contributions to stage literature.

Melodrama was Wilkie Collins's forte, but he worked better as a novelist than as a dramatist. Of the creator of Count Fosco, of Betteredge, of Miss Gwilt, and of Mercy Merrick it cannot be said that he was not a bold and painstaking student of character, and his zeal in eccentric portraiture went so far as to become an infirmity in his later writings. But his best creations were puppets, and he was pre-eminent as a manipulator of marionettes. As a novelist 'with a purpose' he was a disciple of Dickens, preserving his own individuality, and showing some affinity to Poe. As a weaver of plots he has no rival in England, and in certain respects he surpassed, if in others he could not equal and widely differed from, Gaboriau and the rest of the French contrivers of elaborated plots. His mastery of details, all cunningly contrived and ordered with a view to startling and realistic effects, aimed at, and often achieved, more than a verisimilitude of actual life. Whether he was right or wrong, whether he pleaded in fiction for charity towards erring women, or whether he attacked vivisectionists, or whatever else he attempted or did, he never failed to preach what seemed to him some moral doctrine that needed to be enforced. Though many people strongly resented his *Heart and Science* and *I Say No*, and though his art was always crippled by his moralizing, he deservedly holds high rank as a literary artist as well as a zealous moralist, and in both respects is vastly superior to many younger imitators and rivals.

His style of work was peculiarly suited to the serial form of publication which he generally adopted, with great profit to himself, and with less injury to the work itself than usually happens in such cases. No one knew better than he how to arouse and maintain the curiosity of his readers as he doled out his stories to them in weekly or monthly instalments, and how to provide them in each mouthful with something appetizing in itself and suited to whet their appetite for more. Yet readers young enough to read his novels for the first time in volume form, and to swallow them in one prolonged meal, are less likely in his case to notice the jerks and the tricks in the narrative than in the case of Thackeray or George Eliot, or many others who could be named. Jerks and tricks, indeed, were what he most excelled in, and if these are not

the highest form of art, or were essentially inartistic, he managed them
so well that few defects in his method are discernible. His method was
his own, and just such as his talent could best achieve, and in following
it he proved his wisdom and his strength as a novelist.

82. 'Cleverness rather than genius': the excellence and limitations of Wilkie Collins

September 1889

M. W. Townsend, unsigned obituary article, *Spectator*, 28
September 1889, lxiii, 395–6.

Meredith White Townsend (1831–1911) owned and edited the
Spectator jointly with R. H. Hutton from 1860 until Hutton's
death in 1897; it has been estimated that, during a journalistic
career of sixty years, he must have written nearly 10,000 articles.

The position of Mr. Wilkie Collins in literature was a very unusual one.
He was an extremely popular writer—deservedly popular, as we think
—who was not very highly esteemed. Of all the Englishmen who read
novels, few have failed to read some of his best stories; fewer, having
begun them, ever laid them down unfinished; and fewest of all ended
their reading without some criticism of more or less depreciatory
friendliness. That is an odd position, and we do not know that it has
been quite satisfactorily explained. That which Mr. Collins pretended
to do, he did, when he was doing his best work, admirably; and it is by
his best work, and not by his early failures, or the inferior stuff he wrote
after he took, as his friend Mr. Yates explains, to opium-eating on the
grand scale, opium-eating like Coleridge's or De Quincey's, that he
ought to be judged. In four of his books, *The Woman in White*, *No
Name*, *The Moonstone*, and *Man and Wife*, he showed himself exactly as

he was,—that is, as a literary chess-player of the first force, with the power of carrying his plan right through the game and making every move tell. His method was to introduce a certain number of characters, set before them a well-defined object, such as the discovery of a secret, the revindication of a fortune, the tracking of a crime, or the establishment of a doubted marriage, and then bring on other characters to resist and counterplot their efforts. Each side makes moves, almost invariably well-considered and promising moves; the counter-moves are equally good; the interest goes on accumulating till the looker-on—the reader is always placed in that attitude—is rapt out of himself by strained attention; and then there is a sudden and totally unexpected mate. It is chess which is being played; and in the best of all the stories, the one which will live for years, *The Moonstone*, the pretence that it is anything else is openly discarded. There are two games going on at once,—that of the Indians who are seeking their diamond, against the heirs of Major Herncastle; and afterwards that of Frank Blake against his traducers. Both are fought out with a slow skill which enchains the observer, and both end in admirably contrived and most surprising mates. In *The Woman in White*, the deliberate play is less manifest, because all through one side plays blindfold, at the bidding of a higher power or Fate; but in *No Name* the play is again of the most open kind, the players, Margaret Vanstone and Mrs. Lecount, setting to the game with a will, and turning up their faces now and then to see if you admire the skilfulness of their moves.

That skilfulness is exceedingly great. We doubt if there are stories in English in which the plots are more perfect than in the four we have named, in which the situations are more dramatic, or in which the mystery is more perfectly preserved to the very end. The surprise is usually complete, so complete that it excites a kind of involuntary laughter, and usually, in *The Moonstone* in particular, it is led up to with a high degree of artistic skill. Every detail of the story leads up to the *dénouement*, yet not one in a thousand readers guesses it till it has arrived. . . . The story is a very triumph of cleverness, is, in fact, the best detective-story ever written, and there is nothing surprising about its immense success, a success which we believe still continues. The reader has his hunting instinct excited to the full, while he is at the same time amused by the brightness of the narrative, and by an exhibition of humour which, though occasionally farcical, is always genuine and provocative of mirth. Mr. Wilkie Collins's humour was sometimes quite detestable—witness the scenes in the inn in *Man and Wife*, and the

scenes with Mrs. Wragge in *No Name*—but in *The Moonstone*, Betteredge is admirably comic, and so, for the little we see of him, is the
melancholy, rose-growing Inspector of Police. The reader wants to find
that diamond as much as any one of the characters; and to produce that
feeling is, we maintain, of its kind a literary triumph. It is not of the
highest kind, or perhaps of a high kind at all; but still, it is literary skill
quite great in degree. It is all the more remarkable skill because it is not
exactly dramatic, though we have used that word, but something
separate. The plays made from the novels never greatly succeeded, and
it is not difficult to see why. The situations are strong, but as a rule—
there is a remarkable exception in Rachel's denunciation of her lover, in
The Moonstone—they are not dependent for their strength on details
which can be transferred to the stage. It is the idea of the opium as the
cause of the theft which is interesting, not Frank's sleepwalking expedi-
tion after the diamond.

Was there anything in the novelist beyond this chess-playing power?
Yes, decidedly, a great deal, though we should hesitate to admit that he
had genius. There is something very like it occasionally in special
scenes,—such, for instance, as the drawing-master's reception by Mr.
Fairlie, in *The Woman in White*; in Geoffrey's conduct about the bet
after his defeat in the long race; in Magdalen's appeal to the lot to decide
whether she shall die or live; and, above all, in the whole conception of
the child Jicks, in that repertory of wasted cleverness, *Poor Miss Finch*.
We should, however, prefer to assign to Wilkie Collins overflowing
cleverness rather than genius. There is overflowing cleverness everywhere,—in the details of the plots; in the apparently useless hints, each
one so full of meaning; in the vivacious dialogue; in the lightly humorous descriptions; and, above all, in the photographs offered us of a
multitude of distinct and recognisable characters. With the possible
exception of Count Fosco, about whom we are doubtful, Mr. Collins
having not only failed, but consciously failed to find him a governing
motive, he has never created a character; but he has sketched-in an
enormous number, a dozen or two of whom the spectator will never
forget. He does not know them exactly, but he does know the aspect of
them, and that is something. Compare Alfred Jingle with Captain
Wragge, in *No Name*, who is very much the same kind of swindler, and
the difference between genius and cleverness becomes at once apparent;
but still, Captain Wragge is a figure perfectly coloured, and outlined as
it would appear in a looking-glass. So is Mrs. Lecount, in the same
story; so is Betteredge, in *The Moonstone*; so is Frank Blake, though he

lacks natural anger; so is the athletic hero in *Man and Wife*; and in a much higher degree, Sir Patrick Lundy, the kindly cynic, keen as a lancet, yet always a courtly gentleman; and so are the Pedgifts, the lawyers of *Armadale*, a book we have omitted from our list of the works by which Wilkie Collins should be judged, because, in spite of its popularity and of a certain atmosphere of eeriness diffused with exceeding skill, its characters are usually as unnatural as its situations are hopelessly impossible. Mr. Wilkie Collins was no sculptor, but he was a skilful painter, his portraits lacking only that soul which we fancy he not only could not paint, but never clearly saw. The oddly *naïf* attempt, at the end of *The Woman in White*, to account for Count Fosco in three separate ways was, we are persuaded, no accident, but an effort to remedy an indistinctness in his own mind of which the novelist himself was conscious, and at which he was just artist enough to be profoundly annoyed. He just could not vivify, and he knew it; and it is that limitation which will always keep him out of the front rank of English novelists, though in his power of attracting an audience he was, while his powers remained to him, almost unsurpassed. To the last, although it was clear to good critics that his powers had failed, and that his method had become a mannerism, he never lost his charm for the average reader, or his faculty of exciting the impression of amused surprise. There was a hiatus in Mr. Collins's sense of literary taste, a total inability to see when he was and was not almost brutally coarse; but the defect only comes out strongly in the first edition of *Basil*, suppressed practically by himself, and in that extraordinary production of his latest time *Fallen Leaves*, which is to us simply abhorrent; but his writing is, for the most part, full of right feeling, and it is with deep regret that we read of the long-continued physical suffering which in his later years poisoned his life, and drove him to palliatives which lowered his powers, and account, we doubt not, for his occasional literary aberrations.

83. In defence of Collins's artistry

November 1889

A. C. Swinburne, 'Wilkie Collins', *Fortnightly Review*, 1 November 1889, n.s. cclxxv, 589–99.

Algernon Charles Swinburne (1837–1909), poet and critic, wrote essays on various nineteenth-century novelists, including Dickens and Charlotte and Emily Brontë. The present essay was reprinted in his *Studies in Prose and Poetry* (1894).

The ingratitude of kings and the ingratitude of democracies have often supplied the text of historic or political sermons: the ingratitude of readers and spectators, from Shakespeare's day to our own, is at least as notable and memorable. A man who has amused our leisure, relieved our weariness, delighted our fancy, enthralled our attention, refreshed our sympathies, cannot claim a place of equal honour in our grateful estimation with the dullest or the most perverse of historians who ever falsified or stupefied history, of metaphysicians who ever 'darkened counsel' and wasted time and wearied attention by the profitless lucubrations of pseudosophy. To create is nothing: to comment is much. The commentary may be utterly hollow and rotten, the creation thoroughly solid and alive: the one is nothing less than criticism, the other nothing more than fiction. 'Un âne qui ressemble à monsieur Nisard' takes precedence, in the judgment of his kind, of the men on whose works, inventive or creative, it is the business of a Nisard to pass judgment and to bray.

Some few students, whose levity or perversity is duly derided and deplored by the Nisards of our time, are of opinion that the age of Shakespeare is well worth studying even in the minor productions of his day and the humblest professors of his art. And, far as the modern novel at its best is beneath the higher level of the stage in the time of Shakespeare, it must be admitted that the appeal to general imagination or to general sympathy, which then was made only by the dramatist, is now made only by the novelist. Middleton, Heywood, and Rowley would now have to undertake the parts so excellently played by Collins, by Trollope, and by Reade. Culture, in their days, was pleased to ignore the drama with a scorn as academic—in Mr. Carlyle's picturesque and fortunate phrase, as 'high-sniffing' a contempt—as it now can pretend to feel for the novel. And yet the name of Shakespeare is now more widely known than the name of Puttenham. And though Dickens was not a Shakespeare, and though Collins was not a Dickens, it is permissible to anticipate that their names and their works will be familiar to generations unacquainted with the existence and unaware of the eclipse of their most shining, most scornful, and most superior critics. To have written *Basil*, though *Basil* is by no manner of means an impeccable work of imperishable art, is something more than to have demonstrated what needs no demonstration—that a writer must do better than this if he wishes to achieve a serious or a memorable success. But, violent and unlovely and unlikely as it is, this early story had in it something more than promise—the evidence of original and noticeable power to constrain and retain attention of a more serious and perhaps a more reasonable kind than can be evoked by many later and more ambitious or pretentious appeals to the same or a similar source of interest. The horrible heroine, beast as she is, is a credible and conceivable beast; and her hapless young husband is a rather pathetic if a rather incredible figure. But the vindictive paramour is somewhat too much of a stage property; and the book would hardly be remembered for better or for worse if the author had not in his future stories excelled its merits and eschewed its faults. Nor would *Hide and Seek*, though a most ingenious and amusing story, have had much chance of a life as long as it deserves if it had been the best that its teller had to tell. But in *The Dead Secret* Wilkie Collins made his mark for the first time as a writer who could do something that no one else could—and something well worth doing. The skill of the plot, the construction, and the narrative, whatever such skill may be worth, was far beyond the reach of any contemporary, however far above him in the loftier and clearer qualities of genius. Dickens never wrote and Thackeray never tried to write a story so excellent in construction and so persistent in its hold on the reader's curiosity—a curiosity amounting, in the case of its younger and more impressible readers, to absolute anxiety. But, good as it is, this book is the first among many examples of the too undeniable and characteristic fact that the remarkable genius of its author for invention and construction and composition of incidents and effects was limited by an incapacity and dependent on a condition which cannot but be regarded as seriously impairing his claims to consideration as an artist or a student. He could not, as a rule, get forward at all without the help of some physical or moral infirmity in some one of the leading agents or patients of the story. Neither *The Dead Secret* nor *The Woman in White* could have run its course for a single volume if Sarah Leeson or Anne Catherick had been sound in mind—not abnormally and constitutionally deficient in nerve and brain. And the suggested or implied suffering of such poor innocent wretches, the martyrdom of perpetual terror and agony inflicted on the shattered nerves or the shaken brain of a woman or a girl, is surely a cruel and a painful mainspring for a story or a plot. Again, if the hero in this story and the heroine in another [*Poor Miss Finch*] had not been blind, there could have been no story at all. It is in every case a wonderfully ingenious and interesting story that we enjoy; but the ungrateful reader cannot avoid the reflection that there is something unlovely as well as artificial in the condition of its existence. Madge Wildfire is no more the central and indispensable mainspring—the 'cheville ouvrière'—of *The Heart of Midlothian* than Ophelia is of *Hamlet*: their insanity is an important but subordinate point in the working of the story, most skilfully and superbly wrought into the texture of its composition; but in neither case is the story made to depend for its very existence on this insanity.

But from first to last, if allowance be duly made for occasional lapses, it will be admitted that Wilkie Collins was in his way a genuine artist. *Basil*, with all its violence and crudity, has something of sustained though not elevated interest; whereas the most successful imitation ever attempted of its author's method has nothing in it whatever beyond one certainly most ingenious idea—that a blind man should by accident be the only witness (if witness he can be called) of a murder; the rest of the story being but vehement commonplace, of the spasmodically torpid kind—electrified stupidity, if the phrase may be allowed to pass. All the works of Wilkie Collins which we remember with pleasure are works of art as true as his godfather's pictures, and in their own line as complete. His excellent sense, his perfect self-command, his modest devotion to his art, are qualities not more praiseworthy than they are obvious. And if it were but for their rarity they should command no less attention than respect. His most illustrious friend and contemporary did not always show himself at once so loyal and so rational in observance of intellectual or æsthetic propriety. Collins never ventured to fling down among his readers so shapeless or misshapen a piece of work, though doubtless he could not furnish them with a piece of work so splendid and so excellent in parts and sections, as *Little Dorrit*. Dickens, with his usual straightforward dexterity, laid hold of the objection absurdly raised against the catastrophe of *Little Dorrit* by the carpers who averred that it must have been suggested by an actual accident which occurred just before the close of the periodical publication of his story: he pointed out the intimations conveyed again and again of just such an unforeseen peril in the earlier stages of the story—in numbers which had appeared many months before; and he most satisfactorily and triumphantly stamped out that most fatuous and preposterous suggestion. But he did not prove or even try to prove it possible for his most devoted admirer to believe that when he began the story he meant that so much of it should finally be left hanging in the air; that a figure so admirably and so carefully outlined as that of a malignant 'self-tormentor' should have been intended to justify and expound herself by putting into the hands of a stranger to whom she had conceived a rather virulent antipathy the unsolicited and unexplained revelation of her poisoned nature and her cankered life; or that the ill-mated pair whose miserable tragedy had been so darkly foreshadowed and so elaborately sketched in should have been left in the simply uncomfortable condition to which the great novelist, overburdened with an inartistic multiplicity of episodical and incoherent interests, was finally content to condemn them by default. A writer may let his characters slip for the sake of his story, or he may let his story slip for the sake of his characters: Dickens, in *Little Dorrit*, fell alternately into both errors, and yet achieved such success on both lines that the chaotic magnificence of his work may well be held sufficient to strike even the most rational and rightful criticism into silence. Such triumph and such aberration were alike impossible to Collins; the most plausible objection that could be brought against his best books was that the study of character and the modesty of nature must too surely have been subordinated, if not sacrificed, to the exquisitely mechanical ingenuity of so continuously intricate a plot. And now and then it would certainly seem as if the writer had been struck, and had possibly been irritated, by an apprehension that he might be regarded as a mere mechanic or mechanist of fiction, and had been impelled by this apprehension into some not always fortunate or felicitous attempt to relieve the weft of his story and heighten the tone of his work with somewhat crude and over-coloured effects of character or caricature. But it seems to me grossly and glaringly unjust to deny or to question the merit or the truthfulness of his better studies. By far the best, the

most thoughtful, serious, and critical article that appeared on the
occasion of his death, fair and good as it was in the main, may be cited
in example of this injustice. Count Fosco, said the critic, stands revealed
as a mechanical nonentity, an ingenious invention never realized or
vitalized or informed with humanity by the inventor, who felt at last
that he had failed to make a living man of him; the proof of this being
simply that at the close of the story two or three different explanations
of his conduct and his character are suggested as equally plausible and
acceptable. This would be a quite unimpeachable objection if the story
had been told in the third person; but such too intelligent criticism
overlooks the fact that it is not. The author does not tell us what he
thinks of his creature; he gives us the various impressions made on the
fellow-creatures of his imagination by the influence or the impact of
this particular figure. And the consequence is that we see there are more
ways of considering and estimating a man's character than a meaner
artist could have suggested or conceived. And the author's especial
genius is never more distinctly displayed or more happily employed
than in the exposition and the contrast of such varying estimates of
character or explanations of event. At the opening of the story which
seems to be generally regarded as the masterpiece of his art, we are
warned by the worthy old steward who first takes up the narrative to
believe nothing that may be said of him by a lady whose recollections
and reflections are to follow on the record of his own; and when the
Evangelical hag who is one of her creator's most thoroughly and simply
successful creations takes up the tale in turn, and sets forth her opinions
as to the past and the present and the future of her friends and neighbours,
we find that her view of life and character is as dramatically just and
appropriate—from the opposite point of view—as his. It is apparently
the general opinion—an opinion which seems to me incontestable—
that no third book of their author's can be ranked as equal with *The
Woman in White* and *The Moonstone*: two works of not more indisputable than incomparable ability. *No Name* is an only less excellent example
of as curious and original a talent. It is more elaborately ingenious, but
less thoroughly successful, than the finest work of the first Lord Lytton
—a story grounded on the same motive, and starting from the same
point; the imputation of illegitimacy, the struggle against its consequences, and the final triumph over its disadvantages. But there is
nothing—though much is good—so good in the work of the later
novelist as the character of Gawtrey; nor anything so effective and
impressive as his end.

In this story the complication and alternation of interests and incidents are carried as far as they can reasonably be carried: in *Armadale* they are carried further. That curious and laborious romance must be considered, even by those who cannot consider it successful, as a failure which fell short on the verge of a success. The prologue or prelude is so full of interest and promise that the expectations of its readers may have been unduly stimulated; but the sequel, astonishingly ingenious and inventive as it is, is scarcely perhaps in perfect keeping with the anticipations thus ingeniously aroused. To the average reader, judging by my own impressions, I should imagine that the book must on the whole be a little disappointing; but such a reader should ask himself whether this impression of disappointment is reasonable. The criminal heroine who dies of her own will by her own crime, to save the beloved victim whom it has accidentally brought to the verge of death, is a figure which would have aroused the widest and the deepest sympathy of English readers if only she had not been the creation of an Englishman. Had a Frenchman or an American introduced her, no acclamation would have been too vehement to express their gratitude. The signature of Nathaniel Hawthorne or of Octave Feuillet would have sufficed to evoke a rapture of regret that England could produce no such novelist as this. But neither Feuillet nor Hawthorne could have composed and constructed such a story: the ingenuity spent on it may possibly be perverse, but is certainly superb. And the studies of character are fair; the fortunate and amiable young hero and heroine may be rather incredibly boyish and girlish, but the two somewhat loathsome figures of the Pedgifts are as good as any studies of ugly dotage in a father and hideous depravity in a son can be made by any dexterity of arrangement to be or to appear. But the weft of the story is perhaps too dense; the web is perhaps too tightly drawn, and the threads of it are perhaps not always harmonious in colour. The superb success of *The Moonstone* may perhaps make even his most cordial admirers unconsciously if not ungratefully unjust to the less unquestionable and the less unqualified successes of its author; just as any one who has thoroughly enjoyed Lord Digby's incomparable *Elvira*—the one dramatic work in the language which may be said to have anticipated the peculiarly lucid method, and the peculiarly careful evolution of a most amusingly complicated story, which we admire in the best works of Wilkie Collins—will find himself disqualified from enjoying Sir Samuel Tuke's *Adventures of Five Hours*,[1] even when he remembers that the recollection of the

[1] Digby's play, adapted from Calerón, was produced in 1667, Tuke's in 1663.

latter play, recently witnessed on the stage, made Mr. Samuel Pepys reflect, after seeing *Othello*,—a play which he was wont to think well of —that, 'having so lately seen *The Adventures of Five Hours*, it do seem but a mean thing.' In *Elvira*, as in *The Moonstone*, the skill of construction is so exquisite, so complete, so masterly, that we follow the thread of the story with unflagging enjoyment and a perpetually changeful and delightful perplexity of conjecture as to what the upshot is to be; and when this upshot comes it is all that sympathy could have desired, and more than ingenuity could have conceived. Lord Digby lives—if he can be said to live—by grace of his *Elvira* alone, and for fewer readers, I fear, than he seems to me to deserve; there are many, I believe, who think that Wilkie Collins would have a likelier chance of longer life in the memories of more future readers if he had left nothing behind him but his masterpiece *The Moonstone* and the one or two other stories which may fairly be set beside or but a little beneath it. A man who has written much after writing a book of indisputably great merit in its way, and has never again written anything of merit so indisputable and so great, is apt to be thought all the less of on that account: but if these comparatively inferior works have any real and indisputable merit of their own, they surely ought rather to be set down to his credit than to his discredit. And if no good judge of fiction—in other words, of that creative art which alone can entitle a man to be called, not a discoverer or inventor, a commentator or a thinker, but a maker—will affirm that any later work of this able and loyal workman is so good as not to disappoint us when we compare it with *The Moonstone*, none will deny the real and great merit of this later work at its best. And few will differ, I should think, from the suggestion that the inferiority or imperfection which we cannot ignore or deny in it was due to the lamentable illusion of which most unquestionably there are no traces in his earlier work—work which was always modestly, straightforwardly, and thoroughly loyal to the intellectual dictates of his instinct and the intelligent rules of his art. This illusion was the benevolent and maleficent fancy—the 'devout imagination'—that he might do good service, as Dickens had done and was doing, in the line of didactic fiction and reformatory romance. The shades of Mr. Bumble, Mr. Fang, Mr. Nupkins, Mr. Squeers, Mr. Alderman Cute, Mr. Pecksniff, Mr. Creakle, Mr. Kenge, Mr. Vholes, Mr. Bounderby, Mr. Gradgrind, Mr. Merdle, and I know not how many more immortals, may well have disturbed the literary rest of their great creator's friend and disciple; but that was an evil day for his genius on which he bethought himself to try his hand at the correction of abuses, the castigation of follies, and the advocacy of reforms. It is as noble a work as man can undertake, to improve the conditions of life for other men, by writing or by speaking or by example; but in the two former cases, if a man has not the requisite capacity, even the most generous volunteer in the army of progress or reform will be likelier to lose his own way than to lead other men back into theirs.

The first and best of Wilkie Collins's didactic or admonitory novels is so brilliant in exposition of character, so dexterous in construction of incident, so happy in evolution of event, that its place is nearer the better work which preceded than the poorer work which followed it. The subject of marriage law in Scotland is one which it is painfully difficult for any one who has read the most exhaustingly delightful and the most unmercifully side-splitting of all farcical comedies to consider as suggestive of serious or tragic interest. Belinda and her Belvawney, Cheviot and his Minnie, rise up again before the eyes of enraptured if incredulous fancy, in the light—or should we say the limelight?—of inextinguishable and irrepressible laughter: and the woes and wrongs of any couple accidentally or otherwise mismarried on the wrong side of the Border are inevitably invested with a lambent halo of ridicule—an ineffaceable aureole of farce. But if Mr. Gilbert had never written *Engaged*[1] (Momus forbid the lamentable fancy!), it might still be possible to follow the fortunes of the singularly frail and singularly stout-hearted heroine of *Man and Wife* with no sense of incongruity or comicality in the mainspring of the action which directs them: and it is still possible to regret the unexplained if not inexplicable incongruity between the physical or moral weakness which could yield up honour and character to the seduction or attraction of a brainless and soulless brute, and the moral and physical courage which could inspire and sustain the devotion of his victim when aware that her self-sacrifice for the sake of others must expose her to the imminent peril of suffering and terror worse than death. The satire on muscle-worship, though neither unprovoked nor unmerited, might have gained in point and force if the method of attack had been a trifle less heavy-handed. The great objection to the muscular Christians and ethical professors of athleticism, as was once remarked by an undergraduate of my acquaintance, is that they are so unhealthily conscious of their unconscious healthiness. But the satirical or controversial note in this book, if not too finely touched, is touched

[1] W. S. Gilbert's 'farcical comedy' was produced at the Haymarket Theatre on 3 October 1877.

more finely than those which the author attempted to strike in some of his subsequent works. *The New Magdalen* is merely feeble, false, and silly in its sentimental cleverness; but in *The Fallen Leaves* there is something too ludicrously loathsome for comment or endurance. The extreme clumsiness and infelicity of Wilkie Collins as a dramatic teacher or preacher may be tested by comparison with the exquisite skill and tact displayed by M. Alexandre Dumas in his studies of the same or of similar subjects. To the revoltingly ridiculous book just mentioned I am loth to refer again: all readers who feel any gratitude or goodwill towards its author must desire to efface its miserable memory from the record of his works. But take even the comparatively successful *New Magdalen* and set it for instance beside *Les Idées de Mme Aubray*: it is as the scratching of a savage or a child to the drawing of an all but impeccable artist. Even *Une Visite de Noces*, though not exactly a lovely or a lofty study of noble manners and elevated life, is saved by the author's astonishing gift of dexterity in presentation, 'that can make vile things precious:' whereas Mr. Collins, if only by overstating his case, destroys any pathos or plausibility that might otherwise be fancied or be found in it. To the mealy-mouthed modern philopornist the homely and hardy method of the old poet who first discovered or invented the penitent prostitute may seem rough and brutal in its lifelike straightforwardness: but to the wiser eye Bellafront is worth a shoal of her successors in that line of sentimental fiction which provokes from weary humanity the bitter cry of the long-suffering novel-reader: When will the last reformed harlot vanish into space in the arms of the last clerical sceptic—Mercy Merrick and Robert Elsmere destroy each other in a fiery embrace, or in such a duel as that between the princess and the Ifrit, which ended in mutual annihilation?

Less offensive if not less irrational, more amusing if not more convincing, was the childish and harmless onslaught on scientific research attempted if not achieved by the simple-minded and innocent author of *Heart and Science*. The story which bears that most remarkably silly title is the best—after *Man and Wife*, and a good way after—of all its writer's moral or didactic tales. There is a capital child in it, for one thing; her experiences of Scottish life and character, as related on the occasion of her last appearance, are nothing less than delicious.

[Quotes from ch. 61: from 'Carmina could have Zo all to herself...' to '... pick her up again, and clear her'.]

Her father, too, is good; her mother is merely a 'shocking example.'

Not quite so much can be said against the leading character of the story: the relentless lover of knowledge who lives for that love alone is at least *un succès manqué*. Now and then he becomes a really living, interesting, and rather memorable figure. The cynomaniacs with whom the death or the suffering of 'that beast man' is of less account than the death or the suffering of a rabbit or a dog must naturally, one would think, have disapproved of a story in which the awkward champion of their preposterous cause has contrived somehow so to concentrate the serious interest of his book on the person of a vivisector, whom he meant to be an object of mere abhorrence, as to leave him an object of something like sympathy and admiration as well as compassion and respect; none the less deserved if he did once feel a desire to vivisect his vicious and thankless idiot of a brother. The cynical sentimentality—cynical in the metaphorical no less than in the literal sense of the word—which winces and whines at the thought of a benefit conferred on mankind at the price of experiments made on the vile or at any rate the viler body of a beast is worth exactly as much as the humanity and sympathy which inspire the advocates of free trade in the most unspeakable kind of pestilence. And it strikes me that Mr. Godfrey Ablewhite (of *The Moonstone*) would have been a fitter champion of free and independent hydrophobia than the creator of that distinguished philanthropist; who would certainly have been a quite ideal chairman at a meeting of the Ladies' Society for the Propagation of the—well, let us say for the Dissemination of Contagious Disease (Unlimited).

> What brought Sir Visto's ill-got wealth to waste?
> Some demon whispered—'Visto! have a taste.'

A slight change in that famous couplet will express and condense the truth about Wilkie Collins the teacher and preacher more happily and aptly than many pages of analysis.

> What brought good Wilkie's genius nigh perdition?
> Some demon whispered—'Wilkie! have a mission.'

Nothing can be more fatuous than to brand all didactic or missionary fiction as an illegitimate or inferior form of art: the highest works in that line fall short only of the highest ever achieved by man. Many of the very truest and noblest triumphs achieved by the matchless genius of Charles Dickens were achieved in this field: but Collins, I must really be allowed to repeat, was no more a Dickens than Dickens was a

Shakespeare; and if the example of his illustrious friend misled him into emulation or imitation of such labours, we can only regret that he was thus misguided: remembering nevertheless that 'the light which led astray was light from' Dickens.

In some but by no means in all of his later novels there is much of the peculiar and studious ability which distinguishes his best: but his originally remarkable faculty for writing short stories had undergone a total and unaccountable decay. *After Dark* is one of the most delightful books he has left us: each of the stories in it is a little model, a little masterpiece in its kind: but if we compare the admirable story of *The Yellow Mask* with the hideous fiction of *The Haunted Hotel*, we cannot but acknowledge and deplore in the later novelette such an absolute eclipse or collapse of all the qualities which we admired in the earlier that it reads rather like a bad parody than like a bad imitation of its author's better work.

It would seem something less than complimentary to say of an industrious and not unambitious writer that the crowning merit, the most distinctive quality, of his very best work was to be sought and would be found in the construction of an interesting and perplexing story, well conceived, well contrived, and well moulded into lifelike and attractive shape; yet this is what we enjoy—it is all, or almost all, that we find to enjoy, to admire, or to approve—in a work of tragic art so admirable to so many generations as was *The Orphan*; it is the supreme quality of a work so far superior to Otway's as *The Maid's Tragedy*.[1] And both these famous poems are faultier in study of character —more false, incoherent, and incredible—than almost any work by Wilkie Collins. It is but right and reasonable that his abilities should find such favour as they find in France; that so fair an example of his conscientious and ingenious workmanship as the story called *I Say No* should have been honoured by the appearance of a masterly translation in the columns of the *Rappel*. His mannerisms and faults of style are much less obvious and obtrusive in a foreign version: his best qualities are commoner, I regret to think, in French than in English fiction. Such lucidity, such order, such care in the adjustment of parts and the arrangement of the whole, would hardly seem so exceptional to a French reader as to claim for the possessor of these merits a place in the Pantheon; nor can it be supposed that a memorial in Westminster Abbey would not be considered by most Englishmen something more than an

---

1 *The Orphan* (1680), a tragedy by Otway; *The Maid's Tragedy* (1619) by Beaumont and Fletcher.

adequate recognition of his claims. But a friendly and a kindly recollection of them is no more than may be hoped for and expected from a later generation than his own.

84. The minor talent of Wilkie Collins

January 1890

Andrew Lang, 'Mr Wilkie Collins's Novels', *Contemporary Review*, January 1890, lvii, 20–8.

Lang (1844–1912), poet, novelist, historian, folklorist, and translator of Homer, was also an energetic reviewer. On this obituary assessment, see Introduction, p. 30.

Next to reviewing a book without reading it, the most unfair thing one can do is to read it for the purpose of reviewing it. In an ideal world, if books were criticized at all, it would only be by persons who, after reading them, felt constrained to express their delight or their discontent. The critical spectacles almost inevitably distort the object on which you look through them. The beauty of women, the beauty of landscape, would be no longer the same if you were introduced to a lady or a loch-side after being told that you must go straight home and review them. In attempting to estimate the work of Mr. Wilkie Collins, the present reviewer is under the disadvantage of having read several of his books for the first time, with a critical intention. Yet it is fair to say that the impression left on the mind, after a somewhat forced march through several romances, is precisely what it was when the regretted death of Mr. Collins made every one think of his performances as a whole. He still remains a most conscientious, and careful, and ingenious constructor of plots, a writer with a respect for his art, and deeply concerned with its processes. We still find in him a man with an almost bitter sense of human unhappiness, a man whose favourite characters are at odds with the world. We still recognize that, in his best books, he is not incapable of humour, and it must still be added that, in general, he 'jocked wi' deeficulty,' as the Scotch editor confessed about himself. His methods do not cease to force on us the old sense of their difficulties. We cannot accept it as natural that so many persons should write such copious diaries, that criminals should establish minute indictments against themselves by committing every detail of their schemes to paper and ink. Guilty people *do* neglect the sound advice 'Let Letts alone'; but they are not often so elaborate in their confessions. Mr. Collins's method is that of Mr. Browning in *The Ring and the Book*. His characters view the same set of circumstances, but with very different eyes. The method has its obvious advantages and disadvantages; perhaps it is most artfully worked in *The Woman in White*. Again, after reading and re-reading, one keeps one's old opinion—that for a writer so conscientious and careful, Mr. Wilkie Collins was but rarely successful in the full measure of his success. A few of his short stories, his *Woman in White*, his *No Name*, and, above all, doubtless, *The Moonstone*—reach a level of ingenuity and of interest which the many others fall very far short of. The humorous passages, for example, in *Armadale* and *Hide and Seek* are very laboured and melancholy. The unsympathetic quality of his characters is exaggerated in Zack Thorpe, and Matthew Grice, and Midwinter, and Allan Armadale. The very construction becomes a mass of coincidences, which have a cumulative weight of impossibility far more grievous than the frank postulates of fantastic romances, such as *Frankenstein*, or *Avatar*, or *La Peau de Chagrin*. These conclusions are absolutely forced on a dispassionate reader, in spite of all the pleasure and excitement which he derives from Mr. Wilkie Collins at his best. Yet the novels remain most instructive reading, one may suppose, to a novelist who is concerned with the technique of construction, as the author himself was.

There are certain ideas, combinations, and *trucs* which constantly preoccupied the author. He wished to excite and sustain curiosity as to a secret; or, again, he liked to foreshadow the progress of the story, and then to interest the reader in the fulfilment of what had been fore-shadowed. This latter is the process in *No Name* and in *Armadale*; the former is the process in *The Moonstone* and *The Woman in White*. In these aims Mr. Collins competes with M. Gaboriau, and with M. Fortuné du Boisgobey. But he escapes Gaboriau's defect, his habit of first powerfully exciting curiosity, and then explaining inexplicable circumstances by going back almost as far as the First Crusade. Nor does Mr. Collins, like M. Boisgobey, secure his secret by making some person act quite out of character, as in that very clever tale, *Le Crime de l'Opéra*. Perhaps even *The Moonstone* is not more craftily wrought than *Les Esclaves de Paris*, and it would be false patriotism to set Mr. Collins above M. Gaboriau in the qualities that were common to both. But there are defects in M. Gaboriau's manner which Mr. Collins escaped. The vehement admirer of Mr. Collins may object to the comparison, yet it is almost inevitable. Mr. Collins frequently required for his purposes a character of only occasional sanity, or a blind person, or a somnambulist, and he ventured most unsuccessfully on what M. Gaboriau and Edgar Poe never attempted, the introduction of the supernatural. True, he tried to 'hedge' about his supernatural, to leave it hazy, in a dim penumbra. But any one who wishes to see failure here has only to look at *Armadale*, while in Hawthorne he will find the same attempt made with success. Another favourite device was to make one character personate another, as in *Armadale*, and in *The New Magdalen*; but here, again, Mr. Collins did not cope with M. Gaboriau, nor perhaps with Miss Braddon, in *Henry Dunbar*.[1] In all but his very best novels his combinations were apt to be too intricate, too like a very difficult game at chess, and in passing from one coincidence to another, we gradually lose our power of belief, and with it, of course, our interest. That Mr. Collins aims frequently at being didactic and reformatory is, of course, not necessarily a fault. But when he attacks society and social verdicts, in *The New Magdalen*, he is certainly unfair in his handling of the characters. His repentant and beautiful Magdalen does not repent much of her imposture till she gets into an inextricable position, while her respectable and offensive foil is handicapped by ugliness in opposition to the beauty of the woman who has stolen into her place, and thrown her, destitute, wounded, and morally maimed, on the world. As to *Fallen Leaves*, that novel involves much that may excite our partisan feelings in a time of furious debate, and so had better be left out of the question as a work of art. Again, in *Man and Wife*, Mr. Collins attacked 'athleticism' without really knowing what the life of athletes at the universities is like. To any one who knew them well, who had seen so many of them, not debauched and brutal clods, but men of refinement, sometimes scholars, occasionally wits, interested in most of the arts, and capable, as time has declared, of taking and making honourable positions in life, the satire of *Man and Wife* seemed blunt and ignorant. . . .

[1] Published in 1864.

As a didactic writer, Mr. Collins injured his art somewhat, and probably did little to refine athletics, or to make the world more charitable to such a sinner as his New Magdalen; but what has worst served his fame is, doubtless, the flood of later novels, in which he so decidedly fell below his own standard. But these will be forgotten, while his earlier books may long retain their very wide and deserved popularity. We do not think of *The Surgeon's Daughter*, and *Castle Dangerous*, when we think of Scott, nor will the future associate Mr. Collins with *The Guilty River*, and *Little Novels*.

This is not a bibliography, and it is not possible here to examine each of Mr. Collins's novels in detail. His *Antonina* and *Basil* were prior to 1854, when his *Hide and Seek* appeared. He himself speaks of it in his Preface, as 'an advance in Art on his earlier attempts.' If he was right, *Antonina* and *Basil* must be very far indeed below the level which he attained in the middle of his working life.

Mr. Collins had a strong dislike of evangelical religion, or at least of certain developments of it, with which he seems to have been familiar. No one who has met, among people of that faith, the very best, most kindly, and, in spite of the gravest trials, the happiest of his friends, will charge the creed of Miss Clack and Mr. Thorpe with the vices of these two deplorable persons. In *Hide and Seek* the story turns on the early misdeed of a man who appears in the novel as a strict and gloomy sabbatarian fanatic. It is the tale of a secret, and a secret as well kept as it is absurdly discovered. The novel was revised and altered by the author in later editions, but, as now published, it is disagreeable in the drawing of the favoured characters, and in the plot, while it is very far from being well constructed. The deafness and dumbness of the heroine give Mr. Collins a chance of studying the life of a beautiful mute, but her defects lead to nothing. . . .

[The improbabilities of the plot are criticized at length.]

That any writer could rise rapidly from the composition of *Hide and Seek* to that of *The Woman in White* is as extraordinary as that the author of the *Woman in White* should descend to *Armadale*, and, again, should climb to the perfection, in its own class, of *The Moonstone*. Mr. Collins's career was entirely unlike that of his greater contemporaries. Mr. Thackeray slowly prepared himself, by a series of advances in art, for *Vanity Fair*, and then kept 'the crown of the causeway' with a series of masterpieces, till he declined in *The Virginians*. Mr. Dickens began, as far as public recognition went, with the most delightful explosion of humorous high spirits in the world, then distinguished himself by several immortal stories, then had an interval of partial eclipse, and shone out again in new lights with *The Tale of Two Cities* and *Great Expectations*. Mr. Collins, on the other hand, had done a good deal of not particularly noticeable work for ten years or so before he found himself in *The Woman in White*, lost himself in *Armadale*, excelled himself in *The Moonstone*, and, after that, seldom rose much above the level of his earlier essays. His biographer—if he is to have a biographer—may be able partly to explain by reasons of health and circumstance this intermittent brilliance. Whatever its causes, *The Woman in White* is a masterpiece of excitement and ingenuity. From the moment when the white woman flutters across the moonlit heath, within sound of the roar of London, till 'Laura, Lady Glyde,' stands veiled by her own tombstone, and looks across it at her lover, there is hardly a page in this book but lives with its own mysterious life, and beckons you to follow till the end. It is a rare thing among novels of incident, of secret, and of adventure, to find one that you can read several times. But this is part of the merit of *The Woman in White*.

'I have always held,' says Mr. Collins, 'the old-fashioned opinion that the primary object of a work of fiction should be to tell a story.' This opinion will probably outlive most of our perishable institutions. But, Mr. Collins adds, he sees no reason why a novelist who fulfils this condition should neglect character; in fact, he held that, given a story, characters *must* be presented. Necessarily they must; but it is undeniable that a very good story may be told in which little of character, except pluck and endurance, is displayed, the adventures not calling for the exhibition of anything more subtle. In *The Woman in White* some of the characters may border on what are called 'character parts' in acting. Count Fosco has tendencies in this direction, so has the admirable little Italian, Professor Pesca. But certainly Marian Halcombe is also a 'character,' without any touch of caricature, while Anne Catherick herself, with her craze about white, has a high place among the fantastic women of fiction. Even Sir Percival is more than a fair specimen of that favourite *persona*, the bad baronet. He is not so colossally nefarious as the regretted Sir Massingberd, but he will more than pass. *The Woman in White* is, in its way, a masterpiece; it has even humour, in the Foscos and elsewhere, and redeems the terrors of that picnic on the water, which amazes the reader of *Armadale*. Though it is a work which we can never forget, we can often return to it; and it made Mr. Collins for long the most popular favourite in English fiction. It is curious to think over that series of premier novelists who, one after another, have held the top of the market, and been dearest to the booksellers. The reigns of some were long, of others brief indeed. Their throne has occasionally been the mark of envying, hatred, and uncharitableness, and some of the masters of the art have never been crowned there. Hard it is to descend from that perilous eminence. Mr. Collins, at least, was never ungenerous to his successors, the 'new tyrants,' the later dynasties.

The Woman in White was followed by *No Name*. As a novel of the author's central period, it stands far above the common average of his immature and of his later work. The character of Magdalen Vanstone is perhaps the most original and striking in his great family of imaginary people; the most winning at first in her beauty, vivacity, and affection, and much the most pardonable when wrong drove her to revenge. There is something of the Corsican, of Colomba, in Magdalen Vanstone, and we might have preferred for her an end tragic and desperate rather than the haven to which she came. As a mere matter of probability, her constant changes of costume and 'make-up' are less trying to belief than many of Mr. Collins's later devices. The other characters are among the most life-like in his novels, whether we look at the lucky lout, the wretched pretty Frank Clare, or his misanthropic sire, or the governess (Miss Garth), or Mr. Vanstone himself. There are scenes of simple and powerful truth, as where Magdalen tries, in her desperate and outcast fortunes under the roof of a rogue, to repeat the part that she had acted when she was happy, secure, and beloved. . . .

Here, and in the passage where Midwinter declares his love to the beautiful, sinful, battered Miss Gwilt, wakening so many memories of things true and tender, spoiled and betrayed, Mr. Collins, perhaps, comes nearest to the poetry of romance. In this novel, too, are the most humorous of his lighter characters, that esteemed swindler Captain Wragge, and Mrs. Wragge. The scene of Mrs. Wragge's omelette and her struggles with the involved pronouns of the Cookery Book is really diverting.

Mr. Collins acted wisely in not producing *The Moonstone* while *No Name* was fresh in his readers' memories. For the scene of the sleep-walking-admiral, in *No Name*, really contains the key to the mystery of *The Moonstone*, just as Miss Gwilt, *dans la peau d'une autre*, suggests the central idea of *The New Magdalen*. Between *No Name* and *The Moonstone* came *Armadale*, written when the author was at the height of his reputation, to which it added little or nothing.

Few men can follow one prodigious hit by another as great. *Armadale*, which appeared in the *Cornhill Magazine* was, to my own thinking, a terrible descent. Mr. Swinburne, in a recent review, acknowledges its 'superb ingenuity';[1] I must regret that its ingenuity seems to me far too ingenious. I am the last reader to boggle at an impossibility, and to reject *Vice Versâ*,[2] say, because 'miracles do not happen.' We can accept the miracle as a postulate, and few people will censure the *Odyssey* because Calypso is 'an immortal woman living in a cave,' or because sailors are changed to swine. You grant the postulate, and, that done, you believe as you read. But in *Armadale* you read and do not believe. What fancy can accept the unending coincidences of *Armadale*, and the Dream in seventeen distinct compartments, every one of them fulfilled in the future? Who can believe that a little girl of twelve could commit an artful forgery? Yet if Miss Gwilt had been older than twelve, when she forged, she would have been older than thirty-five when all men, from twenty to seventy, fell violently in love with her. There are few Ninons, but Miss Gwilt must have been one of them. As for the characters, the gloom of Midwinter is as oppressive as the mode in which he learned Greek and German is astonishing. Allan Armadale, with his noisy absurdities, is justly censured by Miss Gwilt herself, and the school-girl who makes love to him is not more endurable than her admirer. Miss Gwilt herself saves the story, which becomes alive when she enters it, and, with all her crimes on her head, she is infinitely the most human and agreeable of the persons in this sordid affair. The destruction of three able-bodied heirs in a fortnight, one by an accidental chill, two by an avalanche, rivals some performances with African lightning in its rough and ready slap-dash. The theory of 'hereditary superstition' is strained to breaking, but on it the whole weight of the plot depends. The letters between Mrs. Oldershaw and Miss Gwilt are scarcely more possible than the diary to which the murderess confesses her crimes. There is nobody in the book to like or admire, unless Miss Gwilt be the person, or unless we repose on the bosom of Pedgift the younger. Mr. Collins endeavoured to defend his series of coincidences by an example from real life. In *Armadale* the heir is to be poisoned by sleeping in a room charged with poisoned air, and three men, as the story was running, were actually poisoned by foul air, in a ship called the *Armadale*. Much more astonishing coincidences have occurred than that; but *Armadale* is one tissue of succeeding coincidences. The cumulative effect produces incredulity and indifference, and we are vexed by

[1] See p. 258, where Swinburne's phrase is 'astonishingly ingenious'.
[2] By F. Anstey, published in 1882.

the number of persons who spy, listen, and overhear what was not meant for them. And for humour, we have 'the curate, with a ghastly face, and a hand pressed convulsively over the middle region of his waistcoat'.

Armadale was much more than redeemed by *The Moonstone*. Here we have good romance in the very presence of the Diamond, as fatal a thing as the dwarf Andvari's ring in the Saga. The Indians, wandering in and out, impress one more, I think, than our new Hindoo visitor, Secundra Dass. The sudden appearance of Mr. Godfrey Ablewhite, in the guise of a sailor, was, to myself, the most complete and pleasant surprise in the whole range of the surprises of fiction. When one first read the story, one resented the explanation, the sleep-walking, as a disappointment. Already the idea had been used, when Jack Ingoldsby's breeches vanished night by night, in the *Ingoldsby Legends*.[1] M. Boisgobey has employed it in *L'Affaire Matapan*, and Mr. Collins had used it in *No Name*. Still, probably few readers guessed at the truth, so cunningly were all sorts of false and plausible clues suggested. As for the humour of the story, Miss Clack is somewhat mechanical and exaggerated. Mr. Collins makes her too profuse a writer in 'the *patois* of Zion.' The old butler with his *Robinson Crusoe* is rather a bore, like most characters marked with too pronounced tricks. Mr. Collins did not abuse this method of 'individualizing' his persons nearly so much as Mr. Dickens often did, but he occasionally made the thing wearisome. Of the later novels, it is not my intention to speak. The ingenuity of *Poor Miss Finch* cannot reconcile us to the manifest and grotesque 'machinery' of the blind girl and the blue lover. She is too 'in and out' in her blindness, and he too much excels mankind 'in azure feats,' as Mr. Browning puts it. The unfairness of *The New Magdalen* has already been hinted at: there is interest and great resource, however, in the ups and downs of the central narrative.

Nobody can write romances for thirty-five years without vicissitudes in the fortunes of his works, without varieties in his inspiration and his skill. Mr. Collins was fortunate enough not to attract the attention of the literary wrecker. He may have been saved from the dangers of success by his conscientious endeavour, in each new tale, to do his very best. As to that best, one cannot equal it with the excellence of Dickens, of Thackeray, of George Eliot, of Charles Reade, or even of Anthony Trollope. The *genre* of novel to which Mr. Collins devoted himself was lower than theirs. In even his best work there is, or I seem to be aware

[1] By R. H. Barham, published 1840-7.

of, a kind of professional hardness, for there is no charm in his style, and there is much premeditation in his humour. We cannot all admire all things equally, and it seems a pity that we should quarrel as much as we do over our tastes in fiction. A man can, in the end, only express an honest opinion, and I must own that I read Mr. Collins's greatest books with much pleasure and excitement, but without much enthusiasm; while in his less fortunate novels, his manner wearies me, and his method is too nakedly conspicuous. There are even two or three stories by the comparatively neglected Mr. Sheridan Le Fanu which I would rate as high as Mr. Collins's best; there are scenes of Mr. Le Fanu's far more deeply and terribly stamped on the memory; there are secrets as cunningly hidden; and in the volume *In a Glass Darkly*[1] Mr. Le Fanu's command of the supernatural contrasts gloriously with Mr. Collins's failures. Both men were masters in their school, but by some caprice of taste, some accident of vogue, the author of *Uncle Silas* never won such rewards as fell to the author of *The Woman in White*.

Both are gone; they have left no man to take their precise place in that art which, even in living hands, has diverted the camp-fires of Australian cattle drovers, has consoled the latest hours of statesmen outworn, and dying emperors, which opens to all of us, as the Zulu wizards say, 'the gates of distance,' and gives us the entry of undiscovered lands. For these benefits the least thing we can do, and frequently the last thing we do, is to be grateful.

[1] Published 1872.

85. Plot, character and purpose in Wilkie Collins

August 1890

Edmund Yates, 'The Novels of Wilkie Collins', *Temple Bar*, August 1890, lxxxix, 528–32.

On Yates, see headnote to No. 17.

With the death of Wilkie Collins we have lost almost the last of the great English novelists who made the middle of the nineteenth century memorable in the history of fiction. Thackeray, Dickens, Charles Reade, Trollope, Kingsley, Mrs. Gaskell, Charlotte Brontë, George Eliot; only one of them reached the allotted threescore years and ten. Collins, by a few years the younger of the coterie, has joined them; and the world is the poorer for want of one of the most fearless and honest fictionists who ever fed the public's sensation hunger while seeking to influence the public's serious sentiments. His time, the time not of to-day but of twenty or thirty years ago, was one of straight speaking, when men wrote from their hearts in a way that would be scorned in these days of subtle intellectualism, told their tale, set forth their moral, if there was one, and were content. The complications in which Collins revels are never of the subjective or metaphysical kind. The field of his narratives bristles with ingenious obstacles, but he goes at them like a steeplechaser at a hurdle, and the emotions of his men and women are as simple as those of the *dramatis personæ* of an Adelphi drama.

This was not perhaps what Collins himself wished—probably not what he believed to be the case. Judging from his own prefaces, and other expressions of feeling in his novels, he laid great stress upon his character-drawing; it is intimated that *The Moonstone* is built upon 'the conduct pursued under a sudden emergency by a young girl.' But who stops to consider the psychological problem presented by Rachel Verinder? What we want to find out is, what has become of the

273

diamond? In *No Name* there is a similar reference to the setting forth of a woman's character as a main object of the book; but who spends thought on the complexities of Magdalen Vanstone's nature until, at least, he has got to the end of her escapades? In other tales there is the same thing; the author is engaged, he believes, in tracing the influence of circumstance on character or character on circumstance; and yet the individuals that fix themselves in a reader's memory are not those around whom the labyrinth of plot is constructed; nor would any one think of calling Wilkie Collins a novelist notable for character-drawing. It is the semi-burlesque sketches, which he probably learnt to make from Dickens, that come to mind when we recall the novels: Count Fosco and Miss Clack, Uncle Joseph and the inimitable Captain and Mrs. Wragge, who are among the immortals. There is nothing like analyses of emotions or motives such as those upon which later writers delight to turn a microscopic lens. Even his Wragges and Foscos are not in the same familiar circle of our acquaintance with Mrs. Gamp and Mr. Pecksniff. And it is a little curious that Dickens, who has added more friends to all the world's portrait-gallery than any other writer has done, longed to shine as an elaborator of plots, inspired no doubt by admiration for his friend's genius; while Collins, the past master of the plot, aspired to be a delineator of character. Next to this, Collins had a firm belief in the purpose of his stories; it was characteristic of his frank and earnest nature; but so far as his readers were concerned, it was a mistake. Motives indeed are obvious in not a few—the marriage laws are aimed at in *Man and Wife*, the position of illegitimate children in *No Name*, society's treatment of 'penitents' in *The New Magdalen*, vivisection in *Heart and Science*; and there is a declared intention or object woven in with many others, though it may never be suspected by the reader. Where the moral is evident it is freely forgiven for the sake of the plot which involves it, and that in itself is a tribute to his genius. With Dickens and Reade the same thing may be said, but it takes a master hand to make the public enjoy that powdered jam, fiction with a purpose.

To his position of supremacy as a manufacturer of plots no one denies Wilkie Collins's right, though critics may scorn or sneer at both the art and its master. It is a manufacture; there is no doubt about that. Nobody imagines the misfortunes of *Poor Miss Finch*, and her blue-complexioned lover, the masquerades of Magdalen Vanstone, the machinations of the Romish Church in *The Black Robe*, the remarkable coincidences of *Hide and Seek*, or the melodramatic farrago of *The Frozen Deep*, to be precisely scenes from real life. But, truth being stranger than fiction, possibly they might be; and if a man writes fiction as if it was truth, and it is good fiction into the bargain, there is no reason why the public should not like it as well as the washiest or wickedest realism.

Collins's style is not a thing of literary beauty like Mr. Stevenson's, or a marvel of finish like Mr. Henry James's. It is jerky and absolutely unornamented. There are no elegant extracts to be got out of his stories; it would be no easy matter to compile beauties of Collins, and even birthday-book framers might be in difficulties. The incidents are of the stage stagey, and as for scenic art there is probably never a word given to the description of natural surroundings unless it has a direct bearing on the development of the plot. But he had a story to tell, and he knew how to tell it. He had a strong grip of his story, too; a singularly forcible and vigorous method of unfolding it, and a talent for dramatic situations. Few readers, however much their intelligence may revolt from the strains on probabilities, or however near their heads may be to splitting in the effort to follow the endless complications and mystifications which confront them, lay aside the novel until they have read to the end. In their own peculiar way, *The Woman in White* and *The Moonstone*, it may be safely said, have never been surpassed.

Like the majority of writers, Wilkie Collins wrote his most popular books when in the prime of life. Thackeray was forty-one when he gave *Esmond* to the world; Dickens two or three years younger when *David Copperfield* was written; George Eliot was thirty-nine when *Adam Bede* placed her name among the immortals; and Trollope was forty-two when, with *Barchester Towers*, he made his first success. Collins wrote *The Woman in White*, *No Name*, *Armadale*, and *The Moonstone*, in succession, between the ages of thirty-five and forty-five; and none of his many earlier or later fictions have achieved the same fame as those four brilliant novels. *Antonina*, a story of ancient Rome, was his first, then came *Basil*, a remarkably unpleasant story, which yet showed ample evidence of inherent power and dramatic ability. In its feverish autobiographical mode of telling, and obvious indications of youth in the manner of it, *Basil* may be said to have literary kinship with Mr. William Black's *Kilmeny*, and Mr. Justin McCarthy's *My Enemy's Daughter*. Ingenuity of plot, helped out by useful coincidences, is the feature of the third effort, *Hide and Seek*, with its gentle deaf and dumb heroine; but *The Dead Secret* was really the earliest example of the distinctly Collins method of narration, which has had a world of imitators, and, like most distinct methods, is a dangerous model. A little cheap satire and a great deal of egotism persuade the young writer who cultivates them that he is a second Thackeray; a free use of caricature, especially in proper names, and of capital letters, are expected to convince the world that a second Dickens has arisen. Similarly it is required only to have recourse to a bewildering sequence of events, place the telling of them in the mouths of half-a-dozen narrators, and let the narration be as bald and colloquial as possible, in order that a man may avow himself a disciple of Wilkie Collins. The difficulty lies in the acquirement of Wilkie Collins's talent. Improbabilities, absurdities, long-drawn-out complications of plot, and an almost brutal bluntness of style are, no doubt, among his characteristics; but, on the other hand, there is the singular realistic power which vitalises even the most tiresome of his stories. *The Dead Secret* is melodramatic, and the secret is soon guessed by the reader; a change of children cannot be regarded as an original notion, and the hiding of the confession in the deserted portion of a house whose owner is most concerned in the matter is possibly not an expedient of great literary value; but the schemes of Sarah Leeson to get into the house and abstract the document, the strength with which this part of the book is written, and the humorous atmosphere surrounding Uncle Joseph and his musical box, are almost on a level with Collins's best work. After this came the four already named: *The Woman in White*, with the memorable figure of Count Fosco, best known of all his characters, because no one had before conceived the possibility of a villain who should be fat and comic, and possess pet animals; *No Name*, the history of Magdalen Vanstone's plots to recover her lost home, and entrap her odious Cousin Noel—odious, also, after an original type—and of the counterplots of Mrs. Lecourt, whose cold and slimy reptile pets are a pair to Fosco's white mice; *Armadale*, wherein occurs the curious figure of Miss Gwilt, which took a firm hold of public fancy. For this novel it is said that Wilkie Collins reached his top price; but it may be taken for granted that its predecessors had a considerable effect upon this point; for in plot it is scarcely equal to them or to its successor, though there are other admirable features which lend probability to the statement that it was the author's own favourite work. In skill of plot, conception, and development, without considering other details, *The Moonstone* stands pre-eminent.

Of the dozen or so other novels which the same pen has since given us, *Man and Wife* and *The New Magdalen* made the most sensation. They dealt with delicate questions, and they took a new view of them. *Man and Wife*, indeed, dealt with at least two questions; not only is the injustice of the marriage laws keenly and forcibly insisted on—in itself a sufficiently startling onslaught upon popular conservatism—but a vehement attack is also made upon the excessive value set on athletic sports. In this matter Wilkie Collins ran as directly contrary to public feeling as in the obesity of Fosco, and the devotion to Beethoven of Lydia Gwilt; and he hit it more closely. Various ameliorations have been made in the legal relationship of man and wife; but as to the sports and exercise craze, the current appears to be all the other way, and until people can appreciate the difference between the rational and healthy development of every boy's and every girl's limbs and muscles, and the forcing and straining of one man's physical powers in order that the rest may look on and bet, so long it will be well that such an illustration of the triumph of brute over angel as Geoffry Delamayn should be held up to them. Still more risky is the main idea of *The New Magdalen*, which narrowly misses being a fine story; strong and clever it is, but it misses the higher rank by that want of spirituality which is discernible throughout Collins; we feel that it is Mercy Merrick's beautiful figure and 'grand head' which constitute her saving grace, and influence Julian Gray, and this conviction kills the moral of the story at once. The author's pen was too human for his theme.

One conspicuous trait of Wilkie Collins can scarcely be overlooked —thorough-going manliness; not by any means the manliness which is based on a swaggering assertion of strength, or that which exults especially in man's prowess and pluck. Geoffry Delamayn shows what he thought would be the result of training the physical powers at the expense of the mental and moral capabilities. *Armadale* sets forth his views (we may fairly assume) as to the hunting-field, when Allan horrifies 'the county' by making known his ability 'to enjoy a ride on horseback without galloping after a wretched stinking fox or a poor distracted little hare.' His literary style is indeed distinctively masculine; but the manliness of his nature was revealed by the use he made of his strength for the defence of weakness. It is always on the side of the weak that his voice is raised—the women, the children, the fallen, the desolate, and the oppressed. And it is because of this fearlessness and this nobility of purpose that, however inartistic and inexpedient we may declare purpose of a serious kind to be in fiction, he touches a deeper note in our sympathy than could be reached by the writer whose aim it is to concoct sensational stories only, whether that writer's gifts be greater or less than the high talent which the world has recognized in Wilkie Collins.

86. 'The Master of Constructive Fiction'

April 1891

W. J. Johnston, 'Wilkie Collins and the Novelists of the Day',
Irish Monthly, April 1891, xix, 206–8.

This extract is taken from an article which, surveying Collins's
career, finds that his best work belongs to the decade 1860–70 and
anticipates modern judgments by predicting that the novels which
will survive are *The Woman in White*, *The Moonstone* and *No
Name*. No details are known about the author.

Taking everything into consideration, the three books of this author
that will live are: *The Woman in White*, on account of the admirable
way in which he manages the bewildering sequence of events; *The
Moonstone*, thanks to the originality of the central idea and the artistic
manner in which he works up to the very unexpected climax; and *No
Name*, if only for the sake of that humorous rascal, Captain Wragge. . . .
In spite of all his faults—even because of his faults—he was a great story-
teller. At the time when some of the greatest novelists that the world has
yet seen were depicting men and women of every conceivable variety
and in every conceivable position, he took up his one-sided idea of
inventing, first and above all, a good story, and then fitting it with men
and women. To this peculiar theory he remained true as steel, in spite
of the fashion of the time, and went on constructing his literary labyrinths and giving inexpressible relief to a world surfeited with novels of
character. When Dickens and Thackeray were penning their marvellous experiences of human conduct; when George Eliot was analysing
the workings of the human mind; when Anthony Trollope was showing his infinite knowledge of human trivialities; when Charles Reade
was distributing from his treasure-house of human incidents—obstinate,
one-sided old Wilkie was laboriously planning and putting together
his secrets and surprises, his letter-writing and his telegraph operating, his
strange meetings and his wonderful resemblances, his deaths and his
risings from the dead, and proving his right to be considered the Mastes
of Constructive Fiction.

APPENDIX

Wilkie Collins: Principal Works

Collins's plays and journalism are not included in the following list. For a more comprehensive and detailed listing, see the book by Parrish and Miller, and the article by Andrew, referred to in the Bibliography.

Memoirs of the Life of William Collins, R.A. (November 1848).
Antonina, or the fall of Rome (February 1850).
Rambles Beyond Railways (January 1851).
Mr. Wray's Cash-box (December 1851; 1852 on title-page).
Basil (November 1852; revised edition, 1862).
Hide and Seek (June 1854).
After Dark (February 1856).
The Dead Secret (June 1857; previously serialized in *Household Words*).
The Queen of Hearts (October 1859; some of the stories had been previously serialized in *Household Words* and elsewhere).
The Woman in White (September 1860; revised edition in the following year; previously serialized in *All the Year Round*).
No Name (December 1862; previously serialized in *All the Year Round*).
Armadale (June 1866; previously serialized in the *Cornhill*).
The Moonstone (July 1868; previously serialized in *All the Year Round*).
Man and Wife (June 1870; previously serialized in *Cassell's Magazine*).
Poor Miss Finch (January 1872; previously serialized in *Cassell's Magazine*).
Miss or Mrs.? (January 1873; the stories had previously appeared in various magazines).
The New Magdalen (May 1873; previously serialized in *Temple Bar*).
The Frozen Deep and Other Stories (November 1874; the stories had previously appeared in various magazines).
The Law and the Lady (February 1875).
The Two Destinies (September 1876).

The Haunted Hotel (late 1878; 1879 on title-page; previously serialized in *Belgravia*).

A Rogue's Life (April 1879; previously serialized in *Household Words*).

The Fallen Leaves (July 1879; previously serialized in the *World* and *Rose-Belford's Canadian Monthly & National Review*).

Jezebel's Daughter (March 1880).

The Black Robe (April 1881; previously serialized in *Rose-Belford's Canadian Monthly & National Review*).

Heart and Science (April 1883; previously serialized in *Belgravia*).

'I Say No' (October 1884).

The Evil Genius (September 1886; previously serialized in various provincial newspapers).

The Legacy of Cain (November 1888).

Blind Love (January 1890; previously serialized in the *Illustrated London News*).

Bibliography

Minor sources cited in the headnotes and in the notes to the Introduction are not repeated here.

ANDREW, R. V., 'A Wilkie Collins checklist', *English Studies in Africa*, iii (1960), 79–98: a comprehensive listing which includes the plays and journalism as well as the fiction.

ASHLEY, R. P., 'The career of Wilkie Collins', unpublished doctoral dissertation, Harvard University, 1949.

ASHLEY, R. P., *Wilkie Collins* (1952): brief general study.

ASHLEY, R. P., 'Wilkie Collins', in *Victorian Fiction: A Guide to Research*, ed. L. Stevenson (Cambridge, Mass., 1964), 277–84: useful descriptive listing of secondary material.

CORDASCO, F. and SCOTT, K., *Wilkie Collins and Charles Reade: A Bibliography of Critical Notices and Studies* (New York, 1949): fails to fulfil the promise of its title, being very brief and hopelessly incomplete.

DAVIS, EARLE, *The Flint and the Flame* (New York, 1963): some sections on Collins.

DAVIS, NUEL PHARR, *The Life of Wilkie Collins* (Urbana, 1956): full-scale study, not entirely reliable.

ELLEGÅRD, ALVAR, *The Readership of the Periodical Press in Mid-Victorian Britain* (Gothenburg, 1957).

HARVEY, W. J., Collins bibliography in *New Cambridge Bibliography of English Literature* (*1800–1900*), ed. G. Watson (Cambridge, 1969), 924–8: the most recent listing, but inaccurate in some details and incomplete in its information regarding serialization.

MARE, WALTER DE LA, 'The early novels of Wilkie Collins', in *The Eighteen-Sixties*, ed. J. Drinkwater (Cambridge, 1932), 51–101.

MARSHALL, W. H., *Wilkie Collins* (New York, 1970): short general study.

MILLEY, H. J. W., 'The influence of Wilkie Collins on Dickens and Trollope', unpublished doctoral dissertation, Yale University, 1941.

PARRISH, M. L. and MILLER, E. V., *Wilkie Collins and Charles Reade: First Editions Described with Notes* (1940): a mine of detailed bibliographical information.

ROBINSON, KENNETH, *Wilkie Collins: A Biography* (1951): sound and comprehensive.

SADLEIR, MICHAEL, *Excursions in Victorian Bibliography* (1922), 129–55.

SADLEIR, MICHAEL, *XIXth Century Fiction: A Bibliographical Record* (1951).

WALPOLE, HUGH, 'Novelists of the 'seventies', in *The Eighteen-Seventies*, ed. H. Granville-Barker (Cambridge, 1929), 22–44.

Select Index

References are grouped as follows: I. Wilkie Collins: (a) writings; (b) characteristics discussed; II. Periodicals quoted from or referred to; III. Authors of extracts; IV. General index of names.

I. (a) WILKIE COLLINS: WRITINGS

I. (b) WILKIE COLLINS: CHARACTERISTICS

II. PERIODICALS QUOTED FROM OR REFERRED TO

III. AUTHORS OF EXTRACTS

IV. GENERAL INDEX OF NAMES

THE CRITICAL HERITAGE SERIES

GENERAL EDITOR: B. C. SOUTHAM

Volumes published and forthcoming

Continued